Makers of Ancient Strategy

Makers of
Ancient Strategy

*From the
Persian Wars to the
Fall of Rome*

EDITED AND INTRODUCED BY

Victor Davis Hanson

PRINCETON UNIVERSITY PRESS
PRINCETON AND OXFORD

Published by Princeton University Press,
41 William Street, Princeton, New Jersey 08540

In the United Kingdom:
Princeton University Press,
6 Oxford Street, Woodstock, Oxfordshire OX20 1TW
All Rights Reserved

Library of Congress Cataloging-in-Publication Data

Makers of ancient strategy : from the Persian wars to the
fall of Rome / edited and Introduced by Victor Davis Hanson.
p. cm.
Includes bibliographical references and index.
ISBN 978-0-691-13790-2 (hardcover : alk. paper)
1. Military art and science—History—To 500.
2. Military history, Ancient.
I. Hanson, Victor Davis.
U29.M26 2010
355.409'014—dc22
2009034732

British Library Cataloging-in-Publication Data is available

This book has been composed in Dante MT Std

Printed on acid-free paper. ∞

press.princeton.edu

Printed in the United States of America

1 3 5 7 9 10 8 6 4 2

Contents

Contributors

Victor Davis Hanson is the Martin and Illie Anderson Senior Fellow in Residence in Classics and Military History at the Hoover Institution, Stanford University, and emeritus professor of Classics at California State University, Fresno. He is also the Wayne & Marcia Buske Distinguished Fellow in History, Hillsdale College, where he teaches courses in military history and classical culture. He is the author of many books, including *A War Like No Other: How the Athenians and Spartans Fought the Peloponnesian War* (Random House, 2005); *Carnage and Culture: Landmark Battles in the Rise of Western Power* (Doubleday, 2001); *The Soul of Battle: From Ancient Times to the Present Day, How Three Great Liberators Vanquished Tyranny* (Free Press, 1999); *Hoplites: The Classical Greek Battle Experience* (Routledge, 1993); *The Western Way of War: Infantry Battle in Classical Greece* (Knopf, 1989); *Other Greeks: The Family Farm and the Agrarian Roots of Western Civilization* (Free Press, 1995); and *Warfare and Agriculture in Classical Greece* (University of California Press, 1983).

David L. Berkey is assistant professor in the Department of History at California State University, Fresno. He received his doctorate in Classics and ancient history in 2001 from Yale University and his bachelor's degree from Johns Hopkins University in international studies in 1989.

Adrian Goldsworthy was educated at St. John's College, Oxford, and is currently Visiting Fellow at Newcastle University. His doctoral thesis was published in the Oxford monographs series under the title *The Roman Army at War, 100 BC–AD 200*. He was a Junior Research Fellow at Cardiff University and subsequently an assistant professor in the University of Notre Dame's London program. He now writes full time. His most recent books include *Caesar: The Life of a Colossus*

(Yale University Press, 2006) and *How Rome Fell: The Death of a Super-power* (Yale University Press, 2009).

Peter J. Heather is professor of medieval European history at King's College, London. He was born in Londonderry, Northern Ireland, and educated at Maidstone Grammar School and New College, Oxford. He was awarded a postdoctoral degree by the History Faculty of Oxford University. He has since taught at University College, London, Yale University, and Worcester College, Oxford.

Tom Holland is the author of three highly praised works of history. The first, *Rubicon: The Triumph and Tragedy of the Roman Republic*, won the Hessell-Tiltman Prize for History and was short-listed for the Samuel Johnson Prize. His book on the Greco-Persian wars, *Persian Fire: The First World Empire and the Battle for the West*, won the Anglo-Hellenic League's Runciman Award in 2006. His latest book, *The Forge of Christendom: The End of Days and the Epic Rise of the West*, was published in the spring of 2009. He has adapted Homer, Herodotus, Thucydides, and Virgil for the BBC. He is currently working on a translation of Herodotus for Penguin Classics. In 2007 he was awarded the 2007 Classical Association prize, given to "the individual who has done most to promote the study of the language, literature and civilisation of Ancient Greece and Rome."

Donald Kagan is Sterling Professor of Classics and History at Yale University. He has won teaching awards at Cornell University and at Yale, and was awarded the National Humanities Medal in 2002. He was named the Jefferson Lecturer by the National Endowment for the Humanities in 2004. Among his publications are a four-volume history of the Peloponnesian War, *Pericles of Athens and the Birth of Democracy*, and *On the Origins of War and the Preservation of Peace*. He is also co-author of *The Western Heritage* and *The Heritage of World Civilizations*.

John W. I. Lee is associate professor of history at the University of California, Santa Barbara. He received his Ph.D. in history from Cornell University. He is the author of *A Greek Army on the March: Soldiers and*

Survival in Xenophon's Anabasis (Cambridge University Press, 2007). He has also published on women in ancient Greek armies, on the Persian army in Herodotus, and on ancient soldiers' memoirs. Lee is currently working on a new book that examines warfare and culture in the eastern Aegean and along the west coast of Anatolia, from the Ionian Revolt (499–494 BC) to the fourth century BC.

Susan Mattern is professor of history at the University of Georgia. Her most recent book is *Galen and the Rhetoric of Healing* (Johns Hopkins University Press, 2008), a study of the medical practice of the ancient physician Galen, based on his stories about his patients. She is also the author of *Rome and the Enemy: Imperial Strategy in the Principate* (University of California Press, 1999; now in paperback) and co-author of *The Ancient Mediterranean World from the Stone Age to A.D. 600* (Oxford University Press, 2004). She is now working on a biography of Galen.

Barry Strauss is professor of Classics and history and chair of the History Department at Cornell University, as well as director of the Program on Freedom and Free Societies. He is the author of six books, including *The Battle of Salamis*, named one of the best books of 2004 by the *Washington Post*, and *The Trojan War: A New History*, a main selection of the History Book Club. His most recent book, *The Spartacus War*, appeared in March 2009. He is series editor of Princeton History of the Ancient World and serves on the editorial boards of *MHQ: The Quarterly Journal of Military History*, *Historically Speaking: The Bulletin of the Historical Society*, and the *International Journal of the Classical Tradition*. He is the recipient of the Heinrich Schliemann Fellowship at the American School of Classical Studies at Athens, a National Endowment for the Humanities Fellowship for University Teachers, and Cornell's Clark Award for Excellence in Teaching.

Ian Worthington is Frederick A. Middlebush Professor of History at the University of Missouri. Previously he taught for ten years in the Classics Department at the University of New England and the

University of Tasmania, Australia. He is author or editor of fourteen books and more than eighty articles. His most recent publications include the biographies *Alexander the Great: Man and God* (Pearson, 2004) and *Philip II of Macedonia* (Yale University Press, 2008), and the *Blackwell Companion to Greek Rhetoric* (Oxford University Press, 2006). He is currently writing a book on Demosthenes, editing the *Blackwell Companion to Ancient Macedonia,* and serving as editor-in-chief of Brill's *New Jacoby.* In 2005 he won the Chancellor's Award for Outstanding Research and Creativity in the Humanities and in 2007 the Student-Athlete Advisory Council Most Inspiring Professor Award, both at the University of Missouri.

Makers of Ancient Strategy

Introduction: Makers of Ancient Strategy
From the Persian Wars to the Fall of Rome

VICTOR DAVIS HANSON

MAKERS OF STRATEGY

Makers of Modern Strategy: From Machiavelli to the Nuclear Age, edited by Peter Paret, appeared as a 941-page volume comprising twenty-eight essays, with topics ranging from the sixteenth century to the 1980s. The work was published by Princeton University Press in 1986, as the cold war was drawing to a close. Paret's massive anthology itself updated and expanded upon the classic inaugural Princeton volume of twenty essays, *Makers of Modern Strategy: Military Thought from Machiavelli to Hitler,* edited by Edward M. Earle. The smaller, earlier book had appeared more than forty years before the second, in 1943, in the midst of the Second World War. It focused on individual military theorists and generals; hence the personalized title, "Makers."

Although the theme of both books remained the relevance of the past to military challenges of the present, the 1986 sequel dealt more with American concerns. Its chapters were built not so much around individuals as on larger strategic themes and historical periods. Although both the editors and the authors of these two books by intent did not always explicitly connect their contributions to the ordeals of their times, the Second World War and the cold war are unavoidable presences in the background. Both books cautioned against assuming that the radical changes in war making of their respective ages were signs that the nature of conflict had also changed.

On the contrary, the two works served as reminders that the history of both the immediate and more distant past deals with the same concerns and dangers as exist in the tumultuous present. The study of military history schools us in lessons that are surprisingly apt to contemporary dilemmas, even though they may be largely unknown or forgotten—and all the more so as radically evolving technology fools many into thinking that war itself is reinvented with the novel tools of each age.

WHY THE ANCIENT WORLD?

In what might be thought of as a prequel to those two works, *Makers of Ancient Strategy* resembles in its approach (not to mention its smaller size) the earlier 1943 volume edited by Earle. The ten essays in *Makers of Ancient Strategy* frequently focus on individual leaders, strategists, and generals, among them Xerxes, Pericles, Epaminondas, Alexander, Spartacus, and Caesar. The historical parameters, however, have expanded in the opposite direction to encompass a millennium of history (roughly from 500 BC to AD 500) that, even at its most recent, in the late Roman Empire, is at least 1,500 years from the present. As a point of modern departure, this third work on the makers of strategy appears not merely in the second generation of industrial war, as was true of the 1943 publication, or in a third era of high-tech precision weapons of the nuclear age, as in 1986, but during so-called fourth-generational warfare. The late twentieth century ushered in a baffling time, characterized by instant globalized communications, asymmetrical tactics, and new manifestations of terrorism, with war technology in the form of drones, night-vision goggles, enhanced bodily protection, and computer-guided weapons systems housed from beneath the earth to outer space. Nevertheless, the theme of all three volumes remains constant: the study of history, not recent understanding of technological innovation, remains the better guide to the nature of contemporary warfare

As the formal lines between conventional war and terrorism blur, and as high technology accelerates the pace and dangers of conflict, it has become popular to suggest that war itself has been remade into something never before witnessed by earlier generations. Just as no previous era had to deal with terrorists' communiqués posted on the Internet and instantly accessible to hundreds of millions of viewers, so supposedly we must now conceive of wholly new doctrines and paradigms to counteract such tactics. But as the ten essays in this book show, human nature, which drives conflict, is unchanging. Since war is and will always be conducted by men and women, who reason—or react emotionally—in somewhat expected ways, there is a certain predictability to war.

Makers of Ancient Strategy not only reminds us that the more things change, the more they remain the same, it also argues that the classical worlds of Greece and Rome offer a unique utility in understanding war of any era. The ancient historians and observers were empirical. They often wrote about what they saw and thought, without worrying about contemporary popular opinion and without much concern either that their observations could be at odds with prevailing theories or intellectual trends. So there was an honesty of thought and a clarity of expression not always found in military discussions in the present.

We also know a great deal about warfare in the ancient Western world. The Greek and Roman writers who created the discipline of history defined it largely as the study of wars, as the works of Herodotus, Thucydides, Xenophon, Polybius, and Livy attest. And while much of ancient history has been lost, enough still survives to allow a fairly complete account of a thousand years of fighting in the Greek and Roman worlds. Indeed, we know much more about the battle of Delion (424 BC) or Adrianople (AD 378) than about Poitiers (732) or Ashdown (871). The experience of Greece and Rome also forms the common heritage of modern Europe and the United States, and in a way that is less true of the venerable traditions of ancient Africa, the Americas, and Asia. In that sense, nineteenth- and twentieth-century Western problems of unification, civil war, expansion abroad, colonization, nation building, and counterinsurgency all have clear and well-documented precedents in both Greek and Roman culture.

Makers of Ancient Strategy explores the most ancient examples of our heritage to frame questions of the most recent manifestations of Western warfare. The Greeks were the first to argue that human nature was fixed and, as the historian Thucydides predicted, were confident that the history of their own experiences would still be relevant to subsequent generations, even our own postmodern one in the new millennium.

The contributors were encouraged to develop a topic close to their interests rather than mold material to a thematic template. In general, however, readers will find in each chapter an introduction that sets out the particular historical landscape and its players, followed by an analysis of the relevant ancient "maker"—statesman, general, or theorist—or strategy and an assessment of his, or its, success or failure. The discussion then broadens to consider the relevance of the strategy to later warfare, and especially to the conflicts of our times.

The essays are arrayed in roughly chronological order, moving from the early fifth-century Greco-Persian Wars (490, 480–479 BC) to the final defense of the borders of the Roman Empire (ca. AD 450–500). Of note, the era was one of empires. The extension of military power abroad, and with it often the political control of weaker states, is usually accompanied by official self-justifications. To launch us on empires and justification, in chapter one Tom Holland focuses on the first great clash of civilizations between East and West, the Persian efforts at the beginning of the fifth century BC to conquer the Greek city-states and absorb them into an expanded empire that would reach across the Aegean into Europe. Imperial powers, as Holland shows, create an entire mythology about the morality, necessity, or inevitability of conquest. Their narratives are every bit as important to military planning as men and matériel in the field. Such an imperial drive, he argues, is innate to the human condition and is not culturally determined. Imperial propaganda did not find its way into the later Western DNA merely through the rise of the Athenian Empire or Rome's absorption of the Mediterranean. Instead, imperialism and its contradictions were present from an even earlier time, as Greek pupils learned about the imperial ambitions of their would-be Persian masters and teachers.

The defeat of the Persian Empire in the early fifth century BC opened the way for the rise of the Athenian Empire. Today we assume that empire is an entirely negative notion. We associate it with coercion and more recent nineteenth-century exploitation, and deem it ultimately unsustainable by the ruling power itself. But as Donald Kagan shows in chapter two, rare individuals—and here he focuses on Pericles' thirty-year preeminence in Athenian politics and the contemporary historian Thucydides' appreciation of his singularity—occasionally do make a difference. Empire, especially of the Athenian brand, was not doomed to failure, if moderate and sober leaders like Pericles understood its function and utility. For a brief few decades under his leadership, Athens protected the Greek city-states from Persian retaliation. It tried to keep the general peace, resisted imperial megalomania, and fostered economic growth through a unified and integrated Athenian system of commerce. The success of Pericles and the failure of those who followed him are timely reminders that to the degree that imperial powers can further the generally understood common interest, they are sustainable. When they transform into an instrument only of self-aggrandizement, they inevitably implode.

The physical defense provided by fortifications helped the Athenian Empire retain its military supremacy for as long as it did. We assume that in our age of sophisticated communications and aerial munitions, old-fashioned fortifications are relics of a military past, if not always of questionable military utility. But increasingly we see their reappearance—though often augmented with electronic enhancements—in the Middle East, in Iraq, and along the U.S.-Mexican border. Recent walls and forts have often enhanced interior defense, in instances where seemingly more sophisticated tactics have often failed. David Berkey in chapter three traces the century-long evolution of walls at Athens, from the initial circuit fortifications around the city proper, to the Long Walls leading from Athens to its port city of Piraeus, 6.5 km distant, to the fourth-century attempts to protect the countryside of Attica through a network of border forts. These serial projects reflect diverse economic, political, and military agendas over 100 years of Athenian defense policy. Yet, as Berkey shows, they had in common a utility that kept Athens mostly safe from its enemies and offered additional manifest and ideological support for the notion of both empire and democracy. Statesmen, policies, and technology all change; fortifications of some sort seem to be a constant feature in the age-old cycle of offensive and defensive challenge and response.

Preemption, coercive democratization, and unilateralism in the post-Iraq world are felt recently to be either singularly American notions or by their very nature pernicious concepts that offer prescriptions for failure and misery to all those involved. In fact, these ideas have been around since the beginning of Western civilization and have proven both effective and of dubious utility. Thus, in chapter four I focus on the rather obscure preemptive invasion of the Peloponnese by the Theban general Epaminondas (370–369 BC), who was considered by the ancients themselves to be the most impressive leader Greece and Rome produced, a general seen as a much different moral sort than an Alexander or a Julius Caesar. At his death in 362, Epaminondas had emasculated the Spartan oligarchic hegemony and had led the city-state of Thebes to a new position of prominence. He founded new citadels, freed tens of thousands of the Messenian helots, and changed the political culture of Greece itself by fostering the spread of democratic governments among the city-states. How and why, through failure and success, he accomplished all this reminds us that what we have seen in the contemporary Middle East is hardly unique. Afghanistan and Iraq are not the first or the last we will see of messianic idealism coupled with military force, perceived as part of a larger concern for a nation's national security and long-term interests.

Great generals in the ancient world often became great public figures who forcefully changed the broader political landscape both before and after their military operations. More has been written about Alexander the Great than about any other figure of classical antiquity. Ian Worthington in chapter five reviews his creation of an Asian empire and the difficulty of administering conquered Persian land with ever-shrinking Macedonian resources. He offers a cautionary if not timely tale from the past about the misleading ease of initial Western military conquest over inferior enemy conventional forces, which soon transmogrify into or are replaced by more amorphous and stubborn centers of resistance. Even military geniuses find that consolidating and pacifying what has been brilliantly won on the battlefield proves far more difficult than its original acquisition. Alexander discovered that cultural sensitivity was necessary to win the hearts and minds of occupied Persia. Yet as a professed emissary of Hellenism, Alexander's aims in introducing what he felt was a superior culture that might unify and enlighten conquered peoples proved antithetical to his pragmatic efforts at winning over the population.

The twentieth century saw the superiority of most Westernized conventional militaries. Their superior technology, industrialized supply, and institutionalized discipline gave them innate advantages over most other forces. But when fighting was confined to the congested terrain of urban centers, when it involved ideologies and tribal affinities rather than the interests of nation-states, and when it drew civilians into combat, the outcome was uncertain at best. John Lee in chapter six shows there is also nothing new about contemporary urban fighting and the problems it poses for conventional infantry forces. The same challenges of gaining accurate local intelligence, winning the hearts and minds of civilians, and finding appropriate tactics to use among dense urban populations were of keen interest to Greek military thinkers and generals alike, when fighting frequently moved from the battlefield to inside the polis. Successful urban tactics in the ancient Greek world often required as radical a change in accepted conventional military thinking as the challenges of terrorism, insurgency, and sectarian violence from Gaza to Falluja do today.

There is also nothing really novel in the various ways that powerful imperial states keep the peace among various subject peoples and diverse provinces. Susan Mattern in chapter seven analyzes the various ways Rome kept together its multicultural and racially diverse empire and dealt with serial outbreaks of insurrection, terrorism, and national revolts. What made these events relatively rare in the half-millennium life of the empire, and why they were usually put down, did not hinge just on the superiority of the Roman army or its eventual mastery of counterinsurgency tactics. Equally important was a variety of insidious "hearts and minds" mechanisms that won over or co-opted local populations. Generous material aid, the granting of citizenship, education, a uniform law code equally applied, and indigenous integration and assimilation into Roman culture and life together convinced most tribes that they had more to gain by joining than by opposing Rome.

Terrorism, insurrections, and ethnic or religious revolts often baffle the modern nation-state. Its traditional forces certainly seem ill-equipped to fight on rough terrain or to root out nontraditional fighters amid sympathetic populations. But the dilemma is often a two-way street. In chapter eight Barry Strauss reviews slave revolts of antiquity—especially the well-known case of Spartacus's first-century BC rebellion against the Roman state—to show that the problems can be even worse for the challengers of state authority. If the goals of insurrectionists evolve beyond terror and mayhem to include mass transit through flatland or winning the hearts and minds of local populations, or even carving out large swaths of permanently occupied or secured territory, then at some point they must find parity with state forces in terms of conventional warfare. Despite the romance we associate with Spartacus, his slave revolt was overmatched by the logistics, discipline, and generalship of the Roman legions. His call for mass slave liberation had no real political resonance among Italians to rival the appeal of the Roman state. We may live in an age of incomprehensible terror and insurrection, but we too often forget that the military odds still lie on the side of the nation-state, especially when war breaks out within its own borders.

Western democracies and republics are wary of the proverbial man on the horse. And why not, given the well-known precedents of what Alexander the Great, Julius Caesar, and Napoleon did to their respective consensual societies? Adrian Goldsworthy in chapter nine meticulously shows how the upstart Caesar, through his conquest of Gaul, outfoxed and outmuscled his far more experienced and better-connected Roman rivals. The lesson Goldsworthy draws is that the use of force abroad inevitably has political repercussions at home, and can prove as dangerous to republican societies that field superior armies as to the enemies that fall before them. Any time the citizenry associates victory abroad with the singular genius of one charismatic leader, then even in constitutional states there are likely to be repercussions at home when such popularity translates into political capital.

The Roman Empire—its formation, sustenance in the face of attacks from outside and internal revolts, its generals—often serves as a historical shorthand for the millennium of strategic thinking discussed in this book. Why, in the military sense, did Rome fall in the late fifth century? Most argue over whether its frontier defenses were stationary or more proactively aggressive, and whether such policies were wise or misguided. Peter Heather in chapter ten makes the point that the forces of imperial Rome, at a time when we sometimes think they were ensconced behind forts, walls, and natural obstacles, as a matter of practice ventured into enemy lands to ward off potential invasions. He also reminds us that the so-called barbarians on the borders of Rome by the later empire were becoming sophisticated, more united, and keenly observant of the methods by which Roman armies were raised and financed—and thus could be circumvented. The result is that we learn not only about the sophisticated nature of Roman border protection but, as important, how adept less civilized enemies really were. In short, military sophistication is not always to be accurately calibrated according to our own cultural norms, and Western states can lose as much because of adroit enemies as through their own mistakes and ongoing decline.

As historians of ancient times, the contributors might be dismayed by how little present makers of modern strategy and war making have learned from the classical past, how much ignored its lessons. Yet, in the spirit of the two earlier *Makers*, we avoid inflicting overt ideological characterizations of a contemporary political nature.

THE BURDENS OF THE PAST

Few formal strategic doctrines have survived from antiquity. No college of military historians wrote systematic theoretical treatises on the proper use of military force to further political objectives. Although there are extant tactical treatises on how to defend cities under siege, the proper role of a cavalry commander, and how to arrange and deploy a Macedonian phalanx or a Roman legion, there are no explicit works on the various ways in which national power is to be harnessed for strategic purposes. Great captains did not write memoirs outlining strategic doctrine or military theory in the abstract.

The historian Thucydides informs us of Pericles' strategic thinking, not Pericles. We learn of Epaminondas's preemptive strike against the Peloponnese from what others said he did rather than from what he or his close associates said he did. Caesar's own commentaries were about *how* he conquered much of Western Europe, not *why* its conquest would be beneficial to Rome, or the costs and benefits—and future challenges—of its annexation. Ancient historians chronicled both Alexander's brilliance in taking Persia and the subsequent challenges such occupation posed. Yet these dilemmas were not addressed in the abstract by Alexander himself or his lieutenants. We have a good idea, not from Greek captains but from classical historians, ancient inscriptions, and the archaeological record, of how Greek and Roman commanders dealt with insurrections, urban warfare, and border defense. In other words, unlike makers of modern strategy, the makers of ancient strategy were not abstract thinkers like Machiavelli, Clausewitz, or Delbrück, or even generals who wrote about what they did and wanted to do, such as Napoleon or Schlieffen.

The result is twofold. First, strategy in the ancient world is more often implicit than explicitly expressed. The classical military historian has far more difficulty recovering strategic thinking than does his more modern counterpart, and certainly the ensuing conclusions are far more apt to be questioned and disputed.

Second, as a result of this difficulty of classical scholarship and its frequent neglect, conclusions are often far more novel. We have thousands of books on Napoleon's or Hitler's strategy but only a few dozen on the strategic thinking of Alexander and Caesar. And if there are dozens of book-length studies on the grand strategy of George Marshall or Charles de Gaulle, there are almost none on Epaminondas's. If readers find in these chapters a great deal of supposition, a bothersome need for conjecture, and sometimes foreign citations, they also will discover much that is entirely new—or at least new manifestations of familiar things that they now discover are in fact quite old. The ancient world is sometimes thought to be irrelevant because it is so distant. But in an age of confusing theories, rapidly shifting technologies, and a cacophony of instant communications, the Greeks and Romans, precisely because of their distance and clarity, loom more relevant than ever. These essays are offered in the hope that the next time a statesman or general offers an entirely new solution to what he insists is an entirely new problem, someone can object that is not necessarily so. Rather than offering political assessments of modern military leaders' policies, we instead hope that knowledge of the ancient world will remind us all of the parameters of available choices—and their consequences.

1. From Persia with Love
Propaganda and Imperial Overreach in the Greco-Persian Wars

TOM HOLLAND

THE INVASION OF IRAQ, when it finally came, was merely the climax of an ongoing period of crisis and upheaval in the international order. The stand-off between the two sides had been a geopolitical fixture for years. Both had surely long suspected that open conflict was inevitable. As the invaders crossed into Iraqi territory, they would have known that they faced a regime that was hardly unprepared for war. It had been assiduous in stockpiling reserves of weaponry and provisions; its troops, massed along the border, blocked all the roads that led to the capital; the capital itself, an intimidating blend of grandiose prestige projects and warren-like slums, was darkly rumored to be capable of swallowing up a whole army. Yet all the regime's defenses, in the final reckoning, might as well have been made of sand. What it confronted in its adversary was nothing less than a superpower, the most formidable on the planet. The task force brought to bear by the invaders was a quite devastating display of shock and awe. Those of the defenders who were not left corpses by the first deadly impact of the enemy onslaught simply melted away. Even in the capital itself, the population proved signally unwilling to die for the sake of their beleaguered leader. A bare few weeks after hostilities had begun, the war was effectively over. So it was, on October 12, 539 BC, that the gates of Babylon were flung open "without a battle,"[1] and the greatest city in the world fell into the hands of Cyrus, the king of Persia.

To the Babylonians themselves, the capture of their metropolis by a foreign warlord was only readily explicable as the doing of Marduk, the king of their gods. Over the centuries, Babylon's peerless glamour and pedigree had served to burnish the conceit of its inhabitants to a truly lustrous sheen. Although long subject to the rule of Assyria, a rival kingdom to the north, Babylon had always chafed at its subordination, and in 612 BC, when its armies took the lead in sacking the Assyrian capital of Nineveh, the city had exacted a splendid and bloody revenge. From that moment on, it had found itself positioned to play the role that its people had always seen as its right: as the very fulcrum of world affairs. Although the collapse of the Assyrian Empire had left the Near East divided between Babylon itself and three other kingdoms—Media in northern Iran, Lydia in Anatolia, and Egypt—there had been little doubt as to which among these four great powers ranked as *primus inter pares*. Over the wreckage of Assyrian power the kings of Babylon had soon succeeded in raising their own far-spreading dominion. Upon their lesser neighbors they had imposed "an iron yoke of servitude."[2] Typical of the fate meted out to those who presumed to stand on their independence had been the crushing, in 586, of the valiant but foolhardy little kingdom of Judah. Two years after staging a revolt against Babylonian rule, the Judaeans had been left to mourn their temerity amid the wreckage of all that had previously served to define them. Jerusalem and its Temple had been reduced to a pile of blackened ruins, its king had been obliged to watch the murder of his sons before himself being blinded, and the Judaean elite had been hauled off into exile. There, weeping by the rivers of Babylon, it had seemed to one of their number, a prophet by the name of Ezekiel, that the shadows of Sheol were closing in on the entire global order. Not a great power, but it had been dispatched to the underworld by the king of Babylon: "all of them slain, fallen by the sword, who spread terror in the land of the living."[3]

But now Babylonian supremacy itself was a dead thing. The fall of the great city appeared to contemporaries a veritable earthquake. What rendered it all the more seismic, however, was the identity of its conqueror: for if Babylon could lay claim to a history that stretched back to the very beginnings of time, when the gods had first begun to build cities from the world's primal mud, then the Persians, by contrast, appeared to have come almost from nowhere. Two decades earlier, when Cyrus had ascended to the throne, his kingdom had been not merely inconsequential but politically subordinate, for he had ranked as the vassal of the king of Media. In a world dominated by four great powers, there was little scope, it might have been thought, for any outsider to make his way. Cyrus, however, over the course of his reign had demonstrated the very opposite. The muscle-bound character of the global order confronting him had been turned dazzlingly to his own advantage. Decapitate an empire, he had demonstrated, and all its provinces might be seized as collateral. First to go had been his erstwhile overlord, the king of Media: toppled in 550. Four years later it was the turn of Lydia. By 539, when Babylon too was added to Cyrus's bag of scalps, he was the master of a dominion that stretched from the Aegean to the Hindu Kush, the largest agglomeration of territory the world had ever seen. Well might Cyrus have described his own rule in totalizing, indeed nakedly cosmic terms: he was the King of Kings, the Great King, "the King of the Universe."[4]

How had he pulled it off? It goes without saying, of course, that the building of an empire is rarely achieved without the spilling of a great deal of blood. The Persians, as tough and unyielding as the mountains of their homeland and raised from childhood to an awesome degree of military proficiency, were formidable warriors. Just like the Assyrians and the Babylonians before them, they had brought to the Near East "the tearing down of walls, the tumult of cavalry charges and the overthrow of cities."[5] During the invasion of Babylonia, for instance, all the characteristics of Cyrus's generalship had been on devastating display: the ability to marshal "numbers as immeasurable as the waters of a river,"[6] to crush all those who thought to oppose him, and to move with an utterly disconcerting speed. Certainly, the sword of such a conqueror did not sleep easily in its scabbard. A decade after his triumphant entry into the capital of the world the by now aged Cyrus was still in his saddle, leading his horsemen ever onward. Various stories are told of his end, but most agree that he died in Central Asia, far beyond the bounds of any previous Near Eastern empire. Even though it is evident that his corpse was transported back with full honors to Persia, for burial in a splendid tomb, numerous eerie stories gave a different account. According to one of them, for instance, the queen of the tribe that had killed Cyrus ordered his corpse to be decapitated, then dropped the severed head into a blood-filled wineskin, so that his thirst for slaughter might be glutted at last.[7] Such a tale powerfully suggests the terror that the great conqueror was capable of inspiring in his adversaries, for vampires, demons hungry for human flesh, had long haunted the nightmares of the peoples of the Near East.

Yet a very different tradition also served to keep alive the memory of Cyrus the Great. He had not merely conquered his enemies, he had assiduously wooed them as well. Brutal though he could certainly be in the cause of securing an enemy's speedy surrender, his preference, by and large, had been to live up to the irenic claims of his own brilliantly crafted propaganda. His mastery once established over the corpses of shattered armies, further bloodshed had tended to be kept to the barest minimum. If the Babylonians chose to attribute his conquest of their city to the will of Marduk, then Cyrus was perfectly content to play along. Invading Iraq, he had made sure to proclaim himself the favorite of his enemies' greatest divinity; toppling its native dynasty, he had posed as the heir of its most venerable traditions. Not only in Babylon but in cities and kingdoms across his vast empire he had presented himself as a model of righteousness and his rule as payback from his various subjects' gods. The very peoples he had conquered had duly scrabbled to take him at his own estimation and to hail him as their own. With a brilliant and calculating subtlety, Cyrus had succeeded in demonstrating to his heirs that mercilessness and repression, the keynotes of all previous imperialisms in the region, might be blended with a no less imperious show of graciousness, emancipation, and patronage. War on its own, Cyrus's career appeared to imply, could take an empire only so far. Guarantee peace and order to the dutifully submissive, however, and the world itself might prove the limit.

So it was, for instance, that Cyrus, even as he flattered the Babylonians with the attentions he paid to Marduk, had not ignored the yearnings of the city's deportees—exiles such as the Judaeans. The Persian high command had recognized in these homesick captives a resource of great potential. Judaea was the pivot between the Fertile Crescent and the as yet unconquered kingdom of Egypt; a land of such strategic significance might certainly be considered worth a small investment. Not only had Cyrus permitted the Judaeans to return to the weed-covered rubble of their homeland but funds had even been made available for the rebuilding in Jerusalem of their obliterated Temple. The exiles themselves had responded with undiluted enthusiasm and gratitude. Whereas Ezekiel had portrayed Babylon as merely the agent of Yahweh, the Judaeans' prickly and boastful god, the prophet who wrote under the name of Isaiah cast the Persian king in an altogether more brilliant light. "Thus says the LORD to his anointed, to Cyrus, whose right hand I have grasped, to subdue nations before him and ungird the loins of kings, to open doors before him, that gates may not be closed: 'I will go before you and level the mountains, I will break in pieces the doors of bronze and cut asunder the bars of iron, I will give you the treasures of darkness and the hoards in secret places, that you may know that it is I, the LORD, the god of Israel, who call you by your name.'"[8]

Cyrus himself, had he ever been made aware of this extraordinary brag, would surely have marked it down as what it so clearly was: a signal triumph for his policy of governing through willing collaborators. While the Persians' tolerance of foreigners and their peculiar customs in no way implied respect, their genius as world conquerors was to indulge the instinctive longing of any slave to believe himself the favorite of his master, and to turn it to their own advantage. What greater source of self-contentment for a peripheral and insignificant subject people such as the Judaeans, after all, than to imagine themselves graced by a special relationship with the far-off King of Kings? Cyrus and his successors had grasped a bleak yet strategically momentous truth: the traditions that define a community, that afford it a sense of self-worth and a yearning for independence, can also, if sensitively exploited by a conqueror, serve to reconcile that community to its very subordination. This maxim, applied by the Persians across the vast range of all their many provinces, was one that underpinned their entire philosophy of empire. No ruling class anywhere, they liked to think, could not somehow be seduced into submission.

True, this did presuppose that the ruling classes themselves could all be trusted to stay in power. Fortunately, in regimes such as were to be found across most of the Near East, with their priesthoods, their bureaucracies, and their cadres of the superrich, it took more than a change of overlord to upset the smooth functioning of the elites. Even at the very limits of the empire, where the gravitational pull of the center was naturally at its weakest, there might often be considerable enthusiasm for the undoubted fruits of the Pax Persica. In Sardis, for instance, the capital of Lydia, and so far distant from Persia that it was only a few days' journey from the "bitter sea," as the Persians termed the Aegean, initial teething problems had not prevented collaboration from soon becoming an accepted way of life. Lydian functionaries still dutifully ran the province for their masters, just as they had done under their native kings. Their language, their customs, their gods—all were scrupulously tolerated. Even their taxes, though certainly high, were not set so high as to bleed them dry. Indeed, of one Lydian, a mine owner by the name of Pythius, it would be claimed that only the Great King outranked him on the empire's rich list. Men such as this, to whom Persian rule had opened up unprecedented opportunities, certainly had not the remotest interest in agitating for liberty.

Nevertheless, not everything was quiet on the western front. Beyond Sardis, dotted along the Aegean coastline, were the gleaming cities of a people known to the Persians as the Yauna. Originally from Greece, the Ionians, as they called themselves, remained quite as determinedly and defiantly Greek as any of their countrymen back in the motherland across the Aegean—which meant that, to their masters, they represented both an enigma and a challenge. All the Yauna ever did, it seemed to the Persians, was quarrel. Even when the various cities were not squabbling with one another they were likely to be embroiled in civil strife. This interminable feuding, which had contributed enormously to the initial ease of their conquest back in the time of Cyrus, also made the Ionians a uniquely wearisome people to rule. Where civilized peoples—the Babylonians, the Lydians, even the Judaeans—had their functionaries and priests, the Greeks seemed to have only treacherous and ever-splintering factions.

As a result, despite their genius for psychological profiling, the Persians found it a challenge to get a handle on their Ionian subjects. Whereas in Babylon or Sardis they could raise their administration on the bedrock provided by an efficient and dutiful bureaucracy, in Ionia they had to base it instead on their own talent for intrigue and espionage. The challenge for any Persian governor was to pick winners among the various Ionian power players, back them until they had outgrown their usefulness, and then dispose of them with a minimum of fuss. Such a policy, however, could hardly help but be a treacherous one. By favoring one faction over another, the Persians were inevitably themselves sucked into the swirl of backstabbing and class warfare that constituted Ionian politics. A frustrating and disconcerting experience, and one that appeared to lend credence to a theory much favored by certain Ionians, wise men known as "philosophers," to whom it appeared simply an observable fact of nature that everything in the universe was conflict and tension and change. "All things are constituted from fire," as one of them put it, "and all things will melt back into fire."[9]

Here, to the Ionians' masters, was a truly shocking notion. Fire, in the opinion of the Persians, was the manifestation not of a ceaseless flux but rather of the very opposite, of the immanence of an unchanging principle of righteousness and justice. Promiscuous in their sponsorship of foreign gods they might have been, yet they knew in their hearts—as lesser peoples did not—that without such a principle, the universe would be undone and lost to perpetual night. This was why, so they believed, when Ahura Mazda, the greatest of all the gods, had summoned creation into being at the beginning of time, he had engendered Arta, who was Truth, to give form and order to the cosmos. Nevertheless, chaos had never ceased to threaten the world with ruin, for just as fire cannot burn without the accompaniment of smoke, so Arta, the Persians knew, was inevitably shadowed by Drauga, the Lie. These two principles—the one embodying perfection, the other falsehood—were coiled, so the Persians believed, in a conflict that was ultimately as ancient as time. What should responsible mortals do, then, but take the side of Arta against Drauga, Truth against the Lie, Light against Darkness, lest the universe itself totter and fall?

This was a question that, in 522, would prove to have implications far beyond the dimensions of priestcraft or theodicy, for it had come to affect the very future of the Persian monarchy itself. First Cambyses, the eldest son and heir of Cyrus and the king who had finally succeeded in conquering Egypt, died in mysterious circumstances on the highroad back from the Nile. Then, in the early autumn, his brother, the new king, Bardiya, was ambushed and hacked down amid the mountains of western Iran. Taking his place on the blood-spattered throne was his assassin, a man blatantly guilty of usurpation, and yet Darius I, with a display of nerve so breathtaking that it served to mark him out as a politician of quite spectacular creativity and ruthlessness, claimed that it was Bardiya and not himself who had been the fraud, the fake, the liar.[10] Everything he had done, he claimed, everything he had achieved, was due to the favor of Ahura Mazda. "He bore me aid, the other gods too, because I was not faithless, I was not a follower of the Lie, I was not false in my actions."[11] Darius was protesting too much, of course, but that was ultimately because, as a regicide, he had very little choice. For all that he was quick to claim a close kinship to the house of Cyrus, and to bundle the sisters of Cambyses and Bardiya into his marriage bed, his dynastic claim to the throne was in reality so tenuous that he could hardly rely on it to justify his coup. Other legitimization had to be concocted, and fast. This was why, far more than Cyrus or his sons had ever felt the need to do, Darius insisted on his role as the chosen one of Ahura Mazda: as the standard-bearer of the Truth.

This seamless identification of his own rule with that of a universal god was to prove a development full of moment for the future. Usurpers had been claiming divine sanction for their actions since time immemorial, but never one such as Ahura Mazda could provide. Trampling down his enemies, Darius was not only securing his own rule but also, and with fateful consequences, setting his empire on a potent new footing. At Bisitun, a mountain that rose a few miles from the scene of Bardiya's assassination, the new king commanded his achievements to be recorded on the rock face directly above the main road; the resulting inscription was to prove a radical and telling departure from the norms of Near Eastern self-promotion. When the Assyrian kings had portrayed themselves subduing their foes, they had done so in the most extravagant and blood-bespattered detail, amid the charging of shock troops, the advance of siege engines, the trudging into exile of the defeated. No such specifics were recorded at Bisitun. What mattered to Darius was not the battle but that the battle had been won, not the bloodshed but that the blood had dried, and a new and universal era of peace had dawned. History, so Darius was proclaiming, had in effect been brought to a close. The Persians' empire was both its end and its summation, for what else could a dominion be that contained within it all the limits of the horizon, if not the bulwark of a truly cosmic order? Such a monarchy, now that the new king had succeeded in redeeming it from the Lie, might surely be expected to endure for all eternity: infinite, unshakable, the watchtower of the Truth.

Here, in Darius's vision of empire as a fusion of cosmic, moral, and political order, was a formulation that was destined to prove stunningly fruitful. Significant as the bloody practicalities of imperial rule were to the new king, so also was their shadow, his sacral vision of a universal state, one in which all his vast dominion had been imposed for the conquered's good. The covenant embodied by Persian rule was henceforth to be made clear in every manifestation of royal power, whether palaces or progresses or plans for making war: harmony in exchange for humility, protection for abasement, the blessings of a new world order for obedience. This was, of course, in comparison to the propaganda of Assyria a prescription notably lacking in a relish for slaughter, but it did serve very effectively to justify global conquest without limit. After all, if it was the destiny of the King of Kings to bring peace to a bleeding world, then what were those who defied him to be ranked as if not the agents of anarchy and darkness, of an axis of evil? Tools of Drauga, they menaced not merely Persian power but also the cosmic order that it mirrored.

No wonder, then, that it had ended up an invincible conviction of imperial propagandists that there was no stronghold of Drauga so remote that it might not ultimately be purged and redeemed. The world needed to be made safe for the Truth. Such was the Persian mission. In 518, gazing eastward, Darius duly dispatched a naval squadron to reconnoiter the mysterious lands along the Indus. Invasion swiftly followed; the Punjab was subdued; a tribute of gold dust, elephants, and similar wonders was imposed. Meanwhile, at the opposite end of the empire, in the distant west, a Persian battle fleet had begun to cruise the waters of the Aegean. In 517 Samos was conquered and annexed.[12] Neighboring islands, anxious to forestall the Persian fleet, began to contemplate making a formal submission to the ambassadors of the Great King. Westward as well as eastward, it seemed, the course of empire was taking its way.

And yet, unsuspected though it might be back in the cockpit of Persian power, there was trouble brewing in the region—and not merely in Ionia but beyond the Aegean as well, in Greece. Here, in a land that to the sophisticated agents of a global monarchy could hardly help but appear an impoverished backwater, the quarrelsome and chauvinist character of Ionian public life found itself reflected in a whole multitude of fractious polities. Greece itself was little more than a geographic expression: not a country at all but a patchwork of city-states. True, the Greeks regarded themselves as a single people, united by language, religion, and custom; but as in Ionia, so in the motherland: what the various cities often seemed to have most in common was an addiction to fighting one another. Nevertheless, the same restless propensity for pushing at boundaries that in Ionia was feeding into a momentous intellectual revolution had not been without effect on the states of the mainland as well. Unlike the peoples of the Near East, the Greeks lacked viable models of bureaucracy or centralization to draw on. In their search for *eunomia*—"good governance"—they were, in a sense, on their own. Racked by chronic social tensions, they were nevertheless not entirely oblivious to the freedom that this gave them: to experiment, to innovate, to forge their own distinctive paths. "Better a tiny city perched on a rock," it might even be argued, "so long as it is well governed, than all the splendours of foolish Nineveh."[13] Ludicrous though such a claim would undoubtedly have appeared to the Persians, those masters of a global empire, there were many Greeks who were fiercely proud of their small-town eccentricities. Over the years, repeated political and social upheaval had served to set many cities on paths that were distinctively their own. To a degree unappreciated by the Persians, who were naturally dismissive of lesser breeds in a way that only the representatives of a superpower can be, the Greeks represented a potentially ominous roadblock on the path to continued expansion, for they were not a people to be broken easily to the Great King's formula for conquest. They were, rather, a people who, by the standards of the Near Eastern norm, were unsettlingly different.

And some were more different than others. In Sparta, for instance, the dominant city of the Peloponnese, a people who had once been notorious for the toxic quality of their class hatreds had metamorphosed into *homoioi*: those who were the same. Merciless and universal discipline had served to teach every Spartan, from the moment of his birth, that conformity was all. The citizen would grow up to assume his place in society, the warrior would assume his place in a line of battle. There he would be obliged to remain for the length of his life, "his feet set firmly apart, biting on his lip, taking a stand against his foe,"[14] with only death to redeem him from his duty. No longer, as they had originally done, did the Spartans rank as predators on their own kind, rich upon poor; rather, they had become hunters in a single deadly pack. For their near neighbors in particular, the consequences of this transformation had been devastating. The citizens of one state, Messenia, had been reduced to a condition of brutalized serfdom, those of others in the Peloponnese to one of political subordination. Across the entire Greek world the Spartans had won for themselves a reputation as the foremost warriors in the world. Some Greeks, rather than face the wolf-lords of the Peloponnese on the field of battle, had been known to run away in sheer terror.

And now, in a city that had once been a byword for parochialism and backwardness, an even more far-reaching revolution was stirring. Athens was potentially Sparta's only rival as the dominant power in Greece, for the city was the mistress of a hinterland, Attica, that was by Greek standards immense and that, unlike Sparta, had not been seized from other Greeks. Nevertheless, throughout Athens's history, the city had consistently punched below its weight, and by the mid-sixth century the Athenian people had grown ever more resentful of their own impotence. Crisis had bred reform, reform had bred crisis. Here were the birth pangs, so it was to prove, of a radical and startling new order. For the aristocracy, even as it continued to negotiate the swirl of its own endless rivalries, had found itself increasingly conscious of a new and unsettling cross-current, as ambitious power players began to make play with the support of the *demos*, "the people." In 546, one of these, a successful general by the name of Pisistratus, had succeeded in establishing himself as the city's undisputed strongman—a "tyrant." The word, to the Greeks, did not remotely have the bloodstained connotations that it has for us, for a *tyrannos*, almost by definition, had to have the popular touch. Without it, he could hardly hope to cling to power for long, and so it was that Pisistratus and his heirs would consistently aim to dazzle the *demos* with swagger and imposing public works. Yet increasingly, the Athenians wanted more, and there were certain aristocrats, rivals of the Pisistratids, who found themselves so resentful of their own exclusion from the rule of their city that they were prepared to take the ultimate sanction and see power handed over to the people. In 507 revolution broke out. Hippias, the son of Pisistratus, was sent into exile. *Isonomia*—"equality," equality before the law, equality of participation in the running of the state—was installed as the Athenian ideal. A great and noble experiment was embarked upon: a state in which, for the first time in Attic history, a citizen could feel himself both engaged and in control, a state, perhaps, that might indeed be worth fighting for.

And that, for the upper-class sponsors of their city's revolution, was precisely the point. Such men were no giddy visionaries but rather hard-nosed pragmatists whose goal, quite simply, was to profit as Athenian aristocrats by making their city strong. They had calculated that a people no longer divided among themselves might at last be able to present a united front to their neighbors, by taking their place not in the train of some great clan lord but as the defenders of an ideal, of *isonomia*, of Athens itself. The first year of what later generations would term the *dêmokratia* served to demonstrate that such expectations were not farfetched. As would happen millennia later, in response to the French, the Russian, and the Iranian revolutions, attempts by rival powers to snuff out the alarming new cuckoo in the nest were comprehensively, indeed triumphantly, rebuffed. Goethe's famous words on the battle of Valmy might have been applied with no less justice to the first great victories of the first great democratic state: "From here and today there begins a new epoch in the history of the world."[15]

As in Persia, then, so in Attica: something restless, dangerous, and novel had come into being. Between a global monarchy and a tiny city that prided itself on its people's autochthony there might have appeared few correspondences, and yet, as events were to prove, both were now possessed of an ideology that could have no possible tolerance of the other. Perhaps, had democracy remained confined to Athens, a clash might conceivably have been avoided, but revolutions invariably prove exportable. In 499, a series of uprisings across Ionia succeeded in toppling the tyrants who for decades had been serving the Persians in the role of quislings; democracies were established in their place; one year later, an Athenian task force joined the rebels in putting Sardis to the torch. The Athenians themselves, however, dispirited by their failure to capture the city's acropolis and by their accidental incineration of a celebrated temple, had no sooner burned the Lydian capital than they were scampering back to Attica, gripped by nerves and regret. Yet panicky though they undoubtedly felt at the notion that the far-seeing and pitiless eye of the King of Kings might soon be fixed upon them, they would surely have been even more so had they only appreciated the precise nature of the beast whose tail they had opted so cavalierly to tweak, for nothing could have been more calculated to rouse the fury of the most powerful man on the planet. To Darius, of course, it went without saying that the Ionian insurgency needed urgently to be suppressed, and that the terrorist state beyond the Aegean had to be neutralized if the northwestern flank of the empire were ever to be rendered fully secure. The longer the punishment of Athens was delayed, the greater was the risk that similar nests of rebels might proliferate throughout the mountainous and inaccessible wilds of Greece—a nightmare prospect for any Persian strategist. Geopolitics, however, was far from the only prompting at the back of the Great King's mind. Stronghold of terrorists Athens might be, but it had also stood revealed as a peculiarly viperous stronghold of the Lie. It was for the good of the cosmos, then, as well as for the future stability of Ionia that Darius began to contemplate carrying his divinely appointed mission, his war on terror, to Attica. Staging post in a necessary new phase of imperial expansion and a blow struck against the demonic foes of Ahura Mazda: the burning of Athens promised to be both.

Yet if the Athenians had little understanding of the motives and ideals of the superpower that was now ranged against them, the Persians in turn were fatally ignorant of what they faced in the democracy. To the strategists entrusted with the suppression of the Ionian revolt, there seemed nothing exceptional about the new form of government; if anything, it seemed only to have intensified the factionalism that for so long had made fighting the Yauna akin to shooting fish in a barrel.

In 494, in a climactic confrontation off the tiny island of Lade, it was Persia's spymasters as much as its admirals, and its bribes as much as its battleships, that served to provoke the final disintegration of the Ionian insurgency. Four years on, and the preparations for an expedition against Athens reflected the same core presumption: that rival factions were bound to end up dooming the city's resistance. It was no coincidence, for instance, that Datis, the commander of the Persian task force, should have been a veteran of the Ionian revolt, a general with such a specialist's understanding of how the Yauna functioned that he could actually speak a few words of Greek. Also on the expedition, and whispering honeyed reassurances into Datis's ear as to the welcome that he was bound to receive, was Hippias, the toppled Pisistratid, evidence of the Persians' perennial obsession with securing the collaboration of native elites. Yet on this occasion, as events were to prove, they had miscalculated—and fatally so. For their intelligence was worse than useless; it was out of date.

The Athenian army that confronted the invaders on the plain of Marathon, blocking the road that led to their city some twenty miles to the south, did not, as the Ionian fleet at Lade had, disintegrate. True, Athens had long been perfervid with rumors of fifth columnists and profiteers from the Great King's gold, but it was precisely the Athenians' awareness of the consequent peril that had prompted them to march out from behind their city's walls in the first place. During a siege, after all, there would have been no lack of opportunity for traitors to open the gates, but out on the field of battle, where the Greek style of fighting, warriors advancing side by side in a phalanx, meant that all had to fight as one or else be wiped out, anyone who wished to live, even a would-be traitor, had no option but to handle his spear and hold his shield for the good of all. The battle line at Marathon, in short, could not be bought. It was to the credit of Datis that he eventually came to recognize this, but still he would not abandon his conviction that every Greek city ultimately had its price. In due course, after a stand-off of several days, he resolved to put this to the test. Dividing his army, he embarked a sizable task force—including, almost certainly, his cavalry—and sent it around the Attic coast to see if its appearance in the harbor off Athens would help to unbar the city's gates. Yet it was precisely this same maneuver that gave the Athenian holding force its chance. Against all expectations, moving against a foe widely assumed to be invincible, crossing what many of the Athenians themselves must have dreaded would prove to be a plain of death, they charged an enemy that no Greek army had ever before defeated in open battle. The reward for their courage was a glorious, an immortal victory. Fearful still of treachery, however, the exhausted and blood-streaked victors had no time to savor their triumph. Instead, in the full heat of day they headed straight back for Athens, "as fast as their legs could take them."[16] They arrived in the very nick of time, for not long afterward Persian transport ships began to glide toward the city's harbor. For a few hours they lay stationary beyond its entrance; then, as the sun set at last, they raised anchor, swung around, and sailed away. The threat of invasion was over—for the moment, at any rate.

To be sure, there was no doubt that what had saved Athens on the battlefield of Marathon was first and foremost the prowess of its own citizens: not merely their courage but also the sheer pulverizing impact of their charge, the heavy crunching of spears and shields into opponents wearing, at most, quilted jerkins for protection and armed, perhaps, many of them, only with bows and slings. Yet something more had been in conflict on that fateful day than flesh and metal alone: Marathon had also been a testing of the stereotypes that both sides had of the other. The Athenians, by refusing to play the role allotted them by the Persians' spymasters, had duly served to convince themselves once and for all that the watchwords of the democracy—comradeship, equality, liberty—might indeed be more than slogans. Simultaneously, the superpower that for so long had appeared invincible had been shown to have feet of clay. The Persians might be defeated, after all. "Barbarians," the Ionians had always called them, a people whose language was gibberish, who went "bah, bah, bah"—and now, in the wake of Marathon, the Athenians began to do the same. It was a word that perfectly evoked their dread of what they had been forced to confront on the day of their great victory, an alien, milling numberless horde, jabbering for their destruction. Yet "barbarian," in the wake of such a battle, could also suggest something more: a sneer, a tone of contempt. A self-assurance, in short, more than fit to go nose to nose with that of a superpower.

Here, then, was a measure of the decisiveness of Marathon: that it helped to purge the Athenians of the deep-rooted inferiority complex the Greeks had traditionally felt whenever they compared themselves to the great powers of the Near East. Nor, as the Athenians themselves never wearied of pointing out, had the victory been won on behalf of their city alone. In its wake, even those Greeks who loathed the democracy could walk that little bit taller, confident that the qualities that distinguished them from foreigners might, just perhaps, be the mark of their superiority. Not, of course, that a temporary reverse on the distant frontier of their empire had done anything to diminish the Persians' own conceit and sense of entitlement; and so it was, ten years after Marathon, when Xerxes, Darius's son and heir, embarked on a full-scale invasion of Greece, that the resulting conflict served to provide an authentic clash of ideals. Indeed, on the Persian side, Xerxes' determination to give form to his sense of global mission was such that it took precedence over purely military considerations. So it was that, rather than leading a strike force such as Cyrus would have recognized, capable of descending on the lumbering infantrymen of the enemy with the same murderous speed that had always proved so lethal to the Greeks of Ionia, he opted instead to summon a tribute of contingents from all the manifold subject peoples of his empire, a coalition if not of the willing then of the submissively dutiful, at any rate. Naturally, this swelling of his army with a vast babel of poorly armed levies represented a fearsome headache for his harassed commissariat, but Xerxes judged that it was necessary to the proper maintenance of his dignity. After all, to what did the presence in his train of the full astounding diversity of his tributaries give glorious expression if not his rank as the lieutenant on earth of Ahura Mazda? Nor was that all. The rumor of his approach, assiduously fanned by Persian agents, promised fair to overwhelm the Greeks with sheer terror—or else, at the thought of all the potential pickings on offer, with greed. It must have seemed to Xerxes, as he embarked on his great expedition, that the whole of Greece would end up dropping like overripe fruit into his lap.

But it did not. Indeed, for all the well-honed brilliance of the invaders' propaganda chiefs, they found themselves, over the course of the invasion, being repeatedly outsmarted by the Greeks. What made this all the more striking an upset was that the Persians, in the opening rounds of the campaign, did indeed have genuine triumphs to trumpet. At the mountain pass of Thermopylae, for instance, their achievement in dislodging a force of five thousand heavy infantry from a nearly impregnable position, in wiping out hundreds of the supposedly invincible Spartans, and in killing one of their kings was a thumping one. No wonder that Xerxes invited sailors from his fleet to tour the Hot Gates, "so that they might see how the Great King deals with those lunatics who presume to oppose him."[17] No wonder either that the Peloponnesian land forces, brought the news of Thermopylae, immediately scuttled back behind the line of the Isthmus of Corinth and refused to reemerge from their bolt-hole for almost a year. Clearly, then, for any Greek resolved to continue the fight, it was essential to transmute the disaster at the Hot Gates into a display of heroism sufficiently glorious to inspire the whole of Greece to continued defiance. Indeed, in the immediate wake of Thermopylae, with their city defenseless before the Persian juggernaut, the Athenians had, if anything, an even greater stake than the Spartans in casting the dead king and his bodyguards as martyrs for liberty. Perhaps, then, it is an index of their success that the Peloponnesians, in the wake of the capture of Athens and the burning of the temples on the Acropolis, did not withdraw their fleets as they had previously withdrawn their land forces but were prepared instead to join with the Athenian ships and make a stand in the straits of Salamis. By doing so they demonstrated that the spin of the Greek propagandists had indeed been something more than spin: that the bloody defeat at Thermopylae had been, precisely as they had claimed, a kind of victory.

It was to prove a decisive one as well. At Salamis and at Plataea, on sea and then on land, the Greek allies crushingly repulsed the amphibious task force that had been ranged against them and ensured that the Pax Persica would not be extended to Greece. The failure of the attempt had certainly not been due to Persian effeminacy, or softness, or any lack of courage, "for in bravery and strength," as the Greeks themselves freely acknowledged, "the two sides were evenly matched."[18] Indisputably, however, in man-to-man combat, Greek equipment and training had proven far superior, for Plataea had confirmed the lesson of Marathon, that in pitched battle the Persian infantry was no match

2007). Another key source is Aeschylus's play *The Persians*, with its celebrated description of Salamis, written by a veteran of the Greco-Persian Wars; a useful edition is Edith Hall's (Warminster, UK: Aris and Phillips, 1996). Diodorus and Plutarch provide valuable, though late, supplementary information.

No Persian is known even so much as to have mentioned the invasion of Greece. That does not mean, however, that there are no relevant sources for this period from the Persian side. The definitive collection is Amélie Kuhrt's, published in two volumes as *The Persian Empire: A Corpus of Sources from the Achaemenid Period* (London: Routledge, 2007). The definitive book on the Persian Empire—and an epochal work of scholarship—is by Pierre Briant, translated into English by Peter T. Daniels as *From Cyrus to Alexander: A History of the Persian Empire* (Winona Lake, IN: Eisenbrauns, 2002). Other excellent recent general studies include *Ancient Persia*, by Josef Wiesehöfer (London: Tauris, 2001), and *The Persian Empire*, by Lindsay Allen (Chicago: University of Chicago Press, 2005). The catalogue of a recent exhibition at the British Museum, *Forgotten Empire: The World of Ancient Persia*, edited by John Curtis and Nigel Tallis (Berkeley and Los Angeles: University of California Press, 2005), is sumptuously illustrated.

For Persian involvement in Iraq, see the collection of essays edited by John Curtis, *Mesopotamia and Iran in the Persian Period: Conquest and Imperialism. Proceedings of a Seminar in Memory of Vladimir G. Lukonin* (London: British Museum Press, 1997). For Lydia and Ionia, see *Aspects of Empire in Achaemenid Sardis*, by Elspeth R. M. Dusinberre (Cambridge: Cambridge University Press, 2003), and *Sparda by the Bitter Sea: Imperial Interaction in Western Anatolia*, by Jack Martin Balcer (Chicago: University of Chicago Press, 1984). Balcer is also the author of a fascinating study of Darius's accession to power, *Herodotus and Bisitun: Problems in Ancient Persian Historiography* (Stuttgart: Franz Steiner, 1987). The best study of the notorious academic bog that is Persian religion is by Jean Kellens, a collection of essays translated into English as *Essays on Zarathustra and Zoroastrianism* (Costa Mesa, CA: Mazda, 2000). For the specifics of Persian warfare, see *Shadows in the Desert: Ancient Persia at War*, by Kaveh Farrokh (Oxford: Osprey, 2007). For a valuable overview of Greco-Persian relations all the way from the conquest of Ionia to Alexander, see *The Greek Wars: The Failure of Persia*, by George Cawkwell (Oxford: Oxford University Press, 2005).

The literature on the Greco-Persian Wars themselves is voluminous. Essential studies include A. R. Burns's *Persia and the Greeks: The Defence of the West*, 2nd ed. (London: Duckworth, 1984), and Peter Green's wonderfully written *The Greco-Persian Wars* (Berkeley and Los Angeles: University of California Press, 1970). The best military study is J. F. Lazenby's *The Defence of Greece 490–479 BC* (Warminster, UK: Aris and Phillips, 1993). Recent books on individual battles include *Thermopylae: The Battle That Changed the World*, by Paul Cartledge (London: Overlook Press, 2006), and *Salamis: The Greatest Naval Battle of the Ancient World, 480 BC*, by Barry Strauss (New York: Simon & Schuster, 2004). For the enduring impact of the wars on the popular imagination, see *Cultural Responses to the Persian Wars: Antiquity to the Third Millennium*, edited by Emma Bridges, Edith Hall, and P. J. Rhodes (New York: Oxford University Press, 2007). Modesty, of course, forbids me from recommending my own *Persian Fire: The First World Empire and the Battle for the West* (London: Time Warner Books, 2005).

NOTES

[1] *Nabonidus Chronicle*, col. ii, 15. Cyrus himself entered Babylon two and a half weeks later.

[2] Jeremiah 28.14.

[3] Ezekiel 32.23.

[4] Cyrus Cylinder 20. The titles used by the Persian kings were not original to them but were derived from an assortment of Near Eastern kingdoms, Babylon included.

[5] Aeschylus *The Persians* 104–5.

[6] Cyrus Cylinder 16.

[7] Herodotus 1.214.

[8] Isaiah 45.1–3.

[9] Heracleitus, quoted by Diogenes Laertius, *The Lives and Doctrines of the Eminent Philosophers*, trans. R. D. Hicks, 2 vols., Loeb Classical Library no. 184 (Cambridge, MA: Harvard University Press, 1925), 1.21.

[10] For a concise introduction to the sources that enable the events of 522 to be reconstructed, as well as the sources themselves, see the chapter "From Cambyses to Darius I," in Amélie Kuhrt, *The Persian Empire: A Corpus of Sources from the Achaemenid Period* (London: Routledge, 2007), vol. 1.

[11] Bisitun Inscription 63.

[12] A date that is probable rather than certain.

[13] Phocylides frag. 4. Despite the Assyrian reference, the poem is almost certainly a reflection of the growth of Persian power.

[14] Tyrtaeus 7.31–32.

[15] Quoted by Tim Blanning in *The Pursuit of Glory: Europe 1648–1815* (New York: Viking, 2007), 626.

[16] Herodotus 6.116.

[17] Herodotus 8.24.

[18] Herodotus 9.62.

[19] Lycurgus *Against Leocrates* 81.

2.   Pericles, Thucydides, and the Defense of Empire

DONALD KAGAN

B Y THE MIDDLE OF THE FIFTH CENTURY, when Pericles became the leading figure in Athens, defense of its empire was of the highest importance, because the empire was the key to the defense of Athens itself. It represented security against a renewal of the Persian threat, and it provided the means for warding off any future challenge from Sparta. Beyond that, its revenues were essential to Pericles' plans for making Athens the most prosperous, beautiful, and civilized city the Greeks had ever known. The glory it reflected was an essential part of his vision for Athens.

Pericles and his Athenians regarded their empire as necessary, but it also raised serious questions. Could an empire limit its growth and ambition and maintain itself in safety? Or did rule over others inevitably lead the imperial power to overreach and bring about its own ruin? Was empire, especially by Greek over Greek, morally legitimate? Or was it evidence of *hubris*, the violent arrogance that was sure to bring on the justified destruction of those who dared to rule over others as though they were gods?

It fell to Pericles, as leader of the Athenian people, to guide their policy into safe channels and to justify the empire in the eyes of the other Greeks as well as their own. In both tasks Pericles broke a sharply new path. He put an end to imperial expansion and moderated Athenian ambitions. He also put forward powerful arguments, by word as well as deed, to show that the empire was both legitimate and in the common interest of *all* the Greeks.

It is important to recall that the Athenians did not set out to acquire an empire and that the Delian League that was its forerunner came into being only because of Sparta's default, but the Athenians had good reasons for accepting its leadership. First and foremost was the fear and expectation that the Persians would come again to conquer the Greeks. The Persians had attacked them three times in two decades, and there was no reason to believe they would permanently accept the latest defeat. Second, the Athenians had hardly begun to repair the damage done by the latest Persian attack; they knew another would surely make Athens a target again. In addition, the Aegean and the lands to its east were important to Athenian trade. Their dependence on imported grain from Ukraine, which had to travel from the Black Sea, meant that even a very limited Persian campaign that gained control of the Bosporus or the Dardanelles could cut their lifeline. Finally, the Athenians had ties of common ancestry, religion, and tradition with the Ionian Greeks, who made up most of the endangered cities. Athenian security, prosperity, and sentiment all pointed toward driving the Persians from all the coasts and islands of the Aegean, the Dardanelles, the Sea of Marmora, the Bosporus, and the Black Sea.

The new alliance was one of three interstate organizations in the Greek world, alongside the Peloponnesian League and the Hellenic League formed against Persia, which had by no means lapsed when the Spartans withdrew from the Aegean. After the founding of the Delian League, the Hellenic League had an increasingly shadowy existence and collapsed at the first real test. The important, effective, and active alliances were the Peloponnesian League, led by Sparta, on the mainland and the Delian League, led by Athens, in the Aegean.

From the first, the Delian League was very effective because it was entirely and enthusiastically voluntary, its purposes were essential to its members, and its organization was clear and simple. Athens was the leader: all the members, about 140 in the beginning, swore a perpetual oath to have the same friends and enemies as Athens, in this way forming a permanent offensive and defensive alliance under Athenian leadership. Hegemony, however, was not domination. In the early years of the league, the Athenians were "leaders of autonomous allies who took part in common synods."[1] In those years, those synods determined policy and made decisions at meetings at Delos, where Athens had only one vote. In theory, Athens was only an equal partner in the synod, with the same single vote as Samos, Lesbos, Chios, or even tiny Seriphos. In fact, the system worked in Athens's favor. Athenian military and naval power, the enormous relative size of Athens's contribution, and the city's immense prestige as *hegemon* guaranteed that the many small and powerless states would be under its influence, while the larger states that might have challenged the Athenians were easily outvoted. Many years later, the embittered and rebellious Mytileneans would say, "The allies were unable to unite and defend themselves because of the great number of voters."[2] In the early years, however, there appears to have been harmony and agreement among the members, large and small, and the degree of Athens's influence was proportionate to its contribution. From the beginning, then, Athens was in the happy position of controlling the Delian League without the appearance of illegality or tyranny.

The early actions of the league must have won unanimous and enthusiastic support: the allies drove the Persians from their remaining strongholds in Europe and made the sea lanes of the Aegean safe by expelling a nest of pirates from the island of Scyros. As victory followed victory and the Persian threat seemed more remote, some allies thought the league and its burdensome obligations were no longer needed. The Athenians, however, rightly saw that the Persian threat was not gone and that it would increase to the degree that Greek vigilance waned. Thucydides makes it clear that the chief causes for the later rebellions were the allies' refusal to provide the agreed-upon ships or money and to perform the required military service. The Athenians held them strictly to account and

> were no longer equally pleasant as leaders. They no longer behaved as equals on campaigns, and they found it easy to reduce states that rebelled. The blame for this belonged to the allies themselves: for most of them had themselves assessed in quotas of money instead of ships because they shrank from military service so that they need not be away from home. As a result, the Athenian fleet was increased by means of the money they paid in, while when the allies tried to revolt, they went to war without the means or the experience.[3]

Less than a decade after its formation, perhaps in 469, the forces of the Delian League won smashing victories over the Persian fleet and army at the mouth of the Eurymedon River in Asia Minor. This decisive Persian defeat intensified the restlessness of the allies and the harshness and unpopularity of the Athenians. The rebellion and siege of Thasos from 465 to 463, which arose from a quarrel between the Athenians and the Thasians and had no clear connection with the purposes of the league, must have had a similar effect.

The first Peloponnesian War (ca. 460–445) strained Athenian resources to the limit and encouraged defection. The destruction of the Athenian expedition to Egypt in the mid-450s provided the shock that hastened the transformation from league to empire. To many, it must have seemed the beginning of the collapse of Athenian power, so it provoked new rebellions. The Athenians responded swiftly and effectively to put them down, and then took measures to ensure they would not be repeated. In some places they installed democratic governments friendly to and dependent on themselves. Sometimes they posted military garrisons, sometimes they assigned Athenian officials to oversee the conduct of the formerly rebellious state, and sometimes they used a combination of tactics. All were violations of the autonomy of the subject state.

The Athenians tightened their control of the empire even more in the 440s. They imposed the use of Athenian weights, measures, and coins, closing the local mints and so depriving the allies of a visible symbol of their sovereignty and autonomy. They tightened the rules for collection and delivery of tribute payments, requiring that the trials for those accused of violations be held in Athens. They used military force against states that rebelled or refused to pay tribute. Sometimes the Athenians confiscated territory from the offending state and gave it as a colony to loyal allies or Athenian citizens. When such a colony was composed of Athenians it was called a cleruchy. Its settlers did not form a new, independent city but remained Athenian citizens. When the Athenians suppressed a rebellion, they usually installed a democratic regime and made the natives swear an oath of loyalty. The following is the oath imposed on the people of Colophon:

I will do and say and plan whatever good I can with regard to the people of the Athenians and their allies, and I will not revolt from the people of the Athenians either in word or deed, either myself or in obedience to another. And I will love the people of the Athenians and I will not desert. And I will not destroy the democracy at Colophon, either myself or in obedience to another, either by going off to another city or by intriguing there. I will carry out these things according to the oath truly, without deceit and without harm, by Zeus, Apollo, and Demeter. And if I transgress may I and my descendants be destroyed for all time, but if I keep my oath may great prosperity come to me.[4]

A bit later they imposed a similar oath on the Chalcidians, but in this one allegiance was sworn not to the alliance but to the Athenian people alone.

The association took a critical step in the transition from league to empire in the year 454–453, when the treasury was moved from Delos to the Acropolis in Athens. The formal explanation was the threat that the Persians might send a fleet into the Aegean, following a catastrophic Athenian defeat in Egypt and confronted with a war with Sparta. We do not know whether that fear was real or merely a pretext, but the Athenians did not waste time in turning the transfer to their advantage. From that year until late in the Peloponnesian War, the Athenians took one-sixtieth of the tribute paid by the allies as first fruits for the goddess Athena Polias, patroness of the city and now of the reconstituted league. The Athenians were free to use the goddess's share as they liked, not necessarily for league purposes.

Changes so important and so radical that they transformed a voluntary league of allies into a largely involuntary empire ruled by Athens demanded justification in the ancient world of the Greeks. In most respects the Greeks resembled other ancient peoples in their attitudes toward power, conquest, empire, and the benefits that came with them. They viewed the world as a place of intense competition in which victory and domination, which brought fame and glory, were the highest goals, while defeat and subordination brought ignominy and shame. They always honored the creed espoused by Achilles, the greatest hero of Greek legend: "Always to be the best and foremost over all others." When the legendary world of aristocratic heroes gave way to the world of city-states, the sphere of competition moved up from contests between individuals, households, and clans to contests and wars between cities. In 416, more than a decade after the death of Pericles, Athenian spokesmen explained to some Melian officials their view of international relations: "Of the gods we believe, and of men we know, that by a necessity of their nature they always rule wherever they have the power."[5]

Yet the Melian Dialogue, as this famous passage in Thucydides on international *Realpolitik* in the classical world came to be known, was a dramatic presentation of the morally problematic status of the Athenian Empire. The Athenians' harsh statement is provoked by the Melians' claim that the gods will be on their side, because the Athenians are behaving unjustly toward a neutral state. The Melian complaint may refer to the specific actions taken or contemplated by the Athenians, but it would have struck a deep vein of sympathy among the Greeks. The Greeks were free from the modern prejudice against power and the security and glory it could bring, but their own historical experience was different from that of other ancient nations. Their culture had been shaped not by great empires but by small, autonomous, independent poleis, and they came to think that freedom was the natural condition for men raised in such an environment. Citizens should be free in their persons and free to maintain their own constitutions, laws, and customs, and their cities should be free to conduct their own foreign relations and to compete with others for power and glory. The Greeks also believed that the freedom made possible by the life of the polis created a superior kind of citizen and a special kind of power. The free, autonomous polis, they thought, was greater than the mightiest powers in the world. The sixth-century poet Phocylides was prepared to compare it to the great Assyrian Empire: "A little polis living orderly in a high place is greater than block-headed Nineveh."[6]

When poleis fought one another, the victor typically took control of a piece of borderland that was usually the source of the dispute. The defeated enemy was not normally enslaved, nor was his land annexed or occupied. In such matters, as in many, the Greeks employed a double standard by which they distinguished themselves from alien peoples who did not speak Greek and were not shaped by the Greek cultural tradition. Since they had not been raised as free men in free communities but lived as subjects to a ruler, they were manifestly slaves by nature, so it was perfectly all right to dominate and enslave them in reality. Greeks, on the other hand, were naturally free, as they demonstrated by creating and living in the liberal institutions of the polis. To rule over such people, to deny them their freedom and autonomy, would clearly be wrong.

That was what the Greeks thought, but they did not always act accordingly. At a very early time the Spartans had conquered the Greeks residing in their own region of Laconia and neighboring Messenia and made them slaves of the state. In the sixth century they formed the Peloponnesian League, an alliance that gave the Spartans considerable control over the foreign policy of their allies. But the Spartans generally did not interfere with the internal arrangements of the allied cities, which continued to have the appearance of autonomy. In the two decades after the Persian War, the Argives appear to have obliterated some towns in the Argolid and annexed their territory, yet such deviations from the pattern remained unusual and did not overcome the general expectation that Greeks should live as free men in autonomous poleis, not as subjects in great empires.

The Greeks shared still another belief that interfered with the comfortable enjoyment of great power and empire. They thought that any good thing amassed by men to an excessive degree led, through a series of stages, to what they called *hubris*. Such men were thought to have overstepped the limits established for human beings and thereby to have incurred *nemesis*, divine anger and retribution. These were the main ideas emerging from the oracle at Apollo's shrine at Delphi, where could be found the pair of divine warnings to man to avoid hubris: "know thyself" and "nothing in excess." To the Greeks of the fifth century, the great example of hubris and nemesis was the fate of Xerxes, Great King of the Persian Empire. His power filled him with a blind arrogance that led him to try to extend his rule over the Greek mainland and so brought disaster to himself and his people.

Therefore, when the Athenians undertook the leadership of a Greek alliance after the Persian War, and that leadership brought wealth and power and turned into what was frankly acknowledged as an empire, traditional ways of thinking provided no firm guidelines. The advantages of empire to the Athenians, tangible and intangible, were many. The most obvious was financial. Revenues paid directly by the allies in the form of tribute, indemnities, and other unspecified payments came to 600 talents annually at the beginning of the Peloponnesian War. Of the 400 additional talents of home income that came in each year, a large part also resulted from the empire, for import and other harbor duties at Piraeus and court fees paid by allied citizens whose cases were heard in Athens. Athenians also profited in the private sphere by providing services for the many visitors drawn to Piraeus and Athens by judicial and other imperial business and by the greatness of Athens itself, which the empire made possible.

The imperial revenues are sometimes thought to have been necessary for the maintenance of the democracy, providing the money to pay for the performance of public duties. But the evidence argues otherwise. Pay was introduced, after all, before the Athenians began to keep a sixtieth of the tribute for themselves. Even more telling is the fact that the Athenians continued to pay for these services even after the empire and its revenues were gone—and even introduced compensation for attendance in the Assembly in the early fourth century. On the other hand, it cannot be irrelevant that these payments were inaugurated when the success of the empire had brought great wealth to Athens in the form of booty and increased trade, and that they spread beyond jury pay in the years surrounding the introduction of Athena's tithe. It seems likely, in any case, that in Pericles' time, the people of Athens connected the growth and flourishing of the democracy with the benefits of empire.

Apart from direct financial gain and, as they thought, the financial support for their democracy, the people of Athens also received benefits in what it is now fashionable to call quality of life. The empire, according to the "Old Oligarch," allowed Athenians to mingle with people from many places, and so they discovered

various gastronomic luxuries; the specialties of Sicily, Italy, Cyprus, Egypt, Lydia, Pontus, the Peloponnesus or any other area have all been brought back to Athens because of their control of the sea. They hear all dialects, and pick one thing from one, another from another; the other Greeks tend to adhere to their own dialect and way of life and dress, but the Athenians have mingled elements from all Greeks and foreigners.[7]

A contemporary comic poet provides a more detailed list of the exotic delicacies and useful wares that the empire made available to the Athenians:

From Cyrene silphium and ox hides, from the Hellespont mackerel and all kinds of salted fish, from Italy, salt and ribs of beef . . . from Egypt sails and rope, from Syria frankincense, from Crete cypress for the gods; Libya provides abundant ivory to buy, Rhodes raisins and sweet figs, but from Euboea pears and sweet apples. Slaves from Phrygia . . . Pagasae provides tattooed slaves, Paphlagonia dates and oily almonds, Phoenicia dates and fine wheat-flour, Carthage rugs and many-colored cushions.[8]

These, as the Old Oligarch observes, are "less important matters," but they helped bring home to the Athenians the advantages of empire and the rule of the sea that it made possible.

Perhaps the greatest attraction of the empire was less tangible than any of these things, appealing to an aspect of human nature common to many cultures across the centuries. Most people prefer to think of themselves as leaders rather than followers, as rulers rather than ruled. Each Athenian took pride in the greatness of his state. The Old Oligarch, an anonymous writer who took a caustic view of Athenian self-aggrandizement, in explaining how the Athenians benefited from having allied citizens come to the courts in Athens for justice shows how the ordinary citizen enjoyed such feelings:

If the allies did not come for trials, they would only respect those Athenians who go abroad—the generals, the trierarchs and the ambassadors; but as it is, each individual ally is compelled to flatter the common people of Athens, realizing that, having come to Athens, the penalty or satisfaction that he receives at law depends solely upon the common people; such is the law at Athens.

Therefore he is compelled to plead humbly in the courts and to seize people's hands as a suppliant as they enter. This situation has increased the subjugation of the allies to the people of Athens.[9]

For all the benefits it brought to the Athenians, the imperial ledger was not entirely unbalanced, for the allies also received much value for their participation. Foremost among these advantages was freedom from Persian rule, the chief purpose for which the league had been formed, and the peace that the Athenian Callias, son of Hipponicus, had negotiated with the Persian Empire. Ionian cities had either been under barbarian rule or fighting to be free of it for well over a century, so these achievements were not insignificant. The success of the league and empire had also brought an unprecedented freedom to sail in the waters of the Aegean. In addition, the campaigns against Persia had brought a percentage of booty to the allies who had taken part in them, and the commercial boom that enriched Athens also brought wealth to many of its allies. In short, the Athenians had brought freedom from Persian rule, peace, and prosperity to all Greeks in and around the Aegean Sea.

To many, Athenian intervention also brought democracy, but that was not its aim. Pericles and the Athenians, when they could, left the existing regime in place, even when it was oligarchic or tyrannical. Only when rebellions forced them to intervene did they impose democracies, and even then not always. Pericles' imperial policy was prudent and pragmatic, not ideological. Nevertheless, over the years the Athenians instituted and supported many democracies against oligarchic or tyrannical opponents throughout the empire. From a twentieth-century perspective, this might seem like an unalloyed benefit of the empire, but it was not so viewed by everyone in the time of Pericles. Aristocrats and members of the upper classes in general regarded democracy as a novel, unnatural, unjust, incompetent, and vulgar form of government, and they were not alone in resenting the Athenian role in support of it. In many cities, probably in most, even members of the lower classes regarded Athenian intervention in their political and constitutional affairs as a curtailment of their freedom and autonomy, and would have preferred a nondemocratic constitution without Athenian interference to a democratic government with it.

Modern scholars have tried to argue that this Athenian support for democracy made the empire popular with the masses in the allied cities, and that the hostility with which they reportedly came to view it was the result of distortions caused by the aristocratic bias of the ancient writers. The consensus, however, has rightly continued to emphasize the empire's fundamental unpopularity with all classes except the small groups of democratic politicians who benefited directly from Athenian support. There is no reason to doubt the ancient opinion that Greeks outside, and especially inside, the Athenian Empire were hostile to it. Even some Athenians objected to what they deemed the immorality of Athens's behavior toward the imperial allies.

Pericles undertook to justify to each constituency Athenian rule and Athens's continued collection of the tribute. For the cities in the empire he provided justification by claiming a change in the concept behind the league. From the beginning, some league members were colonies that had been founded by Athens. Among the Greeks, colonial status implied a proud familial relationship, not inferiority. Beyond that, the Athenians had long claimed to be the founders of the Ionian cities; the Ionians not only accepted the claim but had used it to persuade the Athenians to accept the leadership in the first place. The time of the treasury's transfer was the year that had been scheduled for the quadrennial celebration of the Great Panathenaic Festival in Athens; ties between colony and mother city were normally warm and were celebrated by such religious observances. It was customary for Athens's allies to bring a cow and a full suit of armor to this festival, more as a symbol of allegiance than as a burden. It gave the colony the honor of participating in the grand procession to the sacred shrine of Athena on the Acropolis. Henceforth, all the allies of Athens would share the honor.

We need not believe that all were grateful for the honor or that they found the trappings of a colonial relationship a satisfactory reason for continuing their contributions in circumstances so different from what they had been. Their doubts were surely increased by the terms of the peace treaty with the Persian Empire negotiated by Callias in 449: "All the Greek cities of Asia are to be autonomous; no Persian satrap is to come closer than a three days' journey from the sea; no Persian warship is to sail in the waters between Phaselis and the Cyanean rocks; if the King and his generals respect these terms, the Athenians are not to send any expedition against the country over which the King rules."[10] By this agreement, the Persians gave up their claim to the Greek states on the Aegean and its coasts, as well as the Athenian lifeline through the Dardanelles to the Black Sea. The Persian Wars were now truly over, and the Athenians could claim to have completed the victory left unfinished by the Spartans.

It was a great moment, but it raised serious questions. Although Cimon, the indefatigable prosecutor of the war against Persia, was dead, his example, his memory, and his friends remained to raise doubts about a peace with what had become the traditional enemy. If there was peace with Persia, moreover, would that mean the end of allied contributions, of the league, of Athenian hegemony?

To the first problem, a question of Athenian politics, Pericles applied a skillful touch. The choice of Callias as the Athenian negotiator had been significant. He was the brother-in-law of Cimon, the husband of Elpinice. His central role was evidence that the recent friendship between Pericles and Cimon lived on after the latter's death, and he must have done much to help win the Cimonian faction over to the new policy. By various other connections Pericles had associated himself with the Cimonians, and he continued to do so throughout the years. As a modern scholar has put it, "Behind the public politics of the Athenian state was the family-politics of the great houses; here Pericles was an adept."[11]

Pericles' political operations appear to have had a public aspect as well, if the reconstruction of events by a great modern historian is correct. After their victory at Cyprus, the Athenians made a thanksgiving dedication of a tenth of the booty and commissioned the poet Simonides to commemorate the Persian defeat. It "praised the struggles on Cyprus as the most glorious deed that the world had ever seen. At the same time, it was a monument to the whole Persian War, the inclination to which had been embodied in the person of Cimon."[12] We may assume that Pericles was behind this propaganda, which implied that the war had been won by a glorious Athenian victory instead of by a negotiated peace, and which tied Cimon to the new Periclean policy. At the same time, the memorial to Cimon was a gesture meant to attract and conciliate his friends.

Pericles had need of conciliation and unity in Athens. For despite the peace, he had no thoughts of abandoning the league that had become an empire. Nor did he wish to sacrifice the glory, the political and military power, and the money that went with it. Athens needed the empire to protect its own security and to support the creation and maintenance of the great democratic society Pericles had in mind. Part of that greatness would involve a vastly expensive building program that would need to draw on the imperial treasury for nonmilitary and purely Athenian purposes. Pericles and the Athenians therefore needed to justify the continuation of allied payments as well as their diversion to new purposes.

But already there was trouble in the empire. In 454–453, 208 cities appear on the tribute list and are assessed more than 498 talents. Four years later, only 163 cities are assessed at 432 talents; but some made only partial payment, some paid late, and some surely did not pay at all. Hesitation, uncertainty, and resistance threatened the empire's existence. At the same time, the threat of Sparta loomed. The truce negotiated by Cimon would run out in a few years, but he was no longer there to calm Spartan fears. Great differences remained between the two powers, and there was no certainty that they could be overcome without war. Yet Pericles' plans required peace.

Not long after Callias's peace was concluded, Pericles tried to solve his problems with a most imaginative proposal. He introduced a bill

> to invite all Greeks, wherever they lived, whether in Europe or in Asia, whether small cities or large, to send representatives to a congress at Athens, to deliberate about the holy places that the barbarians had destroyed, and about the sacrifices that they [the Greeks] owed, having promised them to the gods when they fought against the barbarians, and about the sea, so that all might sail it without fear and keep the peace.[13]

Messengers were sent to all corners of the Greek world to deliver an invitation to "share in the plans for the peace and common interests of Greece." Pericles, as one scholar has put it, was "calling on the Greek world to set up another organization to do what the Spartan-led Greek alliance of 480 should have done but had failed to do, and to provide for the peacetime needs which the Delian League had hitherto satisfied."[14]

Beyond that, the invitation presented an Athenian claim to Greek leadership on a new foundation. While war had brought the Greeks together originally, the maintenance of peace and security would cement their union from then on. Religious piety, pan-Hellenism, and the common good were now to justify continued loyalty and sacrifice.

Was Pericles sincere? The temples burned by the Persians were almost all in Attica, and the fleet that would keep the peace would be chiefly Athenian. Pericles may therefore have expected the Spartans and their allies to reject his proposal and thus provide him with a new justification for consolidating the empire. On the other hand, Pericles could honestly have been trying to achieve Greek freedom, security, and unity by this device. The cynical view ignores the facts of Pericles' recall of and rapprochement with Cimon, and the truce with Sparta, plainly intended to be a preliminary to a new policy of lasting peace. But the picture of Pericles as a disinterested devotee of pan-Hellenic cooperation neglects the great advantages to Athens if the congress should meet and approve his proposals. Pericles could well have thought there was a chance the Spartans would accept the invitation. The policy of its militant faction had brought disaster to Sparta and raised Athens to new heights. Sparta's agreement to the Five Years' Peace of 451 shows that this faction had been discredited. It was not unreasonable to expect that the peace faction, impressed by Pericles' unexpected alliance with Cimon and his apparent conversion to a new foreign policy, might take advantage of the troubles in Athens's maritime empire to negotiate a lasting peace, as in Cimon's time. Such a development would achieve Pericles' goals and represent a diplomatic victory for his new policy of pacific imperialism.

If Sparta refused, nothing would have been lost and much gained. Athens would have shown its pan-Hellenic spirit, its religious devotion, and its willingness to lead the Greeks for the common benefit; it would thus have gained a clear moral basis for pursuing its own goals without hindrance or complaint from others.

The Spartans declined the invitation to participate in the new plan for international cooperation, and the congress did not go forward. This episode announced to the Greek world that Athens was ready to take the lead in carrying out a sacred responsibility. It also provided

Athens with a justification for rebuilding its own temples. Pericles was now free to restore order to the empire, to continue collecting tribute on a new basis, and to use the revenue for the projects he had in mind.

A mutilated papyrus now located in Strasbourg provides a good idea of these plans. The papyrus apparently reports a decree that Pericles proposed in the summer of 449, soon after the failure of the congress. Five thousand talents were to be taken from the treasury at once to be used for the construction of new temples on the Acropolis, with another two hundred transferred annually for the next fifteen years to complete the work. The building program, however, would not interfere with the maintenance of the fleet, which justified the payment of tribute. The council would see to it that the old ships would be kept in good repair and ten new ships added annually. If there had been any question before, there could be none now: the Delian League, the alliance (*symmachia*) of autonomous states, had become what the Athenians themselves were increasingly willing to call an empire (*archê*), an organization that still produced common benefits but was dominated by the Athenians and brought them unique advantages.

A few years after the new program had begun, Pericles found himself challenged by a formidable political faction led by Thucydides, son of Melesias, a brilliant orator and political organizer. He used the usual personal attacks to win support, alleging that Pericles was trying to establish himself as tyrant. This he cleverly combined with an assault on the use of imperial funds for the Periclean building program. Plutarch reports the essence of the complaints that were made in the assembly:

> The people is dishonored and in bad repute because it has removed the common money of the Hellenes from Delos to Athens. Pericles has deprived it of the most fitting excuse that it was possible to offer to its accusers, that it removed the common funds to this place out of fear of the barbarian and in order to protect it. Hellas certainly is outraged by a terrible arrogance [*hubris*] and is manifestly tyrannized when it sees that we are gilding and adorning our city like a wanton woman, dressing it with expensive stones and statues and temples worth millions, with money extorted from them for fighting a war.[15]

The attack was shrewd, subtle, and broad in its appeal. It was not against the empire itself or the tribute derived from it, which would have alienated most Athenians. Instead it complained, on the one hand, about the misdirection of funds to the domestic program of Pericles. This reminded the friends of Cimon who were now part of the Periclean coalition that the original Cimonian policy had been abandoned and perverted. On the other hand, it reached out to a broader constituency by taking a high moral tone. Employing the language of traditional religion and old-fashioned morality, it played on the ambiguity many Athenians felt toward their rule over fellow Greeks.

Thucydides' attacks forced Pericles to defend the empire and his new imperial policy before the Athenians themselves. In answer to the main complaint he offered no apology. The Athenians, he said, need make no account of the money they received from their allies so long as they protected them from the barbarian:

> They furnish no horse, no ship, no hoplite, but only money, which does not belong to the giver but to the receiver if he carries out his part of the bargain. But now that the city has prepared itself sufficiently with the things necessary for war, it is proper to employ its resources for such works as will bring it eternal fame when they are completed, and while they are being completed will maintain its prosperity, for all kinds of industries and a variety of demands will arise which will waken every art, put in motion every hand, provide a salary for almost the entire city from which at the same time it may be beautified and nourished.[16]

The first part of this rebuttal answered the moral attack. The use of imperial funds for Athenian purposes was not analogous to tyranny, Pericles asserted, but to the untrammeled use of wages or profits by a man who has entered a contract. If there was any moral breach, it must be on the part of any allies that shrank from paying the tribute while Athens continued to provide protection. The second part was aimed especially at the lower classes, who benefited from the empire most directly, and reminded them in the plainest terms what it meant to them.

The Athenians understood Pericles well, and in 443 he called for an ostracism that served both as a vote of confidence in his leadership and as a referendum on his policies. Thucydides was expelled, and Pericles reached new heights of political influence. The people supported him not least because of the powerful stake they had in the empire.

The concept of empire does not win favor in the world today, and the word "imperialism" derived from it has carried a powerfully pejorative meaning from its very invention in the nineteenth century. Both words imply domination imposed by force or the threat of force over an alien people in a system that exploits the ruled for the benefit of the rulers. Although tendentious attempts are made to apply the term "imperialism" to any large and powerful nation that is able to influence weaker ones, a more neutral definition based on historical experience requires political and military control to justify its use.

In holding such views, the people of our time are unique among those who have lived since the birth of civilization. If, however, we are to understand the empire ruled by the Athenians of Pericles' time and their attitudes toward it, we must be alert to the great gap that separates their views from the opinions of our own time. These developments were a source of pride and gratification, but in some respects they also caused embarrassment and, at least to some Athenians, shame. Pericles himself confronted the problem more than once and addressed it with extraordinary honesty and directness, although neither he nor the Athenians were ever able to resolve its ambiguities.

The Athenians repeatedly acknowledged the unpopularity of their rule, and the historian Thucydides, a contemporary of outstanding perceptiveness, makes the point in his own voice. At the beginning of the war, he tells us,

> Good will was thoroughly on the side of the Spartans, especially since they proclaimed that they were liberating Greece. Every individual and every state was powerfully moved to help them by word or deed in any way they could. . . . So great was the anger of the majority against the Athenians, some wanting to be liberated from their rule, the others fearing that they would come under it.[17]

Pericles was fully aware of these feelings, and he understood both the ethical problems and practical dangers they presented. Yet he never wavered in his defense of the empire.

In 432, when the threat of war was imminent, an Athenian embassy arrived at Sparta, ostensibly "on other business," but really to present Athens's position to the Spartans and their assembled allies. Their arguments were fully in accord with those of Pericles. The ambassadors argued that the Athenians acquired their empire as a result of circumstances they did not set in motion and of the natural workings of human nature. On the one hand, they pointed out,

> We did not acquire this empire by force, but only after you [Spartans] refused to stand your ground against what was left of the barbarian, and the allies came to us and begged us to become their leaders. It was the course of events that forced us to develop our empire to its present status, moved chiefly by fear, then by honor, and later by advantage. Then, when we had become hated by most of the allies and some of them had rebelled and been subdued, and you were no longer as friendly to us as you had been but were suspicious and at odds with us, it was no longer safe to let go, for all rebels would go over to your side. And no one can be blamed for looking to his own advantage in the face of the greatest dangers.[18]

On the contrary, they continued, the Athenians had only done as the Spartans would have had to do had they maintained their leadership. In that case, they would have become equally hated. "Thus we have done nothing remarkable or contrary to human nature in accepting the empire when it was offered to us and then refusing to give it up, conquered by the greatest motives, honor, fear, and advantage."[19]

Pericles certainly thought that circumstances had made the empire inevitable, and the mainspring of Athenian action after Plataea and Mycale had been the general fear that the Persians would return. As the league achieved success and the allies' commitment waned, the Athenians feared the dissolution of the league and the return of the Persians. When the Spartans became hostile, the Athenians feared allied defections to the new enemy. The compulsion that was needed to deal with these problems created a degree of hatred that made it too dangerous to give up control, as Pericles would explain to the Athenians later on:

Do not think that we are fighting only over the question of freedom or slavery; on the contrary, the loss of our empire is also at stake and the danger from those in the empire who hate us. And it is no longer possible to give it up, if any among you, moved in the panic of the moment to the abandonment of responsible action, wants to put on the trappings of virtue. For by now you hold this empire as a tyranny, which it may have been wrong to acquire but is too dangerous to let go.[20]

Pericles clearly saw the dangers that argued for the maintenance of the empire, but he was moved by the claims of honor and advantage, as well. In the great Funeral Oration of 431, he called attention to the tangible advantages brought by the empire and its revenues:

We have provided for the spirit many relaxations from labor with games and festivals regularly throughout the year, and our homes are furnished with beauty and good taste, and our enjoyment of them drives away care. All the good things of the earth flow into our city because of its greatness, and we are blessed with the opportunity to enjoy products from the rest of the world no less than those we harvest here at home.[21]

But these pleasures and advantages were far less important to Pericles than the honor and glory the Athenians derived from the empire, rewards that justified the risk of their lives. He asked his fellow citizens "every day to look upon the power of our city and become lovers [erastai] of her, and when you have appreciated her greatness consider that all this has been established by brave men who knew their duty and were moved to great deeds by a sense of honor."[22] At a darker moment, in the next year, when the possibility of ultimate defeat could not be ignored, Pericles once again called the Athenians' attention to the power and glory of their imperial achievement and to its lasting value:

To be sure, the man who does not like our activities will find fault with all this, but the man who, like us, wants to accomplish something will make it his goal, and those who do not achieve it will be jealous of us. To be hated and unpopular for the time being has always been the fate of those who have undertaken to rule over others, but whoever aims at the greatest goals must accept the ill-will and is right to do so. For hatred does not last long, but the brilliance of the present moment is also the glory of the future passed on in everlasting memory. With this foreknowledge of future glory you must behave with honor at this time and by the zeal of your efforts obtain both now.[23]

Such arguments were not mere rhetoric. Pericles spoke at critical moments in Athenian history, reaching out to the deepest and most important values cherished by his fellow citizens, and everything we know of him indicates that he cherished them too. But he also valued the empire for reasons that were not so important and appealing to the average Athenian. He wanted to create a new kind of state, a place for the development of the aesthetic and intellectual greatness inherent in humanity and especially in Greek culture. Athens was to be the "education of Greece," and toward that end the city had to attract the greatest poets, painters, sculptors, philosophers, artists, and teachers of every kind. The power and wealth brought by empire was needed for that purpose and also to pay for the staging and performance of the great poems and plays they wrote, the magnificent buildings they erected, and the beautiful paintings and sculptures with which they enriched the city.

This was a vision that required an empire, but an empire different from any that had ever existed, even from the one created by Cimon. This new kind of empire needed the security and income for nonmilitary purposes that could only come in time of peace. Yet the Athenian Empire, like all its predecessors, had been achieved by war, and many people could not conceive of one without the other. The problem was intensified by the character of the Athenian empire, a power based not on a great army dominating vast stretches of land but on a navy that dominated the sea. This unusual empire dazzled perceptive contemporaries. The Old Oligarch pointed out some of its special advantages:

It is possible for small subject cities on the mainland to unite and form a single army, but in a sea empire it is not possible for islanders to combine their forces, for the sea divides them, and their rulers control the sea. Even if it is possible for islanders to assemble unnoticed on one island, they will die of starvation. Of the mainland cities which Athens controls, the large ones are ruled by fear, the small by sheer necessity; there is no city which does not need to import or export something, but this will not be possible unless they submit to those who control the sea.[24]

Naval powers, moreover, can make hit-and-run raids on enemy territory, doing damage without many casualties; they can travel distances impossible for armies; they can sail past hostile territory safely, while armies must fight their way through; they need not fear crop failure, for they can import what they need. In the Greek world, besides, all their enemies were vulnerable: "every mainland state has either a projecting headland or an offshore island or a narrow strait where it is possible for those who control the sea to put in and harm those who dwell there."[25]

Thucydides admired sea power no less and depicted its importance more profoundly. His reconstruction of early Greek history, describing the ascent of civilization, makes naval power the dynamic, vital element. First comes a navy, then suppression of piracy and safety for commerce. The resulting security permits the accumulation of wealth, which allows the emergence of walled cities. This in turn allows the acquisition of greater wealth and the growth of empire, as the weaker cities trade independence for security and prosperity. The wealth and power so obtained permit the expansion of the imperial city's power. This paradigm perfectly describes the rise of the Athenian Empire. Yet Thucydides presents it as a natural development, inherent in the character of naval power and realized for the first time in the Athens of his day.[26]

Pericles himself fully understood the unique character of the naval empire as the instrument of Athenian greatness, and on the eve of the great Peloponnesian War he encouraged the Athenians with an analysis of its advantages. The war would be won by reserves of money and control of the sea, where the empire gave Athens unquestioned superiority.

If they march against our land with an army, we shall sail against theirs; and the damage we do to the Peloponnesus will be something very different from their devastation of Attica. For they can not get other land in its place without fighting, while we have plenty of land on the islands and the mainland; yes, command of the sea is a great thing.[27]

In the second year of the war, Pericles made the point even more strongly, as he tried to restore the fighting spirit of the discouraged Athenians:

I want to explain this point to you, which I think you have never yet thought about; it is about the greatness of your empire. I have not mentioned it in my previous speeches, nor would I speak of it now, since it sounds rather like boasting, if I did not see that you are discouraged beyond reason. You think you rule only over your allies, but I assert that of the two spheres that are open to man's use, the land and the sea, you are the absolute master of all of one, not only of as much as you now control but of as much more as you like. And there is no one who can prevent you from sailing where you like with the naval force you now have, neither the Great King, nor any nation on earth.[28]

This unprecedented power, however, could be threatened by two weaknesses. The first resulted from an intractable geographic fact: the home of this great naval empire was a city located on the mainland and subject to attacks from land armies. Since they were not islanders, their location was a point of vulnerability, for the landed classes are reluctant to see their houses and estates destroyed.

Pericles made the same point: "Command of the sea is a great thing," he said. "Just think; if we were islanders, who could be less exposed to conquest?"[29] But Pericles was not one to allow problems presented by nature to stand in the way of his goals. Since the Athenians would be invulnerable as islanders, they must become islanders. Accordingly, he asked the Athenians to abandon their fields and homes in the country and move into the city. In the space between the Long Walls they could be fed and supplied from the empire, and could deny a land battle to the enemy. In a particularly stirring speech, Pericles said, "We must not grieve for our homes and land, but for human lives, for they do not make men, but men make them. And if I thought I could persuade you I would ask you to go out and lay waste to them yourselves and show the Peloponnesians that you will not yield to them because of such things."[30]

But not even Pericles could persuade the Athenians to do that in mid-century. The employment of such a strategy based on cold intelligence and reason, flying in the face of tradition and the normal passions of human beings, would require the kind of extraordinary leadership that only he could hope to exercise, and even in the face of a Spartan invasion in 465–446, Pericles was not able to persuade the Athenians to abandon their farms. In 431 he imposed his strategy, and held to it only with great difficulty. But by then he had become strong enough to make it the strategy of Athens.

The second major weakness was less tangible but no less serious, arising from the very dynamism that had brought the naval empire into being. Shrewd observers, both Athenians and foreigners, recognized this characteristic of imperial exuberance and the opportunities and dangers it presented. Many years after Pericles' death, his ward, Alcibiades, arguing for an imperial adventure against Sicily, painted the picture of an empire whose natural dynamism could only be tamed at the cost of its own destruction. Athens should respond to all opportunities for expanding its influence, he said, "for that is the way we obtained our empire, . . . eagerly coming to the aid of those who call on us, whether barbarians or Greeks; if, on the other hand, we keep our peace and draw fine distinctions as to whom we should help, we would add little to what we already have and run the risk of losing the empire itself."[31] Like Pericles, he warned that it was too late for Athens to change its policies; having launched upon the course of empire, the city could not safely give it up: it must rule or be ruled. But Alcibiades went further, asserting that the Athenian Empire had acquired a character that did not permit it to stop expanding—an inner, dynamic force that did not allow for limits or stability: "A State that is naturally active will quickly be destroyed by changing to inactivity, and people live most safely when they accept the character and institutions they already have, even if they are not perfect, and try to differ from them as little as possible."[32]

In 432, when they tried to persuade the Spartans to declare war on Athens, the Corinthians made a similar point from a hostile perspective, connecting the dynamic nature of the empire with the similar nature of the Athenians themselves. They drew a sharp contrast between the placid, immobile, defensive character of the Spartans and the dangerous and aggressive character of the Athenians:

> When they have thought of a plan and failed to carry it through to full success, they think they have been deprived of their own property; when they have acquired what they aimed at, they think it only a small thing compared with what they will acquire in the future. If it happens that an attempt fails, they form a new hope to compensate for the loss. For with them alone it is the same thing to hope and to have, when once they have invented a scheme, because of the swiftness with which they carry out what they have planned. And in this way they wear out their entire lives with labor and dangers, and they enjoy what they have least of all men—because they are always engaged in acquisition and because they think their only holiday is to do what is their duty and also because they consider tranquil peace a greater disaster than painful activity. As a result, one would be correct in saying that it is their nature neither to enjoy peace themselves nor allow it to other men.[33]

Pericles emphatically disputed such analyses. He did not believe that the Athenian naval empire needed to expand without limit or that the democratic constitution and the empire together had shaped an Athenian citizen who could never be quiet and satisfied. This is not to say that he was blind to the dangers of excessive ambition. He knew there were Athenians who wanted to conquer new lands, especially in the western Mediterranean, Sicily, Italy, and even Carthage. But he was firmly against further expansion, as his future actions would clearly demonstrate. During the great Peloponnesian War, he repeatedly warned the Athenians against trying to increase the size of the empire. It is also revealing that he never spoke of the tremendous potential power of the naval empire until the year before his death, when the Athenians were despondent and needed extraordinary encouragement. He held back from this not merely, as he said, to avoid boastfulness, but chiefly to avoid fanning the flames of excessive ambition.

If Pericles ever had planned to expand the empire, the disastrous result of the Egyptian campaign in the 450s seems to have convinced him otherwise. Its failure shook the foundations of the empire and threatened the safety of Athens itself. From that time forward, Pericles worked consistently to resist the desires of ambitious expansionists and avoid undue risks. He plainly believed that intelligence and reason could restrain unruly passions, maintain the empire at its current size, and use its revenues for a different, safer, but possibly even greater glory than the Greeks had yet known. Pericles considered the Athenian Empire large enough and its expansion both unnecessary and dangerous. The war against Persia was over; now the success of Pericles' plans and policies depended on his ability to make and sustain peace with the Spartans.

Thus, Pericles' defense of the Athenian Empire required a complex strategy. The Athenians needed to deter rebellions by the great power of their fleet and the readiness to crush uprisings when they occurred, as Pericles did against Euboea in 446–445 and Samos in 440, and other places at other times. At the same time, the policy of controlling the empire was firm but not brutal, as it became after the death of Pericles in 429. His successors killed all the men and sold the women and children into slavery at Scione and Melos. Neither Cimon nor Pericles ever permitted such atrocities. At the same time as he counseled keeping the allies under firm control, he also resisted the pressure toward further expansion, fearing that it would endanger the empire Athens already had. Finally, he continued to make the effort to persuade Athenian critics and the other Greeks that the Athenian Empire was necessary, justified and no menace to other states. Although Thucydides was doubtful that a democracy could restrain its ambition and conduct an empire with moderation for long, he believed that it could so under an extraordinary leader like Pericles.

FURTHER READING

The nature and elements of the Athenian Empire are best outlined in the classic survey of Russel Meiggs, *The Athenian Empire* (Oxford: Oxford University Press, 1972), updated by Malcom McGregor, *The Athenians and Their Empire* (Vancouver: University of British Columbia Press, 1987), and P. J. Rhodes and the Classical Association, *The Athenian Empire* (Oxford: Oxford University Press, 1985). Controversy arises over whether the

Athenians were exploitive imperialists or enlightened democrats who protected the poor abroad through their advocacy of popular government. The arguments for both views are set out well in Loren J. Samons II, *The Empire of the Owl: Athenian Imperial Finance* (New Haven, CT: Yale University Press, 2000), and Donald W. Bradeen, "The Popularity of the Athenian Empire," *Historia* 9 (1960): 257–69. G.E.M. de Ste. Croix most forcefully advanced the argument of Athens as a well-meaning protector of the underclasses; see "The Character of the Athenian Empire," *Historia* 3 (1954): 1–41, which should be read alongside the classic account of Athenian imperial finance by M. I. Finley, "The Fifth-Century Athenian Empire: A Balance Sheet," in *Imperialism in the Ancient World*, ed. P.D.A. Garnsey and C. R. Whittaker, 103–26 (Cambridge: Cambridge University Press, 1978).

NOTES

[1] Thucydides 1.97.1.

[2] Thucydides 3.10.5.

[3] Thucydides 1.99.2–3.

[4] B. D. Meritt, H. T. Wade-Gery, and M. F. McGregor, *The Athenian Tribute Lists*, vol. 2 (Princeton, NJ: Princeton University Press, 1949), 69.

[5] Thucydides 5.105.

[6] Phocylides frag. 5.

[7] Pseudo-Xenophon *Respublica Atheniensium* 2.7–8. This work was falsely attributed to the historian Xenophon, and its true author is unknown. He is generally referred to as "the Old Oligarch" because of this work's antidemocratic views, but we do not know his age or the purpose of his work, which is usually dated by internal evidence to the 420s.

[8] Hermippus in Athenaeus 1.27e–28a.

[9] Pseudo-Xenophon *Respublica Atheniensium* 1.18.

[10] Diodorus Siculus 12.4.5–6.

[11] Raphael Sealey, "The Entry of Pericles into History," *Hermes* 84 (1956): 247.

[12] Eduard Meyer, *Forschungen zur alten Geschichte*, vol. 2 (Halle: Max Niemeyer, 1899), 19–20.

[13] Plutarch *Pericles* 17.1.

[14] Some scholars have doubted the authenticity of the Congress Decree, as it is called. For a good discussion, see Russel Meiggs, *The Athenian Empire* (Oxford: Oxford University Press, 1972), 151–52, 512–15. Plutarch does not give a date for the decree, but the sequence adopted here is the one chosen by those who accept its reality.

[15] Pericles 12.2.

[16] Pericles 12:3–4.

[17] Thucydides 2.8.4.

[18] Thucydides 1.75.3–5.

[19] Thucydides 1.76.2.

[20] Thucydides 2.63.1–2.

[21] Thucydides 2.38.

[22] Thucydides 2.43.1.
[23] Thucydides 2.64.3–6.
[24] Pseudo-Xenophon 1.2–3.
[25] Pseudo-Xenophon 2.4–6, 11–13.
[26] Thucydides 1.4–19.
[27] Pericles 1.143.4.
[28] Pericles 2.62.1–2.
[29] Pericles 143.4–5.
[30] Pericles 1.143.5.
[31] Thucydides 6.18.2.
[32] Thucydides 6.18.7.
[33] Thucydides 1.70.

3. Why Fortifications Endure
A Case Study of the Walls of Athens during the Classical Period

DAVID L. BERKEY

T HE HISTORY OF ATHENS during the classical period of Greek history is closely related to the building and rebuilding of the city's walls, as well as the extension of its defensive perimeter along the border of Attica. With every phase of construction, the walls transformed the landscape and symbolized Athenian power, both at its peak and at its nadir.[1] Thousands of Athenian citizens and slaves constructed these walls and forts, many of whom toiled incessantly at moments of danger and uncertainty in the polis's history. Throughout the classical period, their construction was a critical public works project of great political and strategic significance to Athens. In our contemporary era of sophisticated technology, fortifications seem to remain ubiquitous, and they reappear in new and innovative forms even as each new generation of military strategists seems to dismiss their utility. A review of the century-long history of Athenian fortifications illustrates why walls endure, and how construction practices evolve over time to meet new diverse military and political agendas.

These grand investments of the city's resources, both human and material, in the defense of Athens are associated with some of the city's most prominent politicians and military commanders, in particular Themistocles, Pericles, and Conon. Following a time of both crisis and triumph at the end of the Persian Wars, Themistocles began the enlargement of Athens's defenses and positioned the city to become the foremost naval power in the Greek world. In the following decades,

Pericles ushered in the next phase in the fortification, the building of the Long Walls. By the end of the century, years of conflict during the Peloponnesian War had led to the destruction of these walls. The resilient Athenian democracy commenced the postwar period with a vehement desire to rehabilitate the city's position within the interstate system. Conon recognized the significance of the polis's walls and turned his attention to bolstering them. All of these leaders recognized the strategic value of strong defensive fortifications, but the circumstances under which these projects were undertaken and their significance to the polis at given points in time are unique. As the political context shifted, the walls served different strategic purposes. By examining their history during the classical period, we are able to ascertain their shifting strategic value and suggest contemporary historical parallels to these ancient relics of Athens's imperial glory.

Themistocles' strategy with regard to the Persian invasion of Attica provided for the safety of Athenian women and children and enabled the men of the polis to stage an aggressive military response. The walls of Athens were inadequate for the passive defense of the polis in the face of the strength of Xerxes' forces. While the Acropolis itself was girded by a wall that employed Cyclopean masonry—so called because the ancient Greeks believed that the massive blocks of stone used to construct fortifications of this type had been placed there by the legendary race of giants—the mass of Athenian citizens would certainly have perished during a direct, let alone prolonged, Persian assault.[2] The decree of Themistocles of 480 bc demonstrates the extraordinary measures that the Athenians took to save their lives, evacuating Attica and abandoning their territory to the barbarians:[3]

The *city* shall be *entrusted* to Athena, Athen||s' [Protectress, and to the] *other* gods, all of them, for protectio|n *and* [defense against the] *Barbarian* on behalf of the country. The Athenian|s [in their entirety and the aliens] who live in Athens | shall place [their children and their women] *in* Troezen | [-21-] the Founder of the land. [T||he elderly and (movable)] property shall (for safety) be deposited at Salamis. | [The Treasurers and] the Priestesses are [to remain] on the Akropoli|s [and guard the possessions of the] gods. The rest of the Athe│[nians in their entirety and those] *aliens* who have reached young manhood shall em│bark [on the readied] two hundred ships and they *shall* repu││lse the [Barbarian for the sake of] liberty, both their │ own [and that of the other Hellenes,] in common with the Lacedaimmonians, Co│rin[thians, Aeginetans] and the others who wis││h *to have a share* [in the danger].

As the Persians approached Attica, they burned the poleis of Thespiae and Plataea, whose citizens had refused to medize (that is, provide assistance to the Persians).[4] Under these desperate circumstances, Herodotus also mentions that in addition to those Athenians who had been entrusted with the defense of the Acropolis,

> some indigent people who, in an effort to ward off the invaders, had barricaded themselves on the Acropolis with a rampart of doors and planks of wood. They had refused to withdraw from their country to Salamis not only because of their poverty but also because of their conviction that they had discovered the true significance of the oracle delivered by the Pythia: the prophecy that the wooden wall would be impregnable was interpreted by them to mean that this very place and not the ships was to be their refuge.[5]

Themistocles' interpretation of Aristonike's oracular response,[6] namely, that the "wooden wall" referred to the Athenians' construction of a fleet of triremes funded with the revenue from their silver mines at Laureion, proved to be correct. The success of Themistocles' naval strategy at Salamis was decisive for the victory of the Greeks over the Persian fleet.[7] In contrast, the Persian army killed those who had remained behind in Athens, plundered the sanctuaries, and set fire to the place.[8]

In the following year, the Persian general Mardonius recaptured the empty city of Athens, and before retreating to Boeotia he demolished its walls and burned the city to the ground: "But since he had had no success in persuading them [the Athenians] to do so [i.e., make an agreement with him], and he had now learned the whole truth, he demolished all walls, buildings, and sanctuaries still standing, leaving everything in a heap of ruins."[9] When the Athenians returned to their city after the defeat of Mardonius at the Battle of Plataea in 479 BC, they encountered the carnage of their ruined homes and desecrated shrines and temples.[10] Thucydides describes the scene to which the Athenians returned:

> Meanwhile the Athenian people, after the departure of the barbarian from their country, at once proceeded to bring over their children and wives, and such property as they had left, from the places where they had deposited them, and prepared to rebuild their city and their walls. For only isolated portions of the circumference had been left standing, and most of the houses were in ruins; though a few remained, in which the Persian grandees had taken up their quarters.[11]

In the wake of this violent destruction, the Athenians' immediate concern was to establish a secure environment in which they could begin to reconstruct their lives. It was not possible for the Athenians to ignore the losses they had suffered. Just as Americans today wrestle with the challenge of developing a fitting tribute to those who perished at Ground Zero in New York City, the question of how to memorialize the dead and commemorate the event was of critical importance to the citizens of Athens.[12] They elected not to reuse the material from their destroyed temples in the construction of new buildings. Rather, they left the stones to commemorate the Persian sack, perhaps in accordance with the Oath of Plataea:[13] "and having defeated the barbarians in war, I will not raze any of the cities that fought against them, and I will rebuild none of the temples that have been burned and cast down, but I will leave them as a monument to men hereafter, a memorial to the impiety of the barbarians."[14] Accordingly, when the Athenians constructed a new wall to guard the northern side of the Acropolis and decided to incorporate architectural fragments from the archaic temple (most strikingly, the temple's old column drums), the effect was to serve as a war memorial that provided a vivid reminder of the Persian destruction of the city.[15]

Thucydides initiates his discussion of the Pentekontaetia with the construction of the Themistoclean walls, recognizing it as an early stage in the growth of Athenian power:[16]

Perceiving what they were going to do, the Spartans sent an embassy to Athens. They would have themselves preferred to see neither her nor any other city in possession of a wall; though here they acted principally at the instigation of their allies, who were alarmed at the strength of her newly acquired navy, and the valor which she had displayed in the war with the Persians. They begged her not only to abstain from building walls for herself, but also to join them in throwing down the remaining walls of the cities outside of the Peloponnesus. They did not express openly the suspicious intention with regard to the Athenians that lay behind this proposal but urged that by these means the barbarians, in the case of a third invasion, would not have any strong place, such as in this invasion they had in Thebes, for their base of operation; and that the Peloponnesus would suffice for all as a base both for retreat and offense. After the Spartans had thus spoken, they were, on the advice of Themistocles, immediately dismissed by the Athenians, with the answer that ambassadors should be sent to Sparta to discuss the question. Themistocles told the Athenians to send him off with all speed to Lacedaemon, but not to dispatch his colleagues as soon as they had selected them, but to wait until they had raised their wall to the height from which defense was possible. Meanwhile the whole population in the city was to labor at the wall, the Athenians, their wives, and their children, sparing no edifice, private or public, which might be of any use to the work, but throwing all down.[17]

Thucydides makes a correlation between Athens's possession of walls and its power. He concludes by commenting that the alacrity with which this circuit was built compromised the quality of its workmanship:

> In this way the Athenians walled their city in a short space of time. To this day the building shows signs of the haste of its execution; the foundations are laid of stones of all kinds, and in some places not wrought or fitted, but placed just in the order in which they were brought by the different hands; and many columns, too, from tombs and sculpted stones were put in with the

rest. For the bounds of the city were extended at every point of the circumference; and so they laid hands on everything without exception in their haste.[18]

The Athenians, therefore, demonstrated firm resolve to defend themselves. Perhaps Thucydides is also drawing a parallel between the city's walls and the rise of the Athenian Empire. Both were formed rapidly, and both marked a rupture with the past. The Athenians incorporated the graves of their ancestors into the wall, and with their imperial power they experienced unprecedented prosperity, thereby transforming both the city and its landscape. The archaeological remains of this circuit of walls, 6.5 km in length, reveal that while it was hastily built,[19] its construction was solid.[20]

Thucydides' discussion of the birth of the Athenian Empire is famous and explains the strategic motivation for the enlargement of the circuit of Athens's walls. It also shows the tenuous nature of the relationship between Athens and Sparta and their history of non-cooperation, which stretched back to before the Persian Wars.[21] The rise of Athenian power also led to the formation of a bipolar structure in the interstate system.[22] Athens and Sparta also differed from each other with respect to matters of defense. Given that walls are a ubiquitous feature of archaic and classical poleis, it is notable that Sparta did not possess them.[23] Militaristic Spartan society saw no valor in its citizens seeking cover behind defensive fortifications,[24] and it was not until Epaminondas's invasions of the Peloponnese in the decade following the Spartan defeat at the Battle of Leuctra (371 BC) that the Spartans were forced to defend their native territory and witness firsthand the construction of hostile walled cities.[25]

Themistocles also pursued his earlier plan of making Piraeus the main harbor of Athens, both in military and in commercial terms, an act that was a logical precondition for the subsequent construction of the Long Walls. With his ostracism in 472 BC and death in 467, Themistocles would never fully realize his intentions. Nevertheless, with increases in the numbers of ships in their fleet and the revenue generated from their empire, the Athenians witnessed the growth of the size and importance of Piraeus. They selected Hippodamus of Miletus to plan the town, presumably during the time of Pericles.[26] Thucydides provides Themistocles' rationale for the importance of fortifying Piraeus, as well as his overall strategic vision:

> Themistocles also persuaded them to finish the walls of the Piraeus, which had been begun before, in his year of office as archon; being influenced alike by the fineness of a locality that has three natural harbors, and by the great start that which the Athenians would gain in the acquisition of power by becoming a naval people. For he first ventured to tell them to stick to the sea and forthwith began to lay the foundations for empire. It was his advice, too, that they built the walls of that thickness which can still be discerned round the Piraeus, the stones being brought up by two wagons meeting each other. Between the walls thus formed there was neither rubble nor mortar, but great stones hewn square and fitted together, cramped to each other on the outside with iron and lead. About half the height that he intended was finished. His idea was that by their size and thickness they would keep off the attacks of an enemy; he thought that they might be adequately defended by a small group of invalids, and the rest be freed for service in the fleet. For the fleet claimed most of his attention. He saw, as I think, that the approach by sea was easier for the King's army than that by land: he also thought the Piraeus more valuable than the upper city; indeed, he was always advising the Athenians, if a day should come when they were hard pressed by land, to go down to the Piraeus, and defy the world with their fleet. In this way, therefore, the Athenians completed their wall, and commenced their other buildings immediately after the retreat of the Persians.[27]

The Athenians' decision to concentrate their military resources on naval warfare and the construction, maintenance, and sailing of triremes would have strategic repercussions throughout the remainder of the classical period, not only in Athens but throughout the Greek world. In particular, they capitalized on the strength of their citizens, the majority of whom were ill-equipped for fighting in the hoplite phalanx. The thetes, the lowest of the four Solonian property classes, now served in the capacity of oarsmen in the Athenian fleet. With the decision to emphasize the fleet, the Athenians enlisted the greatest possible number of citizens in pursuit of the security and prosperity of Athens. And in order to forgo engaging directly with the enemy on land, the fortification of the polis was essential. As the cornerstone in the process of advancing the political power of thousands of poorer Athenians, the walls of Athens—and now those of Piraeus as well—appear to have assumed a new, democratic significance in the minds of some Athenians.[28]

After the construction of the walls of the city and those of Piraeus, the next phase in the history of the fortification of Athens was the building of the Long Walls.[29] This project initially involved the construction of two walls, each 6 km in length, which ran from Athens to the harbors of Phaleron and Piraeus. The first phase of construction was completed early in Pericles' political career,[30] and later he would convince them to build a third wall, which ran parallel to the Piraic walls.[31] In the event of a siege, these walls, which connected the city with the port, would permit the Athenians access to their naval fleet, merchant ships, and the provisions that they supplied. During the Peloponnesian War, the Long Walls also provided a safe haven for the rural citizens of Attica, even though this was likely not their original purpose.[32] Donald Kagan describes Pericles' strategy in the following terms:

> Pericles, however, devised a novel strategy made possible by the unique character and extent of Athens' power. Their navy enabled them to rule over an empire that provided them income with which they could both sustain their supremacy at sea and obtain whatever goods they needed by trade or purchase. Although Attica's lands were vulnerable to attack, Pericles had all but turned Athens itself into an island by constructing the Long Walls that connected the city with its port and naval base at Piraeus. In the current state of Greek siege warfare these walls were invulnerable when defended, so that if the Athenians chose to withdraw within them they could remain there safely, and the Spartans could neither get at them nor defeat them.[33]

Athens's fortifications successfully defended its populace during the war, and it was not until the Spartans blockaded Piraeus that the Athenians were forced to capitulate. Even with the Athenians' success in withstanding the Spartans behind their walls, Pericles' strategy challenged the traditional Greek warrior ethic and failed to deter the Spartans, whose incursions into Attica had sought to compel the Athenians into an infantry battle. For all their utility, the Long Walls contributed to a diminution of traditional notions of deterrence; the Spartans knew in spring 431 that their hoplites would pay no immediate or great price for their violation of Athenian sovereignty. Once the fear of reprisals was removed, the invasions became chronic rather than exceptional, until either the plague or the capture of Spartan prisoners on Sphacteria reestablished the notion of deleterious consequences.[34]

During the Peloponnesian War, Athens had encouraged other democratic poleis to join with them in extending their fortifications from the city to the harbor, as seen, for example, in 417, when Thucydides relates that the Argives renewed their alliance with the Athenians and began construction of long walls to link their city to the sea.[35] This occurred after Argive democrats had already either killed or expelled the leading oligarchs of the city. The walls were built so that "in case of a blockade by land, with the help of the Athenians, they might have the advantage of importing what they wanted by sea. Some of the cities in the Peloponnesus were also privy to the building of these walls; and the Argives with all their people, women and slaves not excepted, applied themselves to the work, while carpenters and masons came to them from Athens."[36] The Athenians provided a manner of support that was familiar to them, helping the Argive democrats to consolidate their leadership and facilitating the alliance between the two poleis. The walls that connected Argos with the coast were designed to permit the city to be supplied in times of siege, and not to serve as the foundation for imperial power. As a corollary, the ruling democrats in Argos granted the Athenians access to their polis. Perhaps most important, however, is the symbolic nature of this action. The walls were synonymous with the Athenian democracy and a symbol of Athenian power. For the Argives to undertake the construction of these walls was for them to reject Sparta.

The recognition of the centrality of the Long Walls to Athenian strategy and their symbolic association with the democracy is perhaps most clearly articulated in the Spartan insistence on destroying them at the conclusion of the Peloponnesian War (404 BC). The terms of surrender levied against the Athenians mandated the destruction of the Long Walls, the reduction of the Athenian fleet to twelve triremes, and the installation of pro-Spartan oligarchs, the Thirty Tyrants, to govern the city. Lysander's victory in the preceding year at the Battle of Aegospotami (405 BC) had elevated Sparta to the height of its power.[37] Xenophon describes the panic of the Athenians when the news of the disaster reached them:

> It was at night that the Paralus arrived at Athens. As the news of the disaster was told, one man passed it on to another, and a sound of wailing arose and extended first from Piraeus, then along the Long Walls until it reached the city. That night no one slept. They mourned for the lost, but still more for their own fate. They thought that they themselves would now be dealt with as they had dealt with others—with the Melians, colonists of Sparta, after they had besieged and conquered Melos, with the people of Histiaea, of Scione, of Torone, of Aegina and many other states. . . . They could see no future for themselves except to suffer what they had made others suffer, people of small states whom they had injured not in retaliation for anything they had done but out of arrogance of power and for no reason except that they were in the Spartan alliance.[38]

Lysander's next action was to complete the encirclement of Athens already achieved on land by now controlling its harbor as well. With their grain supply dwindling, the besieged Athenians recognized that the time for negotiation had arrived.[39] The initial proposal was to join the Spartan alliance on the condition that the treaty permit them to retain their Long Walls and the walls of Piraeus intact. When Athenian ambassadors arrived at Sellasia on the border of Laconia, the ephors refused them entry to Sparta and rejected their terms.[40] A later delegation led by Theramenes would listen to the debate among the victors as to the fate of the vanquished Athenians:

> On their [Theramenes' and the other Athenian ambassadors'] arrival the ephors called an assembly at which many Greek states,

and in particular the Corinthians and the Thebans, opposed making any peace with Athens. The Athenians, they said, should be destroyed. The Spartans, however, said they would not enslave a Greek city which had done such great things for Greece at the time of her supreme danger. They offered to make peace on the following terms: the Long Walls and the fortifications of the Piraeus must be destroyed; all ships except twelve surrendered; the exiles to be recalled; Athens to have the same enemies and the same friends as Sparta had and to follow Spartan leadership in any expedition Sparta might make either by land or sea.[41]

Unwalled, oligarchic Sparta insisted that the walls of Athens be destroyed. Following the Ecclesia's acceptance of the Spartan offer, "Lysander sailed into Piraeus, the exiles returned and the walls were pulled down among scenes of great enthusiasm and to the music of flute girls. It was thought that this day was the beginning of freedom for Greece."[42] This scene of jubilation recalls the celebrations that attended the tearing down of the Berlin Wall, at which joyous crowds gathered both to witness and to participate in the symbolic dismantling of the Iron Curtain, although the Athenian walls were designed to keep enemies out, not citizens in.

Xenophon's account of the fall of Athens marks the end of the political alignment of the Greek poleis that had been in existence during the Peloponnesian War and, in many instances, for decades prior.[43] The Spartans' decision to spare Athens from annihilation was a tribute to the Athenians' service to Greece during the Persian War. It appears to have been especially magnanimous considering the severity and duration of the Peloponnesian War. Perhaps most significant, Sparta chose to ignore the recommendation of its principal allies, Corinth and Thebes, in favor of preserving Athens. Nonetheless, Sparta tried to cripple Athenian democracy by destroying the city's fleet and its walls and ruling the city in a manner that resembled Lysander's model of decarchies, with harmosts and armed garrisons. By having a military presence in Attica, the Spartans could curtail the expansion of Thebes in central Greece, and perhaps some Spartans hoped to employ the Athenians' frontier fortresses for this purpose.[44]

Sparta's victory over Athens changed the structure of the interstate system.[45] The absence of Athenian leadership from what had been a bipolar state system encouraged Sparta to enlarge its ambitions as the leader of the victorious coalition of states. Instead of establishing Sparta as the exclusive leader, however, the years 404–395 produced an uneasy transition from bipolarity to multipolarity. During this period of transition, the structure of the interstate system, being neither bipolar nor multipolar, was inherently unstable. This instability resulted from the elimination of Athens as a major power and the uncertainty of what power or collection of powers would take its place. Following its defeat in the Peloponnesian War, Athens's recovery in part depended on the Athenians' ability to acquire financial resources to refortify their city.[46] Fortunately for the Athenians, they had a willing financier with complementary strategic interests. When the Persian satrap Pharnabazus met with representatives from Thebes, Corinth, and Argos and the Athenian general Conon, whom the Persian king Artaxerxes had appointed to command his fleet in 397,[47] at the Isthmus of Corinth, he supplied them with encouragement and financial support, and (according to Diodorus) formed an alliance with them.[48] Xenophon records Conon's argument to Pharnabazus and the satrap's subsequent actions:

> Conon, however, asked to be allowed to keep the fleet. He said that he could support it by contributions from the islands, and that he proposed to sail to Athens and to help his countrymen rebuild the Long Walls and the walls of the Piraeus. "I can think of no action," he said, "which would hurt the Spartans more. By doing this you will not only have given the Athenians something for which they will be grateful but will have really made the Spartans suffer. You will make null and void that achievement of theirs which cost them more toil and trouble than anything else." This proposal was welcomed by Pharnabazus. He not only sent Conon to Athens but gave him additional money for the rebuilding of the walls. And Conon, when he arrived, erected a great part of the fortifications, using his crews for the work, hiring carpenters and masons and meeting all other necessary expenses.[49]

Pharnabazus thereafter returned to Persia, leaving Conon in command of the fleet. Conon himself returned to Athens, where he undertook the task of rebuilding Athens's fortifications. Ancient sources generally recognize Conon's objectives to have been the overthrow of the Spartan Empire and, in the process, to reestablish Athenian power.[50] Without the support of Persia, it would have been virtually impossible for the Athenians to finance a war against Sparta, the defeat of which reemerged as the primary objective of Athenian foreign policy.[51] The Athenians had already begun to rebuild the walls of Piraeus, and work now proceeded on the Long Walls in earnest.[52]

Amid the rubble of defeat, ancient Athenians sought to reconstitute both their power and their image. Unlike the victors who had constructed the Themistoclean walls at the end of the Persian War, the Athenians who built these walls were the vanquished. This onerous task, which represented continuity with Athens's former military strategy, was not a work of innovation. As a way to project "soft power,"[53] however, the rebuilding of the Long Walls, the symbol of Athens's fifth-century empire, demonstrated the Athenians' urge to restore the status of their polis in the eyes of neighboring city-states that might look for an attractive ally against Sparta.[54] The completed fortifications signaled to other Greek poleis the return of Athenian autonomy and its vibrant democracy.

The desire to revive their empire was alive in Athens, but whether or not this was a realistic goal for the Athenians is another matter. Athens and the other major Greek poleis had failed to wrest hegemony from the Spartans during the Corinthian War. To outfit a fleet to a size commensurate with their past imperial power had proven to be beyond the Athenians' reach. The vital role played by Persia was clear for all to see: the King's Peace contained provisions for an end to hostilities on the basis of Artaxerxes' terms. The treaty stipulated that all the poleis of Asia Minor, as well as the islands of Clazomenae[55] and Cyprus, were to be Persian possessions.[56] All other poleis—with the exception of the Athenian possessions of Lemnos, Imbros, and Skyros, which were strategically vital in their efforts to protect grain shipments destined for Piraeus[57]—were to be autonomous.[58] Any polis that did not accept these terms would be an enemy of the Persian king and subject to attack by Persia and whoever else was willing to join forces.[59]

The conclusion of the war was a Spartan victory. Sparta dissolved the Boeotian League, broke apart the union of Corinth and Argos, regained Corinth as an ally, and halted Athens's expansion. Xenophon recognized that Sparta's victory in the Corinthian War was a diplomatic victory and not a military victory: "In the actual fighting the Spartans had just about held their own, but now, as a result of what is known as 'The Peace of Antalcidas,' they appeared in a much more distinguished light."[60] The fact that the leading Greek poleis accepted the conditions set forth in 387 provides important indications about shifts in the relative power of those states under consideration, and hence in the balance of power.[61]

The King's Peace is considered the first example of the fourth-century phenomenon of common peace treaties.[62] In comparison with their fifth-century predecessors, these treaties were generally multilateral (as opposed to bilateral), were accepted by the leading Greek poleis (even if not formally signed by them), were of theoretically unlimited duration (as opposed to a specified period of time), and adhered to the principle of *autonomia* for all Greek poleis. From this perspective, the King's Peace adequately meets some of these criteria, but it fails in other regards.[63] It is perhaps more accurate to view the King's Peace as a negotiated peace that sought to respond to the shortcomings of earlier treaties. The treaty ending the Peloponnesian War created more antagonism among the contestants—and thereby generated more problems than it solved—in large measure as a result of its bilateral nature. The Peloponnesian War was a hegemonic struggle that engulfed the entirety of the Greek world. Sparta's treaty with Athens put an end to the conflict between the two leading powers but did not address the myriad concerns of the other participants. Bilateral negotiations were insufficient to address the complexity of fourth-century interstate relations, which often involved numerous poleis with competing foreign policy objectives. The King's Peace, although it purported to involve all Greek poleis, was nonetheless a product of similar bilateral negotiation.[64]

The autonomy clause of the King's Peace (387–386 BC) precluded the formation of an empire along the fifth-century model, but the Athenians implemented a clever solution to the problem of how to return themselves to a prominent position in the Greek interstate system. Perhaps shortly after Sphodrias's raid on Piraeus in 378, the Athenians founded the Second Athenian League.[65] His advance through the Attic countryside to the Thriasian plain alerted the Athenians to his presence, and they subsequently mobilized. After laying waste to the plain of Thria, Sphodrias retreated without having gained his objective, although the Athenians sensed their own vulnerability. They would again need to rely on the stability of the city's network of fortifications if they hoped to restore their former imperial glory, and they appealed to their allies to join together for the sake of common freedom.[66] They recognized that while the King's Peace deprived them of overseas possessions (excluding the islands of Lemnos, Imbros, and Skyros), it also provided them with some measure of protection. They carefully abided by the terms of the peace settlement and exploited the Spartans' transgressions of it. In promulgating the King's Peace, the Athenians sought to restore their reputation among the poleis of Greece and with Persia by serving as a counterbalance to the tyrannical rule of Sparta. The stele of Aristoteles records the league's provisions and is an expression of Athenian policy. It assures both current and future member poleis that their freedom and autonomy are guaranteed, that Athens will not place garrisons or military officials in their poleis, that Athens will not exact tribute from them,[67] and that Athens will restore all land, both publicly and privately held by Athenians, to the league's member poleis and halt the formation of cleruchies. The stele then lists the members of the Second Athenian League.

Athens needed to distance this new league from its old empire and to make concessions to its allies in order to acquire and subsequently retain them. This alliance is an example of weaker states joining together to balance the power of a stronger state. It provided protection for Thebes and Athens with its deterrent force: Sparta would not control central Greece without a major confrontation involving a large coalition of poleis. Both the Athenians, with their bold plan to form a new league, and the recently liberated Thebans needed to acquire basic security from wanton Spartan encroachment if they were to rehabilitate their respective poleis.[68] The incentive for the smaller Aegean poleis to join the league would be the grant of collective security that the newly formed league offered and the restitution of properties that were in Athenian hands. The stated purpose of the league was to protect the autonomy of its members from Sparta. This is somewhat surprising given that, of the league's first members (with the exception of Athens and Thebes), the potential threat to their freedom came primarily from Persia and not Sparta. Athens was gaining control of the role of *prostates* of the King's Peace from Sparta. The seizure of the Cadmeia and the raid of Sphodrias demonstrated to all Greek poleis, however, that Sparta was the violator of the King's Peace and not its guarantor. The immediate threat to Athens and mainland Greece was Sparta, not Persia.

The restoration of Athens as a credible naval power was significant for the interstate system in that the poleis of Asia Minor and the Aegean did not have to rely solely on Sparta for their safety from Persia. Unless the Athenians were to abandon their city, any strategy emphasizing naval power necessitated the maintenance of the Long Walls. Yet without a substantial fleet, there was little merit in the Athenians depending on the defenses of Piraeus and the Long Walls to ensure their survival. In this highly competitive multipolar environment, the Athenians also decided to invest in the defense of their borders.[69] Because of the problematic nature of dating ancient walls,[70] it has not been possible to date this array of fortifications with any great degree of precision,[71] although they are plausibly dated in general terms to the fourth century. By enlarging their defensive works, the Athenians distinguished between their desire to exercise power over others and their need to control their own territory.

Josiah Ober emphasizes the fourth-century Athenians' defensive mentality,[72] and yet their fortification of the city and its frontiers coincided with a period during which they pursued an aggressive foreign policy, particularly given the limitations imposed on them by the newly configured state system. As a result of their experiences during the Peloponnesian War, it seems only natural that the defense of Attica would be of importance to the Athenians.[73] They were determined to resist encroachments on their territory, such as the Spartan devastation of the countryside of Attica at the outset of the Peloponnesian War, the subsequent occupation of Decelea in its final phases, and the recent raid of Sphodrias. Again, adopting an apparently defensive mentality, the Athenians sought to establish control over their territory, and in so doing to position themselves as attractive allies to like-minded poleis in the struggle first against Spartan hegemony, then that of Thebes.

In order for the Athenians to regain their security and advance their interests, they fixed on a new strategy that required the fortification of the polis and its surrounding territory. In this context, Aristotle's later description in the *Politics* of the use of walls and fortifications, while not necessarily referring to Athens specifically, is pertinent to the mentality of fourth-century military planners:

> The fortification of cities by walls is a matter of dispute. It is sometimes argued that states which lay claim to military excellence ought to dispense with any such aids. This is a singularly antiquated notion—all the more as it is plain to the eye that states which prided themselves on this point are being refuted by the logic of fact. When the question at issue is one of coping with an enemy state of a similar character, which is only slightly superior in numbers, there is little honour to be got from an attempt to attain security by the erection of a barrier of walls. But it sometimes happens—and it is always possible—that the superiority of an assailant may be more than a match for mere courage, human or superhuman; and then, if a state is to avoid destruction, and to escape from suffering and humiliation, the securest possible barrier of walls should be deemed the best of military methods—especially to-day, when the invention of catapults and other engines for the siege of cities has attained such a high degree of precision. To demand that a city should be left undefended by walls is much the same as to want to have the territory of the state left open to invasion, and to lay every elevation level with the ground. It is like refusing to have walls for the exterior of a private house, for fear that they will make its inhabitants cowards. We have also to remember that a people with a city defended by walls has a choice of alternatives—to treat its city as walled [and therefore to act on the defensive], or to treat it as if it were unwalled [and therefore to take the offensive]—but a people without any walls is a people without any choice. If this argument be accepted, the conclusion will not only be that a city ought to be

surrounded by walls; it will also be that the walls should always be kept in good order, and be made to satisfy both the claims of beauty and the needs of military utility—especially the needs revealed by recent military inventions. It is always the concern of the offensive to discover new methods by which it may seize the advantage; but it is equally the concern of the defensive, which has already made some inventions, to search and think out others. An assailant will not even attempt to make an attack on men who are well prepared.[74]

The fortification of the city and its borders was critical to the defense of their polis not only against foreign enemies but also against those within the city's walls who might wish to breach its security through sedition. In this vein, the fourth-century manual *Poliorcetica* by Aeneas the Tactician urges the city's commanders to be vigilant against treason from within, thereby demonstrating how a city's reliance on its walls also necessitates the use of controls over the local population.[75]

The walls of Athens, always central to the city's defense, played a number of roles throughout the history of the polis. Beginning with Themistocles, the construction of the city's walls provided safety from future invasion. This in turn helped to launch the Athenians' path to empire, and allowed the democracy to flourish in a particular fashion that enhanced sea power and the thousands of poor who were essential to and benefited from it. Under Pericles, the Athenians continued to develop their defensive works and secure their imperial power, and the walls were integral to this strategy. During the Peloponnesian War, Pericles' strategy underestimated the devastation that would be wrought by bringing thousands of its citizens behind these walls in the abandonment of the Attic countryside, thereby fostering a virulent plague that wrought havoc from within. And he seems to have discounted the consequences of the loss of military deterrence—that by de facto making it clear that there were no immediate consequences, through armed infantry resistance, for invading the soil of Attica, a war was more likely to follow.

After the defeat of Athens and the destruction of the city's walls, these walls were rebuilt by Conon for practical and symbolic purposes as well. This strategy, however, failed as a result of the changes that had occurred in the transition of the larger Greek state system. In response to these changes and fighting during the Corinthian War, the Athenians realized that their former strategy was insufficient and tried to bolster their ability to control their territory with the construction of elaborate border defenses that would expand their options beyond passive infantry defense. The second half of the fourth century would usher in profound changes in siege warfare and the use of artillery, changes that go beyond the scope of the present discussion.[76] In Athens, the walls of the city and its frontier defenses were no match for Phillip and his Macedonian army, and the Athenians would submit to his rule without ever testing the strength of their costly and expansive networks of border defense.

For well over a hundred years, Athenian democracy experimented with a variety of fortifications—urban walls, long walls to the sea, networks of border fortifications—both to offer military utility and to express prevailing political and economic agendas. The single Athenian constant seems to have been to construct stone ramparts of some sort to meet almost every diverse need imaginable that arose. And in the last half-century of the free Greek city-state, even more ambitious and novel fortifications emerged outside Athens, as the enormous circuits in the Peloponnese at Mantineia, Megalopolis, and Messene demonstrate: huge new walled citadels designed to incorporate agricultural lands inside the city and to offer protection for the consolidation of scattered towns into new unified democratic states.

Even to this day, in the era of high technology, walls and fortifications continue to play important if less critical roles in defense and strategy. While exponential advances in weapons technology and the advent of air and space power have greatly reduced their effectiveness as lines of defense, they still perform valuable functions in certain circumstances, which emphasizes how the challenge-response cycle of the offensive and defensive is continuous and timeless.

In recent years, the dangerous conditions in Iraq precipitated the construction of security zones and walls to separate warring communities.[77] U.S. forces installed barricades in Baghdad to enhance the ability of Iraqi citizens to conduct their lives with some semblance of normalcy, and the gradual removal of these huge concrete walls perhaps indicates an easing of tension between these contending groups in that war-torn city.[78] In Israel, an interlinking series of walls and barriers constructed to prevent suicide bombers from entering the country has proven an effective means of limiting terrorist attacks, even as an array of experts predicted that such an apparently retrograde solution could hardly be successful. The contemporary Saudi Wall separating Saudi Arabia from Iraq provides yet another example. To address the threat of foreign fighters flooding across their borders, the Saudis have erected an expensive network of defenses along this perimeter to alert them to this threat. The United States is currently constructing a massive, multi-billion-dollar "fence" of concrete and metal intended to fortify the U.S.-Mexican border. Its first stage, from San Diego, California, to El Paso, Texas, is nearly complete, and seems to have drastically reduced illegal border crossings—in a manner at least as effective as increased patrols, electronic sensors, "virtual fences," and employer sanctions. Apparently concurrent with satellite communications, aerial drones, and sophisticated computer-based sensors, metal fences and concrete barriers worldwide continue to offer protection in a way that other high-tech alternatives cannot. The more sophisticated the technology to go over, through, and under walls, the more sophisticated the counterresponses that evolve to enhance the age-old advantages of fortifications, which continue either to stop outright entry (and occasionally to stop exit as well) or to make the attackers' efforts so costly as to be counterproductive.

As with any element of warfare, the functions and purposes of walls shift with the times, but the notion of material obstacles has not ended. Unlike moats and drawbridges, however, they remain in ever expanded and imaginative uses.[79] For Athenians in the classical period, walls represented more than lines of defense; they were also symbols of power and pride that helped shape the strategic landscape in the interstate system and, in the case of the Long Walls to Piraeus, enhanced the autonomy of the lower classes, who were so essential to the vitality of Athenian democracy and its maritime empire.

These fortifications created strategic opportunity for a rising power; their destruction signaled unquestionable defeat; and their reconstruction helped reestablish Athens as a strong potential ally for poleis that shared a common interest in containing Sparta. Just as British sea power served a variety of purposes at different points during the rise and fall of the British Empire—guarantor of commerce, promoter of colonial expansion, and enforcer of rough justice on the high seas—so the walls of Athens had many masters, many builders, and many purposes. All that is certain in our high-technology future is that the more that walls and fortifications are dismissed as ossified relics of our military past, the more they will reappear in new and unique manifestations, and the more we will need to look to the past for time-honored explanations of why and how they endure.

FURTHER READING

For the history of Athens and of its walls, the histories of Herodotus and Thucydides are essential. In addition, the text of the fourth-century BC writer Aeneas the Tactician has been translated into English and annotated by David Whitehead, *Aineias the Tactician: How to Survive Under Siege, A Historical Commentary, with Translation and introduction,* 2nd ed. (London: Bristol Classical Press, 2001).

Perhaps because of their ubiquity throughout the Greek world, walls and fortifications have received a great deal of scholarly attention. In addition to numerous articles and archaeological reports, several major monographs have treated the subject of fortifications and civic defense throughout various phases of Greek history. The challenge of identifying and tracing the chronological development of different masonry techniques and types of construction is discussed in Robert Lorentz Scranton's *Greek Walls* (Cambridge, MA: Harvard University Press, 1941). F. E. Winter's *Greek Fortifications* (London: Routledge & Kegan Paul, 1971) and A. W. Lawrence's *Greek Aims in Fortification* (Oxford: Clarendon Press, 1979) each provide a valuable overview of fortifications in Greece. Y. Garlan's *Recherches de poliocétique greque,* fasc. 223, (Paris: Bibliothèque des écoles françaises d'Athènes et de Rome, 1974) is vital to understanding the role of ramparts in classical Greek municipal defense. J.-P. Adam's *L'architecture militaire Greque* (Paris: J. Picard, 1982) provides excellent photographs and detailed drawings of fortifications throughout the ancient Greek world. The increasing complexity of these constructions also reflects developments in the offensive tactics used to overcome them, and on this topic see E. W. Marsden, *Greek and Roman Artillery: Historical Development* (Oxford: Clarendon Press, 1969). For the period of the Peloponnesian War, Victor Davis Hanson devotes a chapter (chap. 6, "Walls [Sieges (431–415)]," pp. 163–99) to the subject of fortifications and siegecraft in *A War Like No Other: How the Athenians and Spartans Fought the Peloponnesian War* (New York: Random House, 2005).

Turning specifically to Athens, the archaeological remains of the city's walls are discussed by R. E. Wycherley, *The Stones of Athens* (Princeton: Princeton University Press, 1978); see especially chapter 1, "The Walls," pp. 7–26. More recently, John Camp has published an excellent survey of the archaeology of the Athenian civic construction in *The Archaeology of Athens* (New Haven: Yale University Press, 2001). It is only recently that a full-length study of the Long Walls has been undertaken. David H. Conwell has done an admirable job of compiling all relevant information—literary, epigraphical, and archaeological—in *Connecting a City to the Sea: The History of the Athenian Long Walls*, Mnemosyne Supplements, vol. 293 (Leiden: Brill, 2008). Moving beyond the walls of the urban center to the plains of Attica, three major studies have examined the history of Athenian rural defenses: J. R. McCredie, *Fortified Military Camps in Attica*, Hesperia Supplement 11 (Princeton: Princeton University Press, 1966), Josiah Ober, *Fortress Attica: Defense of the Athenian Land Frontier, 404–322 BC* (Leiden: E. J. Brill, 1982), and Mark H. Munn, *The Defense of Attica: The Dema Wall and the Boiotian War of 378–375 BC* (Berkeley: University of California Press, 1993). The latter two works have produced a lively exchange of opinion between the authors over the date, purpose, and efficacy of the ancient Athenian system of rural fortifications.

NOTES

I am grateful to my friend, Matthew B. Kohut, for reading and commenting on several drafts of this essay.

[1] R. E. Wycherley, in *The Stones of Athens* (Princeton, NJ: Princeton University Press, 1978), writes (7):

> The history of the walls of Athens is the history of the expansion and contraction of the city in its successive phases of growth and decline, in victory, disaster, and recovery. This was a dominant feature of the city in her greatest days, an object of immense expenditure of effort and resources by the Athenian Demos, a symbol of the power of Athens, and a notable example of Greek military architecture; and, with repeated repair and reconstruction of course, it remained more or less in being for sixteen centuries of varying fortunes, rising again and again after severe dilapidation.

In a non-Athenian context—an event perhaps related to that described by Herodotus (1.168)—Anacreon wrote (frag. 100 [Bruno Gentili, *Anacreon* (Rome: Edizioni dell'Ateneo, 1958); Bergk 72; Diehl 67, p. 391]): "Now the crown of the city has been destroyed." The Scholiast to Pindar, *Olympian* 8.42c, explains the reference by quoting this line of Anacreon's poetry, adding that "the walls of cities are like a crown." Mogens Herman Hansen in *Polis: An Introduction to the Ancient Greek City-State* (Oxford: Oxford University Press, 2006) describes the general purpose of a Greek polis's wall (104):

> By contrast [i.e., with the Middle Ages], in the ancient Greek *polis* the city wall served only military purposes, and no tolls were levied at city gates. In time of war, of course, the walls and gates were guarded, but in peacetime anyone could pass through the gates in the daytime. The gates were perhaps closed at night, but they were not guarded, and people could still enter and leave the city. In the *polis* the walls were not seen as a barrier between city and country, but rather as a monument for the citizens to take pride in.

[2] Prior to the Persian invasion, the Athenian Acropolis was guarded by the Pelasgic Wall. In addition to this wall, some scholars have postulated that the city was further

fortified by a surrounding wall. Wycherley, *The Stones of Athens*, 9 (see also n. 4), draws attention to the dispute concerning the existence of a pre-Persian wall. The ancient literary testimonia for the wall's existence are ambiguous and the archaeological evidence for its course is lacking. Nonetheless, E. Vanderpool ("The Date of the Pre-Persian City-Wall of Athens," in *Φόρος: Tribute to Benjamin Dean Meritt*, ed. D. W. Bradeen and M. F. McGregor, 156–60 [Locust Valley, NY: J. J. Augustin, 1974]) concludes there was a pre-Persian city wall in Athens with a terminus post quem of 566 BC.

[3] Fornara 55, *GHI* 23. The translation is from Charles W. Fornara, *Archaic Times to the End of the Peloponnesian War*, vol. 1 of *Translated Documents of Greece and Rome*, 2nd ed. (Cambridge: Cambridge University Press, 1983), 53–55. The inscription recording this decree is of a later date, thereby calling its authenticity into question. Fornara provides references both in favor of and opposed to its authenticity on p. 54. See also Herodotus 8.41 and Demosthenes 19.303.

[4] Herodotus 8.50.

[5] Herodotus 8.51. Translations of Herodotus are by Andrea L. Purvis, *The Landmark Herodotus: The Histories*, ed. Robert B. Strassler (New York: Pantheon Books, 2007).

[6] See Herodotus 7.141.3.

[7] For a discussion of Themistocles' preparations for the Persian invasion and the Athenians' subsequent evacuation of Attica, see Barry Strauss, *The Battle of Salamis: The Naval Encounter That Saved Greece—and Western Civilization* (New York: Simon & Schuster, 2004), 61–72.

[8] Herodotus 8.53.

[9] Herodotus 9.3. The quotation is from 9.13.2.

[10] John M. Camp, *The Archaeology of Athens* (New Haven, CT: Yale University Press, 2001), 56–58.

[11] Thucydides 1.89.3.

[12] In this context, it is interesting to compare the construction of the walls of Athens with the construction of the Freedom Tower in New York City. See the commentary of Nicolai Ouroussoff, architectural critic for the *New York Times*, in "A Tower That Sends a Message of Anxiety, Not Ambition," February 19, 2007, and "Medieval Modern: Design Strikes a Defensive Posture," March 4, 2007:

> Four years after the American invasion of Iraq, this state of siege is beginning to look more and more like a permanent reality, exhibited in an architectural style we might refer to as 21st-century medievalism. Like their 13th- to 15th-century counterparts, contemporary architects are being enlisted to create not only major civic landmarks but lines of civic defense, with aesthetically pleasing features like elegantly sculpted barriers around public plazas or decorative cladding for bulky protective concrete walls. . . . The most chilling example of the new medievalism is New York's Freedom Tower, which was once touted as a symbol of enlightenment. Designed by David Childs of Skidmore, Owings & Merrill, it rests on a 20-story windowless fortified concrete base decorated in prismatic glass panels in a grotesque attempt to disguise its underlying paranoia. And the brooding, obelisk-like form above is more of an expression of American hubris than of freedom.

[13] Diodorus 11.29.3.

¹⁴ The translation is by C. H. Oldfather in the Loeb Classical Library. See also Tod, *GHI* 2.204, 21–51, Lycurgus *Against Leocrates* 80–81. Contra: Theopompus, *FGrHist* 115 F153. Russell Meiggs, *The Athenian Empire* (Oxford: Oxford University Press, 1972), 504–7, accepts the validity of the Oath of Plataea, while P. J. Rhodes, *CAH* 5².34, doubts the existence of a clause requiring temples to be left in ruins.

¹⁵ Jeffrey M. Hurwit, *The Athenian Acropolis: History, Mythology, and Archaeology from the Neolithic Era to the Present* (Cambridge: Cambridge University Press, 1999), 135–42. The archaeological evidence of the Persian sack of Athens, and the Agora in particular, is presented in T. Leslie Shear Jr., "The Persian Destruction of Athens," *Hesperia* 62 (1993): 383–482. See also Homer A. Thompson, "Athens Faces Adversity," *Hesperia* 50 (1981): 343–55. He writes (346), "To sum up: their triumphs in the Persian Wars undoubtedly stimulated the Athenians in some of their finest achievements in art, literature and international affairs. But the evidence of the excavations reminds us that the sack of 480/79 BC caused a long and distressed disruption of the domestic, civic, and religious life of the city."

¹⁶ Simon Hornblower (*A Commentary on Thucydides*, I [Oxford: Clarendon Press, 1991], s.v. 1.89.3–1.93.2, 135) cites R. A. McNeal ("Historical Methods and Thucydides 1.103.1," *Historia* 19 [1970]: 306–25) on the significance of walls in Thucydides. McNeal writes (312), "In Thucydides' elaborate theory of power, a fleet permits commerce, commerce brings revenues, revenues create treasure, treasure means stability and walls, and walls permit political domination of weaker states. For Thucydides the wall is the ultimate symbol of power." See also Hornblower's commentary on 1.2.2, where he quotes from Yvon Garlan ("Fortifications et histoire Greque," in *Problèmes de la guerre en Grèce ancienne*, ed. Jean-Pierre Vernant, 245–60 [Paris: Mouton, 1968], quotation at 255) that "la notion d'enceinte urbaine est inseparable du concept de cite."

The author of the *Athenaion Politeia* credits both Themistocles and Aristides in the construction of the circuit walls (23.3–4, trans. P. J. Rhodes [Aristotle, *The Athenian Constitution* (London: Penguin Books, 1984)]):

> (3) The champions of the people at this time were Aristides son of Lysimachus and Themistocles son of Neocles: Themistocles practised the military arts, while Aristides was skilled in the political arts and was outstanding among his contemporaries for his uprightness, so the Athenians used the first as a general and the second as an adviser. (4) The two men were jointly responsible for the rebuilding of the walls, in spite of being personal opponents; and it was Aristides who saw that the Spartans had gained a bad reputation because of Pausanias and urged the Ionians to break away from the Spartan alliance.

For a discussion of this passage, see P. J. Rhodes, *A Commentary on the Aristotelian Athenaion Politeia* (Oxford: Oxford University Press, 1981), 292–95.

See Diodorus 11.39–40 (incorrectly dated 478–477 BC). Plutarch also emphasizes the clever manner in which the Athenians launched their ambitious quest for empire (*Themistocles* 19):

> No sooner were these great achievements behind him, than he immediately took in hand the rebuilding and fortification of Athens; according to Theopompus's account he bribed the Spartan ephors not to oppose his plans, but most

writers agree that he outwitted them. He arranged a visit to Sparta, giving himself the title of ambassador, and the Spartans then complained to him that the Athenians were fortifying their city, while Polyarchus was sent expressly from Aegina to confront him with this charge. Themistocles, however, denied it and told them to send men to Athens to see for themselves; this delay, he calculated, would gain time for the fortifications to be built, and he was also anxious that the Athenians should hold the envoys as hostages for his own safety. This was just how things turned out. The Spartans, when they discovered the truth, did not retaliate against him, but concealed their resentment and sent him away.

[17] Thucydides 1.90.1–3.

[18] Thucydides 1.93.1–2.

[19] John M. Camp, *The Archaeology of Athens* (New Haven, CT: Yale University Press, 2001), 59–60; Gomme, *HCT*, s.v. 1.93.2, 260–61; Hornblower, *A Commentary on Thucydides*, I, s.v. 1.93.2, 137–38.

[20] For a description of these walls, see Wycherley, *The Stones of Athens*, 13. The Athenians placed unbaked bricks on top of a stone socle, which was "composed of several courses of massive well-shaped bricks on either face of a core of rougher stone. The material was poros or harder limestone, with increasing use of conglomerate in later phases."

[21] Gomme, *HCT*, s.v. 1.92, 260.

[22] See T. 1.1.1: "The preparations of both the combatants were in every department in the last state of perfection; and he [Thucydides] could see the rest of the Hellenic race taking sides in the quarrel; those who delayed doing so at once having it in contemplation" (1.18.3):

For a short time the league [the Hellenic League of 481] held together, till the Spartans and the Athenians quarreled, and made war upon each other with their allies, a duel into which all the Hellenes sooner or later were drawn, though some at first might remain neutral. So that the whole period from the Median war to this, with some peaceful intervals, was spent by each power in war, either with its rival, or with its own revolted allies, and consequently afforded them constant practice in military matters, and that experience which is learnt in the school of danger.

[23] Hansen, in *Polis,* writes (95–96):

Already in the Archaic period, then, walls were an important aspect of the Greek perception of what a *polis* was, and an overview of surviving walls only serves to strengthen that point. . . . In the written sources, 222 *poleis* in all are referred to as walled in the Archaic and Classical periods, and only in nineteen cases is it expressly said that a city is unwalled; there are only four *poleis* of which we know positively that they did not have any walls at the end of the Classical period: namely, Delphi, Delos, Gortyn and Sparta.

[24] Plato *Laws* 778d–779b (trans. A. E. Taylor):

As for walls, Megillus, I am of the same mind as your own Sparta. I would leave them to slumber peacefully in the earth without waking them, and here are my reasons. As the oft-quoted line of the poet happily words it, a city's walls should be of bronze and iron, not of stone, and we in particular shall cover ourselves with well-merited ridicule, after taking our young men in annual procession to the open country to block an enemy's path by ditches, entrenchments, and actual buildings of various kinds—all, if you please, with the notion of keeping the foe well outside our borders—if we shut ourselves in behind a wall. A wall is, in the first place, far from conducive to the health of town life and, what is more, commonly breeds of certain softness of soul in the townsmen; it invites inhabitants to seek shelter within it and leave the enemy unrepulsed, tempts them to neglect effecting their deliverance by unrelaxing nightly and daily watching, and to fancy they will find a way to real safety by locking themselves in and going to sleep behind ramparts and bars as though they had been born to shirk toil, and did not know that the true ease must come from it, whereas dishonorable ease and sloth will bring forth toil and trouble, or am I much mistaken.

[25] Victor Davis Hanson, *The Soul of Battle: From Ancient Times to the Present Day. How Three Great Liberators Vanquished Tyranny* (New York: Free Press, 1999), 72–104. On 101–2, he writes,

Again, modern students of Greek history, to gain full insight into the real contemporary view of Spartan culture, must visit the remains of Messenê, Megalopolis, and Mantinea. That such vast circuits could arise so quickly after the Spartan defeat at Leuctra and subsequent invasion of Laconia should tell us exactly what Sparta's neighbors thought about Spartan society. Battlements—the Berlin Wall and the current fieldworks arising on the American-Mexican border are good examples—often provide more honest testimony than literary sources and government proclamation about the respective apprehensions, fears, and ideologies of the cultures on either side of the ramparts. Just as tremors in the Soviet Union caused walls to crash in Germany, so too the check on Sparta offered by Epaminondas immediately prompted thousands to go out into the Peloponnesian countryside to cut and raise stone while they still had the chance.

[26] Aristotle *Politica* 2.8 (1267b22–30). See R. E. Wycherley, *CAH* 5².203–8, and M. Ostwald, *CAH* 5².315.

[27] Thucydides 1.93.3–7.

[28] See also the comments of Plutarch on the impact of this policy for the Athenians (*Themistocles* 19):

After this he proceeded to develop the Piraeus as a port, for he had already taken note of the natural advantages of its harbors and it was his ambition to unite the whole city to the sea. In this he was to some extent reversing the policy of the ancient kings of Attica, for they are said to have aimed at drawing the citizens away from the sea and accustoming them to live not by seafaring but by tilling and planting the soil. It was they who had spread the legend about Athena, how when she and Poseidon were contesting the possession of the country, she produced the sacred olive tree of the Acropolis before the judges and so when the verdict. Themistocles, however, did not, as Aristophanes the comic poet puts it, 'knead the Piraeus on to the city'; on the contrary, he attached the city to the Piraeus and made the land population dependent on the sea. The effect of this was to increase the influence of the people at the expense of the nobility and to fill them with confidence, since the control of policy now passed into the hands of sailors and boatswains and pilots. This was also the reason why the platform of the people's Assembly in the Pnyx, which had been built so as to look out to sea, was later turned round by the Thirty Tyrants, so that it faced inland, for they believed that Athens' naval empire had proved to be the mother of democracy and that an oligarchy was more easily accepted by men who tilled the soil.

[29] See the new study of the Long Walls by David H. Conwell, *Connecting a City to the Sea: The History of the Athenian Long Walls, Mnemosyne Supplements*, vol. 293 (Leiden: Brill, 2008). After describing the walls' physical characteristics, nomenclature, and the local topography where they were situated, Conwell provides a chronological narrative of the walls' construction and purpose during four phases. He concludes with a strategic analysis of the Long Walls in Athenian history from their initial construction to the end of the fourth century.

[30] Thucydides 1.107,108.2. Conwell conjectures that the construction was begun as early as 462–461 and completed in 458–457. His argument (*Connecting a City to the Sea*, 39–54), which attempts to confirm the involvement of Cimon in the project and thereby substantiate a remark in Plutarch (*Cimon* 13.5-7)—that is, in contradiction to Thucydides' admittedly imprecise chronology (1.107)—and also thereby propose an early date for the start of construction, fails to address adequately the democratic thrust of this initiative. The Athenians' commitment to build the Long Walls reinforced the polis's reliance on the masses of citizens who serviced the fleet. For Cimon to favor this segment of the Athenian citizen body seems inconsistent with his political views. Cimon, who had recently suffered dishonor stemming from his pro-Spartan policies, was not in a position of sufficient trust with his fellow citizens to suggest a project involving so much of the city's resources. His involvement in building the walls, which involved dumping "vast quantities of rubble and heavy stones into the swamps" at his own expense, may represent little more, as Conwell himself writes, than the desperate attempt of a politician "seeking to stave off political extinction" (49). He was ostracized from Athens in 461 BC.

[31] Plato *Gorgas* 455d–e. Our written sources only permit us to date this wall to the years 452–431. Conwell (64–78) conjectures that their construction took place around 443–442.

[32] Conwell, *Connecting a City to the Sea*, writes (60):

Given their purpose, the Long Walls (Ia) were at once both conventional and radical. On the one hand, however impressive their dimensions, the structures simply secured the maritime orientation typical of cities in classical Greece. On the other hand, while many fortifications were simply passive barriers defending an urban zone against invasion, the Long Walls had a more ambitious role. Built to defend the connection between Athens and its ships, they were land-oriented structures with a decidedly maritime purpose.

[33] Donald Kagan, *The Peloponnesian War* (New York: Viking, 2003), 51. See also chapter two in this book, in which he delineates the objectives of Athenian foreign policy. The walls of Athens facilitated the pursuit of a naval strategy designed to achieve these objectives.

[34] Kagan, *The Peloponnesian War*, 52–54. Kagan writes (52):

This plan was much better suited to Athens than the traditional one of confrontation between phalanxes of infantry, but it did contain serious flaws, and reliance on it helped cause the failure of Pericles' diplomatic strategy of deterrence. . . . The Athenians would, for example, have to tolerate the insults and accusations of cowardice the enemy would hurl at them from beneath their walls. That would represent a violation of the entire Greek cultural experience, the heroic tradition that placed bravery in warfare at the peak of Greek virtues. Most of the Athenians, moreover, lived in the country, and they would have to watch passively from the protection of the city's walls while the enemy destroyed their crops, damaged their trees and vines, and looted and burned their homes. No Greeks who had ever any chance of resisting had been willing to do that, and little more than a decade earlier the Athenians had come out to fight rather than allow such devastation.

[35] Long walls had also been constructed before the war, most importantly at Megara and oligarchic Corinth.

[36] Thucydides 5.82.1–2.

[37] See Xenophon 2.1.17–32; Diodorus 13.104.8–106.8. At the Battle of Aegospotami, the victorious Spartans, under the leadership of Lysander and Eteonikos, had destroyed or captured 170 of the 180 Athenian triremes and executed perhaps as many as 3,500 Athenian prisoners. See Barry S. Strauss, "Aegospotami Reexamined," *AJP* 104 (1983): 24–35, esp. 32–34. Donald Kagan describes the plight of the Athenians (*The Fall of the Athenian Empire* [Ithaca, NY: Cornell University Press, 1987], 393): "The Athenians' resources were exhausted; they could not again build a fleet to replace the one lost at Aegospotami. Athens had lost the war; the only questions that remained were how long it would hold out before surrendering and what terms the Athenians could obtain."

[38] Xenophon 2.2.3, 10. Unless otherwise noted, all references to Xenophon are from the *Hellenica*. The translation used throughout is that of Rex Warner, *A History of My Times* (Harmondsworth, UK: Penguin, 1966).

[39] Xenophon 2.2.11.

[40] Xenophon (2.2.15) mentions that an earlier Spartan proposal, the origin and date of which are unclear, brought back by the Athenian ambassador Archestratus, which required the Athenians to tear down the Long Walls, had been angrily refused in the Ecclesia. The Ecclesia imprisoned Archestratus and passed a law that forbid further mention of such a term.

[41] Xenophon 2.2.19–20. See also Diodorus 13.107.4, 14.3.2; Plutarch *Lysander* 14.4; Andocides 3.11–12, 39; Lysias 13.14. Against the testimony of Xenophon, the writer of the *Athenaion Politeia* states (34.3):

The peace terms specified that the Athenians should be governed by their ancestral constitution (*patrios politeia*); on this basis the democrats tried to preserve the democracy, while the nobles who belonged to the political clubs and the exiles who had returned after the peace wanted an oligarchy. . . . Lysander sided with the oligarchs, overawed the people, and forced them to vote an oligarchy into power on the proposal of Dracontides of Aphidna.

The translation is that of J. M. Moore, *Aristotle and Xenophon on Democracy and Oligarchy* (Berkeley and Los Angeles: University of California Press, 1975). In accord with *Athenaion Politeia:* Diodorus 14.3.2–3 and Justine 5.8.5. The Athenians disputed the definition of "the ancestral constitution," and the interpretation of the term pitted those favoring democracy against those favoring oligarchy. Lysander, whom the Spartans recalled from the eastern Aegean to Athens, was instrumental in settling the dispute for the time being by appointing Theramenes and the Thirty. For an excellent study of Lysander's policy, see Charles D. Hamilton, "Spartan Politics and Policy, 405–401 BC," *AJP* 91 (1970): 294–314.

[42] Xenophon 2.2.23.

[43] J. K. Davies (*Democracy and Classical* Greece, 2nd ed. [Cambridge, MA: Harvard University Press, 1993], 129) argues against viewing the end of the Peloponnesian War as a pivotal moment in the stability of Greek interstate politics: "The first two phases (i.e. 431–421, 421–413) belong together, but there is a very real break in the years 413–411, when Athenian superiority had been broken, Persia entered the war, and Sparta became a sea-power. Thereafter the new configuration of international politics remained stable for a generation till the 370s, and the actual ends of wars in 404 and 386 were comparatively unimportant." See also 147: "Greek politics after 413 kept the same configuration for a generation." In my opinion, Davies' interpretation fails to acknowledge that the period extending from the end of the Peloponnesian War to the King's Peace (and the treaties that concluded those conflicts) constitutes a transition of the structure of the interstate system from bipolarity to multipolarity. Furthermore, I find it difficult to deny the significance of the treaty that ended the war in 404, which brought a formal end to the Athenian Empire, or the treaty of 387–386 that ushered in the height of the Spartan hegemony. Kagan, *The Fall of the Athenian Empire*, 416:

In spite of its apparently decisive outcome, the war did not establish a stable balance of power to replace the uneasy one that had evolved after the end of the Persian War. The great Peloponnesian War was not the type of war that, for all its costs, creates a new order that permits general peace for a generation or more. The peace treaty of 404 reflected a temporary growth of Spartan influence far beyond its normal strength.

[44] The remains of the fortifications along the border of Attica date mainly to the first half of the fourth century BC; however, it is likely that some defensive structures had been established earlier in the preceding century.

[45] See my 2001 Yale University dissertation, "The Struggle for Hegemony: Greek Interstate Politics and Foreign Policy, 404–371 BC," and Arthur Eckstein, *Mediterranean Anarchy, Interstate War, and the Rise of Rome* (Berkeley and Los Angeles: University of California Press, 2007), chap. 2.

[46] The traditional assumption has been that Athens was utterly devastated after the war (e.g., H. Bengston, *Griechische Geschichte* [Munich: Beck, 1960], 259, Claude Mossé,

Athens in Decline: 404–86 B.C., trans. Jean Stewart [London: Routledge and Kegan Paul, 1973], 12–17). More recent scholarship supports the view that Athens's recovery, both economic and political, occurred more rapidly than previously believed (e.g., G.E.M. de Ste. Croix, *The Class Struggle in the Ancient World from the Archaic Age to the Arab Conquests* [London: Duckworth, 1981], 291–92). Barry S. Strauss (*Athens After the Peloponnesian War: Class, Faction and Policy, 404–386 B.C.* [London: Croon Helm, 1986], passim) provides a detailed analysis of social and economic conditions after the Peloponnesian War. In 395, however, Athens was in a much more compromised position than during the period of its fifth-century empire.

[47] For the collected testimonia of Conon's activities (397–396 to 394–393), see Harding 12, 22–26. In the second half of the fourth century, Athenians viewed Conon's military victories against Sparta as victories for Greece, even though he was an Athenian in the service of Persia. See, e.g., Dinarchus, 1.14 [dated 323], trans. Ian Worthington, *A Historical Commentary on Dinarchus: Rhetoric and Conspiracy in Later Fourth-Century Athens* (Ann Arbor: University of Michigan Press, 1992), 87:

> Athenians, you did not take into account the actions of Timotheus, who sailed around the Peloponnese and defeated the Spartans in a naval battle off Corcyra. He was the son of Conon who freed the Greeks, and he took Samos, Methone, Pydna, Potidaea, and twenty other cities as well. You did not take these deeds into account either at his trial or for the oaths that affirmed the votes you cast, but you fined him one hundred talents because Aristophon said he took money from Chios and Rhodes.

See also 3.17.

[48] Xenophon 4.8.7–11; Diodorus 14.84.4ff.

[49] Xenophon 4.8.9–10.

[50] Isocrates 4.154, 5.63–64, 7.12, 65, 9.52f; Demosthenes 20.68; Dinarchus 1.14, 75, 3.17; Diodorus 14.39.3; Nepos *Conon* 2.1, 5.1f; Justin 6.3.4. An excellent treatment of the issue of Athenian imperialism during the Corinthian War is Robin Seager's "Thrasybulus, Conon and Athenian Imperialism, 396–386 B.C.," *JHS* 87 (1967): 95–115. In summarizing the results of his research, Seager writes (115):

> Thus it appears that the constant determining factor of Athenian policy between the restoration of the democracy and the Peace of Antalcidas is the refusal of the mass of Athenians to accept the fact that the empire had been lost and their desire to attempt to recreate it in fact as soon as or even before the time was ripe. . . . It was this longing for empire on the part of the people which determined the actions of Athens throughout the period, not the divergent views of individual statesmen or political groups, who attempted no more than to restrain or encourage the people in accordance with the dictates of patriotism or personal advantage.

Seager is right to minimize the effects that politicians in Athens exerted in the debate about Athenian foreign policy. The issue of empire was of general concern to all Athenians during these years, and the ability to restore Athens to a prominent position was largely in the hands of outside actors in the interstate arena.

[51] The Athenians, however, remained wary of war with Sparta. The Oxyrhynchus Historian, in the description of the Damainetos affair of 396, remarks that the fear of Sparta united the factions of Athenian society that were customarily divided with regard to foreign policy matters (John Wickersham and Gerald Verbrugghe, *Greek Historical Documents: The Fourth Century B.C.: Hellenic Oxyrhynchia* [Toronto: Hakkert, 1973], §6):

> Launching a ship, he [Demainetos] sailed away from the docks and headed for Conon. An uproar followed, and the prominent upper-class politicians were enraged. They accused the Council of throwing the city into a war with Sparta; the Councilors were frightened and called an assembly. . . . The respectable and wealthy Athenians were not inclined to upset matters anyway, but even the masses and demagogues were on this occasion so frightened as to follow the advice. They sent to Milon, the harmost in Aigina, telling him to punish Demainetos, since he was acting without authority. Previously the masses and demagogues had spent all their time stirring up trouble and crossing the Spartans in many ways.

[52] *IG* II² 1656–64. In addition, see the commentary on selected inscriptions from Piraeus dated to this period by Franz Georg Maier, *Griechische Mauerbauinschriften*, vol. 1 (Heidelberg: Quelle and Meyer, 1959), 15–36. Xenophon 4.8.10. Conwell (*Connecting a City to the Sea*, 109–22, 130–31) dates this phase of construction to the years 395–390.

[53] For a definition and explanation of soft power, see Joseph S. Nye Jr., *The Paradox of American Power: Why the World's Only Superpower Can't Go It Alone* (Oxford: Oxford University Press, 2002), and idem, *Soft Power: The Means to Success in World Politics* (New York: Perseus, 2005).

[54] Andocides, 3.37, trans. Douglas M. MacDowell, *Antiphon and Andocides* (Austin: University of Texas Press, 1998), 157: "There was once a time, Athenians, when we had no walls or ships, but it was when we acquired them that our successes began. So if you want success again now, those are what you must have. With this foundation our fathers built up greater power for Athens than any city has ever had." See also R. Seager, "Thrasybulus, Conon and Athenian Imperialism 396–386 B.C.," *JHS* 87 (1967): 95–115.

[55] Prior to the ratification of the King's Peace, Athens had honored the Klazomenians for their good will toward them: *IG* II² 28 (Tod 114; Harding 26, 40–41).

[56] R. J. Seager and C. J. Tuplin ("The Freedom of the Greeks in Asia: On the Origins of a Concept and the Creation of a Slogan," *JHS* 100 [1980]: 145f.), maintain that this provision of the King's Peace is vital to the establishment of the concept of the Greeks of Asia Minor as a single community, with subsequent value as a propagandistic slogan.

[57] Alfonso Moreno, *Feeding the Democracy: The Athenian Grain Supply in the Fifth and Fourth Centuries BC* (Oxford: Oxford University Press, 2007).

[58] Simon Hornblower, *OCD*³, s.v. "autonomy" (224):

> In internal affairs it means the state of affairs where a community is responsible for its own laws; in this sense it is opposed to tyranny (Hdt. 1.96.1) and means self-determination, whereas freedom (*eleutheria*) means absence of external constraint. But *autonomia* is also regularly used in the context of interstate

relations, where it indicates a limited independence permitted by a stronger power to a weaker.

[59] The precise terms of the King's Peace are unknown. For an admittedly speculative reconstruction, see G. L. Cawkwell, "The King's Peace," *CQ* 31 (1981): 69–83. See also Robert K. Sinclair, "The King's Peace and the Employment of Military and Naval Forces 387–378," *Chiron* 8 (1978): 29–37. In summary, he writes (37):

> While the King's Peace might be criticized for vagueness and <deficiencies> in formulation, these may have been due in part to the novelty of a koine eirene, but are particularly to be related to the objectives of the Persians and Spartans who could more effectively exploit a settlement that was not too precisely defined. The other Greek states recognised the realities of the situation and in particular the dominant position of Sparta, and their reactions in the next decade can be adequately explained in terms of that recognition without invoking specific provisions in the Peace of 387/6.

[60] Xenophon 5.1.36.

[61] Robin Seager, "The King's Peace and the Balance of Power in Greece, 386–362 B.C.," *Athenaeum* 52 (1974): 36–63, esp. 38–39:

> The royal prescript did not assign to Sparta or to any other city the rôle of *prostates* of the peace [n. 9, Xenophon *Hellenica* 5.1.31]. The King himself appeared as the sole guarantor of the peace and as the self-appointed leader of those who would fight to bring it into being [n. 10, the emphasis is clearly on the period before the peace was actually made; see Hampl, *Staatsverträge*, 11]. Yet Persia showed herself ready and willing to let Sparta assume the *prostasia* of the treaty, for those implications of the peace that came at once to occupy the foreground and needed a *prostates* to enforce them were of vital importance to Sparta but of no direct concern to the King, who thus had no reason to become involved [see S. Accame, *La lega ateniese del secolo IV a.C.*, 6]. [. . .] Sparta had then succeeded in exploiting the terms of the peace to considerable effect before the peace was actually concluded. The uses to which she had put it had been entirely retrospective. Her aim had been to put an end to the revival of Athenian imperialism, Theban control of Boeotia and Argive dominion over Corinth—all of which she had been unable to do anything about in the course of the Corinthian War itself. In this sense it was certainly true, as Xenophon says, that although Sparta drew the war, she won the peace [n. 16, Xenophon *Hellenica* 5.1.36].

[62] Ryder, *Koine Eirene: General Peace and Local Independence in Ancient Greece* (Oxford: Oxford University Press for the University of Hull, 1965).

[63] The most glaring exception found in the King's Peace is in regard to the issue of autonomy. See J.A.O. Larsen's review of *Koine Eirene* (*Gnomon* 38 [1966]: 256–60): "Though R[yder] has referred to the fate of the Greek cities in Asia, as well as Lemnos, Imbros, and Scyros, he, nevertheless, states that 'for the first time the autonomy of all cities . . . had been recognized in a treaty ratified by the leading states and by the King' (41). It was rather all cities *except those which some great power wished to keep in subjection*"

(my italics). Later Larsen writes, "Yet it should be a warning to anyone tending to idealize the movement, that the treaties sometimes included a clause which limited the application of the freedom proclaimed in the treaty. This is clearest in the King's Peace, where, apparently, the exceptions were listed before the autonomy of the other poleis was proclaimed (Xen. Hell. 5, 1, 31)."

[64] See the criticism of Ryder in W. G. Forrest's review of *Koine Eirene*, *CR* 19/83 (1969): 211–12:

> More important, there is a failure to ram home (not to state, for who could fail to state it) that the Peace of 387 was an arrangement by which Sparta took control of Greece. Agesilaus said it: *pros ton eiponta tous Lakedaimonious medizein . . . apekrinato mallon tous Medous lakonizein*, and against the background of Spartan behaviour in the years that followed, "autonomy" and words like it must be treated as empty slogans—so too must *koine eirene*.

[65] The principal works devoted to the Second Athenian League are F. W. Marshall, *The Second Athenian Confederacy* (Cambridge: Cambridge University Press, 1905); S. Accame, *La lege atheniese del secolo IV a.C.* (Rome: Signorelli, 1940); and Jack Cargill, *The Second Athenian League: Empire or Free Alliance?* (Berkeley and Los Angeles: University of California Press, 1981). The relative chronology of the foundation of the Second Athenian League and the raid of Sphodrias is highly controversial. The *communis opinion*—and the one adopted in this work—is that Athens responded to the raid of Sphodrias with the formation of the Second Athenian League. This view is held by Ryder, *Koine Eirene*, 53–55; D. G. Rice, "Xenophon, Diodorus and the Year 379–378 B.C.," *YCS* 24 (1975): 112–27; Robert K. Sinclair, "The King's Peace and the Employment of Military and Naval Forces 387–378," *Chiron* 8 (1978): 52–54; John Buckler, *The Theban Hegemony, 371–362 B.C.* (Cambridge, MA: Harvard University Press, 1980), 17; Charles D. Hamilton, *Agesilaus and the Failure of Spartan Hegemony* (Ithaca, NY: Cornell University Press, 1991), 167–74, esp. 173; Ernst Badian, "The Ghost of Empire," 89–90, nn. 33–34. Contra: G. L. Cawkwell, "The Foundation of the Second Athenian Confederacy," *CQ* 23 (1973): 47–60; Raphael Sealey, *A History of the Greek City-States, ca. 700–338 B.C.* (Berkeley and Los Angeles: University of California Press, 1976), 410–412; Cargill, *Second Athenian Empire*; Robert Morstein Kalet-Marx, "Athens, Thebes, and the Foundation of the Second Athenian League," *CA* 4 (1985): 127–51; Robin Seager, *CAH*[2] 6.166f.

[66] Diodorus 15.28.2; see Plutarch *Pelopidas* 14.1. See *IG* II[2] 43 (Tod 123, 59–70; Harding 35, 48–52; *SV* 2.257, 207–211), which reiterated the reason for the formation of the League (ll. 7–12): "Aristoteles *made the motion*: To the good *fortune* of the A|thenians and *of the allies* of the Athenia|ns, in order that (the) Laced[aemo]nians may allow the Helle| |nes, free and autonomous, to live | in peace, holding in security the [land] (that is) *the | ir* [own]."

[67] Callistratus of Aphidna proposed substituting the term "contributions" (*syntaxeis*) for "tribute" (*phoroi*); see Harpokration, *Lexicon,* s.v. "syntaxis" (Theopompus, *FGrHist* 115F98).

[68] For Thebes, this entailed enrollment in an alliance whose strategic interests were vastly different from its own. Buckler maintains that the necessity to strengthen itself in relation to Sparta overrode all other Theban concerns. It was sufficient for Athens

and Thebes to share a common enemy. He writes (*The Theban Hegemony, 371–362 B.C.* [Cambridge, MA: Harvard University Press, 1980], 17–18): "Yet the military support of Athens was so vital to Thebes that submerging itself in the confederacy was a small price to pay for that support. . . . Once either state had attained a degree of security, the disparate goals and concerns of the two powers would drive them apart."

[69] For detailed discussions of Attica's border fortifications, see the major studies of J. R. McCredie, *Fortified Military Camps in Attica*, Hesperia, Suppl. 11 (Princeton, NJ: Princeton University Press, 1966), Josiah Ober, *Fortress Attica: Defense of the Athenian Land Frontier, 404–322 B.C.* (Leiden: Brill, 1982), and Mark H. Munn, *The Defense of Attica: The Dema Wall and the Boiotian War of 378–375 B.C.* (Berkeley and Los Angeles: University of California Press, 1993). The Athenians' investment in fortifications likely went beyond mere economic calculations. Victor Hanson, in a forthcoming review of Jurgen Brauer and Hubert Van Tuyll, *Castles, Battles, and Bombs: How Economics Explains Military History* (Chicago: University of Chicago Press, 2008), writes (email to author in advance of publication):

> Did the Athenians invest in Attic border forts in the fourth century BC because it was the most economical way to protect Athenian territory, and made more economic sense than hoplite armies, cavalry, light-armed skirmishers, or navies? Or, as losers in a twenty-seven-year-long Peloponnesian War, were they so traumatized from land invasion that fortifications seemed to be the most reassuring tactics of keeping out any more armies advancing from Boiotia and the Peloponnese?

[70] For the problems of dating walls in general, see, e.g., the detailed work of Robert Lorentz Scranton, *Greek Walls* (Cambridge, MA: Harvard University Press, 1941).

[71] Munn's attempt at a precise dating of the Dema Wall to the spring of 378 B.C. by the Athenian general Chabrias is an exception. See the review of Munn by Josiah Ober in *AJA* 98 (1994): 374–75 and by Victor Davis Hanson in *AHR* 99 (1994): 1662–63.

[72] Josiah Ober, *Fortress Attica: Defense of the Athenian Land Frontier, 404–322 B.C.* (Leiden: Brill, 1982), 64–65: "Rejection of the Periclean city defense strategy, fear of invasion, determination to protect Attica, and reluctance to send citizen armies to distant theaters of war are the major components of the defensive mentality which grew up in fourth-century Athens. It was this mentality that chiefly determined the course of Athens' defense policy in the period between the Peloponnesian and Lamian Wars." See also his fourth chapter, "The Theory of Defense," 69–86. See the review article of Ober by P. Harding, "Athenian Defensive Strategy in the Fourth Century," *Phoenix* 42 (1988): 61–71; Ober's response, *Phoenix* 43 (1989): 294–301; and Harding's response to Ober, *Phoenix* 44 (1990): 377–80. Munn also takes issue with Ober (see esp. 18–25), arguing (25), "Given the inherent implausibility of the hypothetical system together with the silence of the orators, the silence of Xenophon, the silence of Plato, and of all other sources, we must conclude that Ober and his predecessors have created *e silentio* a fabulous structure. Ober's 'preclusive defense system' never existed except as a modern figment." See also his review of *Fortress Attica* in *AJA* 90 (1986): 363–65. Victor Davis Hanson, "The Status of Ancient Military History: Traditional Work, Recent Research, and On-going Controversies," *The Journal of Military History* 63 (1999), writes (25):

J. Ober's *Fortress Attica* is a superb catalogue of the system of forts and towers built on the borders of Attica in the fourth century as part of a more flexible policy of response that replaced hoplite exclusivity. M. Munn, *The Defense of Attica*, has questioned some of Ober's interpretations of these forts, but his helpful ancillary volume is really more complementary than revisionist, and likewise emphasizes the Greeks' emphasis on border defense during the fourth century B.C., often in preference to open hoplite battles.

[73] See Y. Garlan (*CAH*[2] 6.678–92), who points to an increase in the use of mercenary soldiers and also the professionalism of military operations (679):

> For even though the final outcome was still frequently determined by pitched battles in open country, henceforth they constituted only one element in a strategy which was more complex than it had been in the past, being both differentiated and progressive, aimed at establishing control not only over useful territory but also over walled cities and increasingly well-fortified frontier zones. Hence more sophisticated and varied tactics were evolved, requiring the combined use of specialized forces (integrated on the model of the human body) and based on a professional concept of military leadership and prowess.

[74] Aristotle, *Politics*, 1330b–1331, trans. and ed. Ernest Barker, in *The Politics of Aristotle* (Oxford: Clarendon Press, 1946).

[75] David Whitehead, *Aineias the Tactician: How to Survive Under Siege. A Historical Commentary, with Translation and Introduction*, 2nd ed. (London: Bristol Classical Press, 2001). See his remarks in the Introduction, 25–33.

[76] E. W. Marsden, *Greek and Roman Artillery: Historical Development* (Oxford: Clarendon Press, 1969); A. W. McNicoll, *Hellenistic Fortifications from the Aegean to the Euphrates* (Oxford: Clarendon Press, 1997).

[77] Edward Wong and David S. Cloud, "U.S. Erects Baghdad Wall to Keep Sects Apart," *New York Times*, April 21, 2007.

[78] Alissa J. Rubin, Stephen Farrell, and Erica Goode, "As Fears Ease, Baghdad Sees Walls Tumble," *New York Times*, October 9, 2008.

[79] Note that in the first Gulf War, Saddam Hussein protected his troops in the field by enormous sand bunkers, and in the second Iraq War (2003) used canals of burning petroleum to cover Baghdad with protective smoke. In the 1973 Yom Kippur War, invading Egyptian commandos employed water cannons to knock down towering sand fortifications that the Israelis had constructed to block attack from the Suez Canal. The recent Russian invasion and occupation of Georgia was followed almost immediately by the erection of walls surrounding annexed territories in Ossetia.

4. Epaminondas the Theban and the Doctrine of Preemptive War

VICTOR DAVIS HANSON

THE SIXTEENTH-CENTURY FRENCH RENAISSANCE ESSAYIST Michel de Montaigne once compared what he thought were the three great captains of antiquity. He strangely concluded that the now rather obscure Epaminondas the Theban (d. 362 BC), not Alexander the Great or Julius Caesar, was the most preeminent because of his character, the ethical nature of his military career, and the lasting consequences of his victories.

Montaigne, a keen student of classical antiquity, was hardly eccentric in judging an obscure liberator of serfs in the southwestern Peloponnese superior to two imperialists who had respectively conquered much of the Persian Empire and Western Europe. Instead, he simply reflected the general sentiment of the Greeks and Romans themselves, who put a high premium on military brilliance in service to political idealism. For example, the Roman statesman Cicero, archfoe of Julius Caesar and Marc Antony, three centuries after the Theban general's death saw a kindred defender of republican liberty in Epaminondas, and similarly dubbed him *princeps Graecia*—"first man of Greece." The lost fourth-century BC historian Ephorus, a contemporary of the Theban hegemony, who wrote in the shadow of the autocrat Philip II, in hagiographic fashion considered Epaminondas the greatest of *all* Greeks, a military genius who fought for a cause other than personal aggrandizement.[1]

But while the ancients saw the Theban destruction of Spartan power and liberation of the Messenian helots as one of the landmark moral events in their collective memory, we know little today about the career of the Theban general and statesman Epaminondas, and even less about his accomplishments, strategic thinking, and controversial doctrines of preemption and democratization. His present-day obscurity is partly a result of the fragmentary nature of the extant sources, but it is also a reflection of the ancient and modern emphasis on Athens and Sparta and the general reputation of the Thebans for backwardness.[2]

Yet in little more than two years (371–369 BC), Epaminondas humiliated the Spartan military state, something neither the Persians nor the Athenians had ever accomplished in protracted wars. He freed many of the hundred thousand Messenian helots, fostered democracy for tens of thousands of Greeks, helped to found new fortified and autonomous cities, and waged a brilliant preemptory military campaign against the Spartan Empire—events eerily relevant nearly 2,400 years later to what followed from the terrorist attack on the United States on September 11, 2001.

FOURTH-CENTURY BOEOTIA

We usually associate ancient Greek democracy with the fifth-century Athens of Pericles—its enormous fleet, energized landless poor, maritime empire, and the brilliant cultural achievements of Pericles' contemporaries, such as Aristophanes, Euripides, Pheidias, Socrates, Sophocles, and Thucydides. In contrast, the later emergence of fourth-century Theban democratic hegemony is often ignored and less well understood, despite its unusual nature and political weight. Boeotian democratic culture certainly did not produce either a Thucydides or a Euripides. And it did not, as most elsewhere in the case of ancient democracies, reflect the influence of the landless naval crowd, pejoratively called the *ochlos*, or seek to redistribute income or enforce a radical egalitarianism on its citizenry that transcended mere political equality. Rather, the Boeotian democratic movement was likely more limited to expanding political participation and championed by conservative hoplite farmers. Similarly, in terms of empire, Theban reformist democrats seemed to have questioned the entire existing polis order of hundreds of autonomous city-states rather than creating, in

characteristic imperial fashion, an exploitive empire of subservient subject cities abroad.³

If the defeat of Persia in 479 proved the catalyst for the rise of the
Athenian imperium, the Greek allied victory over Athens in 404 in
turn helped usher in the gradual ascension of Thebes. After the conclusion of the Peloponnesian War (431–404 BC), the former victorious
allies, Thebes and Sparta, quickly turned on each other in squabbles
over booty, the treatment of defeated Athens, and respective spheres of
influence. Indeed, for most of the ensuing half-century (403–362), the
two rivals were in a near-constant state of conflict marked by pitched
battles, frequent Spartan invasions of Boeotia, and brief armistices.
Contemporaries largely viewed their early struggle as a sometimes lop-
sided contest between a traditionally superior Spartan phalanx and an
upstart Theban infantry hitherto considered formidable, but hardly an
instrument capable of projecting Theban power beyond the confines
of a cultural Boeotian backwater with a questionable history.⁴

The on-again, off-again decades-long struggles, however, took a radically different turn in 379 BC. In that year a remarkable group of Theban
democrats overthrew the ruling oligarchs under Leontiades, who was
propped up by Spartan overseers. In place of oligarchy, the reformers
instituted a Boeotian confederate democracy freed from outside influence and bent on ensuring a permanent end to Spartan meddling in the
affairs of the Greek city-states. Not only did the ongoing war between
the two rivals now assume a new ideological dimension, democracy
versus oligarchy, but the conflict was energized by this new group of
Theban firebrands, who were not quite doctrinaire in accepting traditional notions of a balance of power between the city-states. Instead,
led most notably by Pelopidas and, later, Epaminondas, Theban democrats came to the fore determined to eliminate permanently the source
of the Spartan threat.

In reaction, for much of the next eight years the Spartans were
bent on revenge for their own expulsion from Boeotia. King Agesilaus
rightly feared that the new Boeotian democracy under Epaminondas was no longer just a rival polis but rather a unique revolutionary
agent of change that could eventually threaten Sparta's own interests
in the Peloponnese, as well as refashion altogether the traditional

autonomous network of small individual city-states into larger and far more hostile democratic blocs and confederations. As a result of these apprehensions, between 379 and 375, on at least four occasions Spartan kings invaded, or attempted to invade, Boeotia to dismantle its new democratic Boeotian confederation.[5]

Aside from occasional military alliances with Athens, the Boeotians turned to a variety of both passive and active strategies to blunt these serial Spartan offensives. At various times they resorted to erecting an extensive wooden stockade around their most fertile farmland. Sometimes they harassed the invaders with both light-armed and mounted patrols. On rarer occasions they managed to draw them into skirmishes and small pitched battles, such as the surprisingly successful engagement at Tegyra in 375.

This Theban democratic and Spartan oligarchic rivalry initially played out in limited fashion, according to traditional Greek protocols of annual invasions in which the invader tried to harm the agricultural infrastructure of the invaded state. While King Agesilaus, the architect of the Theban invasions, almost succeeded for a season or two in bringing near famine to Thebes, and had established forts in a number of Boeotian cities—Plataea, Orchomenos, Tanagra, and Thespiae—the Spartans in their nearly decade-long efforts failed to end Theban democratic control of Boeotia. These years of serial and inconclusive fighting in Boeotia explain not only Epaminondas's later radical decision to meet the Spartans in pitched battle at Leuctra but also his subsequent, even larger gamble to attack Sparta itself. At some point in this decade, Epaminondas apparently saw there would be no end to the normal pattern of serial invasion and battle other than an end to Sparta as the Greeks had known it for the prior 300 years.[6]

THE INVASION OF WINTER AND SPRING 370–369

The pulse of this long war of attrition changed radically a second time sometime in midsummer 371, when the Spartans broke the general armistice of 375 and once again invaded Boeotia. But this time, under the leadership of the Theban general Epaminondas, the outnumbered Boeotian army at last chose to engage decisively the Spartan invaders in a dramatic pitched battle amid the rolling hills of Leuctra, not far from Thebes itself. There, in brilliant fashion, the Boeotian army nearly wrecked the invading force, killed the Spartan king Kleombrotos and about 400 of his elite 700 Spartan hoplites, as well as hundreds more of allied Peloponnesians, and sent the scattered survivors back home in shame and defeat, at once redefining the strategic balance of the Greek city-states and presaging a permanent end to what had been nearly annual Spartan invasions in the north.[7]

Most prior decisive victories in Greek hoplite battle—First Coronea (447), Delion (424), or First Mantineia (418)—had led to a regional cessation of major fighting for a few years. But the win at Leuctra, despite its decisive nature, soon led to a resurgence of, not an end to, Theban–Spartan hostilities, and proved to be a precursor of a vast reordering of the Peloponnese. If the Sicilian expedition of 415–413, in which some 40,000 imperial Athenian soldiers and allies were lost, captured, or killed, ended the dream of an expanding Athenian empire, the loss of about 1,000 Peloponnesians and the humiliation of the legendary Spartan military prowess at Leuctra had a similar effect of ending the idea of Spartan expansionary policy and questioning the stability of its very rule beyond the vale of Laconia.

About eighteen months after the battle (which occurred in July 371 BC), during December 370–369 BC, the general Epaminondas convinced the Boeotian leadership to embark on a preemptory strike to the south. The ostensible reason for intervention was a call for help to the Thebans from the newly consolidated Arcadian city of Mantineia to ward off the threat of constant Spartan invasion by King Agesilaus. Epaminondas seems to have concluded that even after Leuctra, the Spartan army still threatened large democratic states, and that it would only be a matter of time until the Spartans regrouped and attempted yet another annual incursion into Boeotia. The timely invitation from the Arcadians and other Peloponnesians to intervene on their behalf seems to have galvanized Epaminondas into envisioning an even larger—and final—plan to end the Spartan hegemony of the Peloponnese altogether.[8]

Epaminondas's huge allied army included thousands of Peloponnesians who joined the invasion at various places south of the Corinthian Isthmus, among them perhaps some of those Peloponnesians spared over a year earlier at Leuctra. The march followed a nearly 200-mile route into the heart of the Spartan state, a legendarily inviolate landscape said to have been untouched by enemies for some 350 years. After ravaging the Spartan homeland and bottling the Spartan army up inside the city across the icy Eurotas, the Boeotians failed to storm the acropolis. Instead, after burning the Spartan port at Gytheion twenty-seven miles to the south, Epaminondas's Boeotians, along with some contingents of their victorious Peloponnesian allies, decided to head west in midwinter across the range of Mt. Taygetos into Messenia, the historical breadbasket of the Spartan state, where indentured serfs, known as helots, supplied foodstuffs and manpower for the Spartan state.[9]

The Boeotians probably descended from the uplands of Taygetos sometime after the first of the year 369 BC, routed the Spartans from their rich protectorate in Messenia, freed most of the helots there, and helped to found the vast citadel of Messene. Before they departed the following spring, Epaminondas had ensured a new autonomous and democratic state of Messenia, its fortified capital at Messene now essentially immune from Spartan reprisals. And by the time Epaminondas had marched home, he had humiliated the Spartan state and ended its parasitical reliance on Messenian food, a relationship essential to freeing up the Spartan warrior-citizen caste to focus on warfare. His dream of an anti-Spartan axis anchored by Messene, the new fortified Mantineia, and the rising Megalopolis seemed to be approaching reality.[10]

The remarkable invasion itself was an anomaly in a variety of ways. Early fourth-century Greek armies, even after the innovative tactics that emerged during the Peloponnesian War (431–404), still usually marched in late spring, preferably around the time of the grain harvest, to ensure good weather and secure adequate rations in the field, as well as to have a better chance at burning the ripening and drying wheat and barley crops of the invaded. Such seasonal armies usually were not absent for more than a few days or weeks because of their own harvesttime obligations. As nonprofessionals, they had little ability to provision themselves for extended stays abroad, whether judged by distance or by time away from home. Usually the target was a nearby enemy army or the agricultural resources of a neighboring hostile power rather than the utter defeat of a more distant adversity and the end of its existence as an autonomous state. Total war intended to destroy a relatively large state was rare.[11]

Epaminondas in remarkable fashion ignored most of such past protocol of internecine Greek warfare. He chose to leave Thebes in December, when there were no standing crops in the field, the roads were muddy, and his one-year tenure as Boeotarch was set to expire within days of his departure at the first of the Boeotian year. He may have remained gone for as long as five to six months, until near late spring harvesttime, 369. And Epaminondas faced certain trial on his return for violating the terms of his one-year tenure of command. His aims were not just the defeat of the Spartan military or even occupation of the Spartan acropolis but apparently, either before or after he arrived in the Peloponnese, a sustained effort to end the Spartan state itself.[12]

Clearly, there was a sense of urgency in his decision to wage such an unprecedented preemptive war in midwinter, and that anomaly raises a number of critical questions. Was such a preemptive strike unusual in Greek history? What were the larger aims of Epaminondas, and did he achieve his long-term objectives? Or did his Boeotians simply widen an already long and costly struggle between two former allies? Was such a preemptive war sustainable, given domestic political opposition at home and the finite resources available for such costly and lengthy commitments abroad? And does the Theban experience with preemptive war and spreading democracy have any lessons for the present?

Before answering those questions, it should be noted again that while the classical world considered Epaminondas among its most preeminent heroes, we have very little information about his career, and we know even less about the details of his great first invasion of the Peloponnese and the founding of Messene. There are no surviving in-depth ancient speeches that reflect his plans, or much editorializing on the part of historians about his intentions. Xenophon, the only extant contemporary historian of the era who chronicled the Theban invasions, either did not appreciate the magnitude of Epaminondas's achievement (Epaminondas is not mentioned by name in the *Hellenica* until his final campaign and death at Mantineia; see 7.5.4–25) or harbored a generic prejudice against all things Theban. Plutarch's life of Epaminondas is lost. As a result, we rely on bits and pieces in Diodorus,

Plutarch's *Pelopidas* and *Agesilaus*, Pausanias, and later compilers such as Nepos. To a large degree, the motivations and aims of Epaminondas are difficult to recover and remain seemingly iconoclastic and not easy to fathom.[13]

PREEMPTIVE AND PREVENTIVE WARS

Both preemptive and preventive wars in varying degrees are justified as defensive acts, and thus supposedly differ from wars of outright aggression or blatantly punitive strikes. No one, for example, suggests that the Persian king Xerxes invaded Greece in 480 to prevent an impending major Hellenic attack on the Persian Empire. Nor did Alexander the Great cross the Hellespont to stop Darius III from striking Greece first. For all the talk of "the brotherhood of man," he was bent on aggression, plunder, and conquest, under the banner of paying the Persians back for more than a century of meddling in Greek affairs.

Despite the Athenian rhetoric of 415, on the eve of the disastrous Sicilian Expedition, about past grievances and future dangers emanating from the West, such as Alcibiades's warning that "Men do not rest content with parrying the attacks of a superior, but often strike the first blow to prevent the attack being made," few Athenians probably believed the pretense that the expedition against Syracuse anticipated, either in the short or the long term, a Sicilian attack on the Athenian Empire. Instead, this too was a clear case of imperial aggression, aimed at finding strategic advantage during a hiatus in the Peloponnesian War. The list of such unambiguously aggressive wars could easily be expanded in the Greek world and would include such episodes as the Persian invasions of Greek territory in 492 and 490, Agesilaus's attack on Asia Minor in 396 to liberate the Greek city-states of Ionia, and Philip's descent into Greece in 338, which culminated in the Greek defeat at Chaeronea.[14]

In contrast, among the so-called defensive wars, preemption is usually distinguished from preventive war by the apparent perception—or at least claim—of a credibly imminent threat. The reality of that assertion determines whether an attack is generally accepted as genuinely defensive. When a state—often one considered the traditionally weaker side—preempts and strikes first, it is supposedly convinced that otherwise an existentially hostile target itself will surely soon attack, and will do so with much greater advantage. Again, this initial aggression of preemptive wars is usually framed as defensive in nature, if the presence of a looming danger is generally recognized. And the argument is strengthened further if there is a past history of conflict between the two belligerents.[15]

Truly preventive wars, on the other hand, such as the Iraq War of 2003 or the German invasion of the Soviet Union in June 1941, are much more controversial. The attacker—now usually assumed to be the stronger power—claims that time will increasingly favor the geopolitical status of an innately aggressive and strengthening adversary that sooner or later might strike and change the status quo. Thus the instigator believes that its own inevitably declining position vis-à-vis a belligerent rival can be aborted by weakening or eliminating a potential threat before such an action proves less promising or impossible in the future. But because the imminence of danger is usually far less likely to be universally recognized than is true in cases of preemption, and since the initiator is usually the currently more militarily powerful, preventive wars are far more often easily criticized as wars of aggression.

The Japanese, for example, convinced no one that their "preventive" Pearl Harbor strike of December 7, 1941, was aimed at weakening an enemy that otherwise would only have one day become stronger in an inevitable American-Japanese war to come. Most felt it was the first step in a westward expansion across the Pacific to augment the preexisting Japanese-led Asian Co-Prosperity Sphere. In turn, the United States did not seek to strike Japan first, out of fear that such an attack might *not* be seen as an understandable *preemptive* war to ward off an imminent Japanese aggression but rather at best as a more controversial *preventive* war that would be denounced by many isolationist Americans as optional, bellicose, and imperial rather than defensive and necessary.

A beleaguered Israel, to general world approval, preempted by mere hours its Arab enemies during the Six-Day War of June 1967 by striking Egyptian airfields before its neighbors were expected to invade Israel. But in contrast, any contemporary strike on Iranian nuclear facilities by a stronger Israeli military, in the manner of its 1981 bombing of the Iraqi reactor at Osirak, would be widely criticized. It would be interpreted as the first act of a more dubiously preventive war, undertaken on the more controversial premise not that Iran was planning an immediate launch against Israel but that Teheran's acquisition of a nuclear weapon, coupled with its much publicized promises to end the Jewish state, would someday mean a dramatic threat to Israeli security and a future weakening of its unquestioned military superiority in the region.

Of course, the fine distinction between the rare preventive war and the more common preemptive war is not always clear. What constitutes an imminent threat is always in dispute and in the eye of the beholder. Nearly every state that initiates actual hostilities denies that it is acting offensively and claims that it is simply forced to go to war for its own self-defense, the initial details of the hostility soon becoming largely irrelevant. When the Bush administration chose to focus just on Iraq's weapons of mass destruction threat to justify the preventive invasion of Iraq, despite the U.S. Congress in October 2002 authorizing twenty-three writs for the removal of the Hussein regime in Iraq, world opinion and soon American public opinion turned against the controversial war. The subsequent absence of stockpiles of dangerous weapons meant the most publicized official justification for a war to remove a genocidal tyrant had proven false. Yet even after such stockpiles were not found, criticism largely mounted only in summer 2003, when the administration could not maintain peace after a brilliant three-week victory over the Baathist regime once a terrorist insurgency had prompted a new dirty war.

In the ancient Greek world, we can find clear examples of both preemptive and preventive strategies. The generally recognized stronger Spartans crossed the Athenian border in 431 claiming they had the right of preventive invasion to start the Peloponnesian War. Sparta was convinced not that Athens was about to attack it that year but rather that, as Thucydides relates, without such a first strike, the unstoppable growth of a hostile Athenian empire would soon lead to Sparta's inevitable decline. The Spartans were justifiably terrified: "They then felt that they could endure it no longer, but that the time had come for them to throw themselves heart and soul upon the hostile power, and break it, if they could, by commencing the present war."[16]

In the same manner, shortly before the Spartan king Archidamaus reached Attica, his ally Thebes attacked the nearby Boeotian city of Plataea. Again, the Thebans were not so worried that the tiny city was about to help launch an Athenian attack. Instead, the attackers figured that Athenian-backed democratic movements in Boeotia, charged by the zeal and wealth of imperial Athens and the example of an independent Plataea, would eventually weaken the relative position of Thebes.

In fact, a frequent tactic of ancient Greek armies was to attack without warning a nearby suspicious city-state and destroy its walls, as the unfortunate history of the much-invaded polis of Thespiae attests. Perhaps the defense of preemptive attack was best articulated by the Theban general Pagondas moments before the battle of Delium (424 BC): "People who, like the Athenians in the present instance, are tempted by pride of strength to attack their neighbors, usually march most confidently against those who keep still, and only defend themselves in their own country, but think twice before they grapple with those who meet them outside their frontier and strike the first blow if opportunity offers."[17]

Epaminondas's strike of 369 should be seen more as a preemptive than as a preventive war. True, while Sparta had been defeated a little more than a year earlier at Leuctra and was not planning for an immediate invasion of Boeotia, it was nevertheless busy invading the territories of other city-states while rebuilding its own forces. Indeed, Sparta had just entered Mantineia in summer 370 to undermine the establishment of a new united democratic polis. Thebes was seen by other Greek states to be the traditionally weaker power, and it could reasonably be expected that the Spartans would soon, as they had done in the Peloponnesian War, attack first, in an effort to try to reverse the verdict of Leuctra and reestablish the Spartan supremacy of the 380s.

While the defeat at Leuctra in midsummer 371 proved the beginning of the end for Spartan power, much of the enduring trauma was psychological, as the army itself probably suffered not much more than 1,000 combined Spartiate and allied hoplites killed. That was a grievous loss, but nevertheless, 90 percent of the composite army survived and made it back to the Peloponnese. Most city-states would have agreed with Epaminondas that the Spartan danger to the Boeotian confederacy from the traditionally more powerful Sparta in 370 was still real and indeed imminent, rather than long term and theoretical.

THE LONGER-TERM AIMS OF EPAMINONDAS

It was the plan of Epaminondas—no doubt subject to some opposition from his fellow Boeotarchs—to preempt Sparta by invading the Peloponnese, and then to take the unprecedented step of advancing into the Laconian homeland. The unusual decision to accept the invitation of the Mantineians and embark on a winter invasion suggests two further considerations. First, Epaminondas probably felt that Sparta might soon strike well beyond its invasion of the territory of Mantineia, perhaps during the campaign season the ensuing late spring or summer. Hitting the Spartans first, whether near Mantineia or in Laconia itself, by leaving in winter would preclude that, and offer some measure of surprise. The Boeotians' conjecture was strengthened when other states in the Peloponnese sent money to defray the cost of the preemptive invasion.[18]

Second, at some point in early 370, if indeed not before, the invasion was envisioned as part of a larger expedition to reorder the Peloponnese by humiliating or defeating the Spartan military, assuring the new Arcadian cities of Mantineia and Megalopolis of Boeotian protection, freeing the helots of Messenia, and founding the new city of Messene on Mt. Ithome. All that would require months abroad, and made it preferable to leave in winter so that the army of mostly farmers could return to Boeotia by at least harvesttime 369.[19]

Despite the meager contemporary descriptions of the Boeotian invasion, we can assume that Epaminondas desperately sought to draw the Spartan phalanx out to battle; and then, barring that, to cross the Eurotas River and storm the Spartan acropolis and physically destroy the center of the Spartan rule. His desire was not the defeat but the apparent end of the Spartan land empire in the Peloponnese. But once those immediate goals failed and the Boeotians proved unable either to annihilate the Spartan army or to capture the city, in the new year 369 Epaminondas ignored the legal end of his tenure as general. He instead kept the army in the Peloponnese and, after brief deliberations in Arcadia, moved on to his second objective of freeing the helots of Messenia, apparently in the belief that the end of Messenian serfdom eventually might emasculate Sparta, which he was so far unable to destroy outright.[20]

This was a far more ambitious goal. It required his army to cross the spurs of Mt. Taygetos in early winter, rid Messenia of its Spartan garrison, marshal the serfs into work forces, immediately begin the construction of a vast new city, and assume that Messenian nationalists would be reliable democratic allies, all while holding the forces of King Agesilaus to his rear at bay. The apparent dream of Epaminondas was a confederation of three huge Peloponnesian citadels at Mantineia, Megalopolis, and Messene, all fortified and democratic, that, under the guidance of Thebes, would constrain Spartan adventurism while slowly eroding the power of the Spartan state, shed of its helot laborers and subservient allies. Although Epaminondas was not adverse to making occasional alliances of convenience with oligarchic states in the Peloponnese, he seems to have assumed that the new confederated democracies in Arcadia and Messenia would, by their natural political interests, remain intrinsically hostile to Sparta and sympathetic to kindred democratic Boeotia.[21]

AFTERMATH

Was Epaminondas's preemptive attack of 370–369 successful in the long run?

If it was intended solely to stop four decades of serial Spartan invasions of Boeotia, the answer is unequivocally yes. The Spartan army never again went north of the isthmus in force to attack another Greek city-state. If the strike was aimed at undermining the foundations of the Spartan Empire and its power, the goals were likewise unambiguously achieved. While the Spartan army still on occasion defeated regional rival states in battle, most notably in the famous "tearless battle" and rout of the Arcadians in 368, Sparta's land empire in the Peloponnese slowly dissolved with the creation of the autonomous states at Mantineia, Messene, and Megalopolis, coupled with the freeing of the Messenian helots and the loss of Spartan farmland in Messenia. In its twilight, Sparta struggled to remain one among equal Peloponnesian powers, but, as a strategically insignificant state, Sparta was notably absent thirty years later in the pan-Hellenic effort to stop the Macedonians at Chaeronea.[22]

Second, did the invasion of 369 end the war outright with Sparta?

Hardly. The oligarchy and empire of Sparta had created a sort of stability within the Peloponnese since the Athenian war ended at the close of the fifth century. Following the Theban liberation of the helot and allied cities from Spartan domination, an upheaval ensued that prompted three more Boeotian invasions of the Peloponnese in 369, 368, and 362, before culminating in the final indecisive battle of Mantineia (362). At that engagement Epaminondas was killed at the moment of Boeotian victory. As the historian Xenophon famously remarked, "There was even more confusion and upheaval in Greece after than before the battle." Diodorus used the occasion to offer his eulogy of Epaminondas in the context that his death meant an end to the brief Theban hegemony altogether.[23]

Apparently the original visions of Epaminondas, at whatever point they were reified, may not have been merely to keep Sparta out of Boeotia but also to reorder the Greek world in such a way as to preclude any chance of Spartan reemergence, an undertaking that would have meant for distant Thebes an almost continual military presence in the Peloponnese. Such a mammoth enterprise would have required capital reserves, some sea power, and political unity—requisites beyond the resources of a deeply divided, rural democratic Thebes. Epaminondas himself seemed finally to have grasped the limits of Boeotian power and the growth of political opposition to his grandiose plans abroad when in 362 he aimed once again at invading Laconia and capturing the Spartan acropolis, as if his previous accomplishments of freeing the helots and establishing fortified democratic cities were not having the desired effect of promptly ending Sparta altogether as a player in regional Greek politics.[24]

Autonomia—local political independence—was a Hellenic ideal held even higher than *dêmokratia*. Once the democratic federated states of Arcadia gained their independence from both Sparta and Thebes, there was no assurance that their assemblies, out of gratitude to Epaminondas, would continue to privilege the Boeotian alliance. By 362 Epaminondas was invading the Peloponnese not just to finish off Sparta but also to fight Mantineia, the democratic ally whose plight had prompted his initial invasion nearly a decade earlier.

Apparently by 362, the Mantineians had calculated that a now weakened, nearby, and Doric Sparta was a better pragmatic, balance-of-power ally than was an aggressive Boeotian hegemon to the north. Thebes had served to ensure democracy to the Mantineians and weakened its traditional ally, Sparta; the Mantineians in turn reciprocated by judging an aggressive, though kindred, democratic Thebes far more a bother to the traditional autonomy of the Greek city-state.

LESSONS FROM EPAMINONDAS'S PREEMPTIVE WAR

Where Does This End?

While successful preemptive war may result in an immediate strategic advantage, the dividends of such a risky enterprise are squandered if there is not a well-planned effort to incorporate military success into a larger political framework that results in some sort of advantageous peace. By its very definition, an optional preemptive war must be short, a sort of decapitation of enemy power that stuns it into paralysis and forces it to grant political concessions. In democratic states, such a controversial gamble cannot garner continued domestic public support if the attack instead leads to a drawn-out, deracinating struggle, the very sort of quagmire that preemption was originally intended to preclude. Like it or not, when successful and followed by a period of quiet, preemption is often ultimately considered moral, justified, and defensive; when costly and unsuccessful in securing peace, in hindsight it always looks optional, foolhardy, and aggressive.

Epaminondas grasped the paradox that he was fighting against both the Spartans and time, given uncertain public opinion back home, and thus, once he failed to destroy the Spartan acropolis and its political and military elite, he turned to two contingency plans that might nevertheless have ended the hostilities with a permanently weakened Sparta on terms favorable to Thebes with a definitive cessation of fighting. Had Epaminondas before venturing into Messenia been able to cross the Eurotas and burn Sparta, defeat its remaining hoplites inside Laconia, and free all the Laconian helots as well, it is very likely that Sparta would have disappeared altogether as a major polis in the winter of 370–369, without need for further invasions of the Boeotian army in subsequent years.

In contrast, the democratization of the Peloponnese was a longer-term project. If successful, it meant the slow recession of the Spartan oligarchic empire, as it could never reconstruct its Peloponnesian alliance under its own auspices, given the presence of three huge fortified rivals and its own ineptness in the art of siegecraft.[25]

Second, the end to Messenian helotage would eventually require the Spartans to produce more of their own food and would insidiously erode the notion of a state-supported military caste, whose preeminence in hoplite battle had in the past substituted for a lack of manpower. The vestiges of local Laconian helotage apparently did not supply enough food to ensure successful continuation of the traditional elite Spartan military culture.

When Epaminondas died, his military goals had been largely achieved, even though there was no longer much Boeotian support, after his death, for once more invading the Peloponnese to complete his original intention of destroying Sparta itself. This suggests that the tragedy of Epaminondas may have been his inability to recognize that by 362, the Thebans had already achieved his objectives in permanently weakening Spartan influence. In some sense, Epaminondas's continued efforts in the Peloponnese were merely trying to hasten, in somewhat dangerous and ultimately unnecessary fashion, the end of Spartan hegemony that was already inevitable given his prior labors. If Thebes was unable to continue its military preeminence after the death of Epaminondas, at least the diminution of Sparta proved permanent.

Means and Ends

The initial failure to destroy Sparta itself in 369 meant that a short preemptive war transmogrified into a decade-long slog, requiring far more resources than originally envisioned. The beguiling attraction of preemptive war is that it is seen as an economical means to solve a problem of a dangerous and disadvantageous peace, without leading to a drawn-out, exhausting war. So it is unlikely that Epaminondas envisioned in 370 that his initial winter invasion would almost immediately be followed by a second late summer return in 369, and two more within the next seven years, with the endpoint his own death in battle against the Spartans eight years later at Mantineia.

Similarly, after the 2003 war, the United States and its allies apparently understood that their preemptive effort to remove Saddam Hussein would immediately require some sort of occupation. The coalition's fostering of civil, democratic society was designed to preclude the reemergence of a similarly autocratic leader like Saddam Hussein who might likewise translate Iraqi's enormous petroleum wealth into military arsenals, regional aggression, and threats to a great deal of the world's oil reserves.

The premise at first appeared sound. But the calculation of the degree of difficulty in bringing the first constitutional government to the Arab Islamic Middle East, in the heart of the ancient caliphate, was overly optimistic, for neither Iraq nor the Middle East in general proved immediately receptive to foreign-imposed democratic government following the end of Saddam Hussein. Given the nature of the modern democratic consumer capitalist society, the American public and its European allies were far less willing to tolerate a five-year occupation, costing more than 4,200 dead and nearly a trillion dollars in expenditures, than a tiny Boeotia was to support the nine-year plan of Epaminondas, which, from the victory at Leuctra to the defeat at Mantineia, meant nearly constant fighting and an endless financial and human drain on a poor agricultural state. The enemies of Epaminondas no doubt made some of the identical arguments against a foreign preemptive war that antiwar opponents brought against the Iraq conflict, among them that the long-term gains were uncertain, while the immediate costs were undeniable.

To be successful, then, preemption, like preventive wars, must change the conditions for the original hostility, and rather promptly, either by destroying an enemy altogether, as was the case of Carthage in Rome's Third Punic War, or by altering its politics to create an ally in place of an enemy. And while a preemptive strike may weaken an enemy, it is risky to leave a wounded target, angry and with a desire and a legal basis for retaliation.

In the end, preemptive war is a paradox. It is attractive because it offers a quick, sudden means of eliminating a threat and assumes that the enemy will not have the military means to withstand attack, but to be successful in the long run, it often involves a postwar investment at odds with its original attraction of quick, surprise, and limited attacks.

Democratic Irony

In both the ancient Peloponnese and contemporary Iraq, preemptive war was intended to lead to the creation of new democratic states that in turn would enhance regional stability and evolve into like-minded democratic parties. To a large extent this was true of the consequences of Epaminondas's invasion of 370–369, as Mantineia, Megalopolis, and Messene for a time became the fetters that prevented the Spartan army from either reconstituting the Spartan land empire or marching northward toward the isthmus. That said, as democratic autonomous states, their own foreign policies reflected local concerns that sometimes could transcend ideological solidarity and hinge more on balance-of-power considerations. By 362 Mantineia, for example, was back on the side of oligarchic Sparta and fighting kindred democratic Thebes.

Again, the irony is that unleashing the democratic genie hardly ensures perpetual allegiance to its liberator, as the United States discovered through much of 2008 in acrimonious negotiations with the Iraqi government over everything from future security guarantees to relations with Iran. That said, it was a truism in the ancient world, as it is in the modern world, that democratic states are less likely than oligarchies to fight other democracies, a fact that eventually works to the long-term advantage of democratic liberators.

ANCIENT PREEMPTION AND MODERN IRAQ

By 2004 many observers were citing the infamous Athenian expedition to Sicily of 415–413, launched during a lull in the Peloponnesian War—200 Athenian imperial ships lost, tens of thousands of coalition troops lost or unaccounted for—as the proper warning about the Iraq War. Both the United States and ancient Athens, it was argued, with plenty of enemies in an ongoing war, had foolishly "taken their eye off the ball" and had preempted and unilaterally begun yet another optional conflict, this time unnecessarily against an enemy that posed no elemental threat. Many commentators pointed to the hysterical warmongering in the Athenian assembly on the eve of the war, graphically related by the historian Thucydides, as an eerie reminder of how rhetors, generals, and politicians can whip up public sentiment for foolhardy disastrous imperial schemes.[26]

But on closer examination, many of the apparent similarities collapse. The democratic Athenians attacked the largest democracy in the ancient world, at a time when Syracuse had a larger resident population than Athens itself. To keep such a dubious ancient–modern analogy proper, it would be instead as if the United States, in a relative truce with radical Islam, suddenly invaded a distant and democratic India, a multi-religious state that was not a threat but was far distant, and larger than the United States itself.

More problematic still is Thucydides' analytical assessment of the Sicilian disaster, in some ways at odds with his own prior narrative of events. Defeat at Syracuse, he says, was not preordained. It arose not necessarily from poor planning or flawed thinking, although his own history in books VI and VII often suggests just that. The real culprit, the historian argues in his summation, was the inability of the Athenians at home to fully support the war they had authorized—a theme he sounds frequently in his history, especially in the speeches of the Athenian statesman Pericles, who chastised the fickle Athenians for being for the Peloponnesian War when they thought it would be easy and short, and then blaming him for sole responsibility when the struggle proved difficult and long.[27]

Instead, for rough parallels in the ancient world that better serve as reminders about the complexities of the preemptive war and its aftermath—with special reference to Iraq in particular—none is more telling than Epaminondas's invasion of 370–369. The Boeotians' preemptive war was aimed at eliminating a longstanding hostile regime in hopes of ensuring stability and alliance by fostering democracy in the region. Prior to the preemptive attack, Boeotia had been in an on-and-off war with Sparta even longer than the twelve-year hostility between the United

States and Iraq that began in 1990 with the Iraqi attack on Kuwait and continued with the subsequent American enforcement of no-fly zones within Iraqi airspace. Epaminondas and his advisers, both at home and abroad, were seen to have been democratic zealots, eager to enact far-reaching goals that were both beyond the resources of Boeotia and without reliable long-term public support. Indeed, Pythagorean utopian zealots supposedly surrounded Epaminondas in the same manner that neoconservative idealists purportedly influenced George W. Bush.[28]

To judge whether either the American or Boeotian efforts were wise, or achieved results that justified the ensuing expense, in some sense depends on how one adjudicates the ensuing strategic calculus, the relative human and material costs of the respective invasions, and the number of lives that were helped or hurt by the enterprise. Before Epaminondas, the Peloponnese was largely oligarchic and at the mercy of Spartan influence, a hundred thousand or more Messenian helots were enslaved, and Sparta had a long record of invading democratic states in northern Greece. After nine years of a long and expensive war (we have no records of the aggregate numbers of Boeotian dead and wounded), the Peloponnese emerged largely democratic, the helots of Messenia enjoyed an autonomous and democratic state, Sparta was permanently emasculated, and the Greek city-states to the north stayed free from Spartan attack.[29]

By the end of 2008, the long ordeal in Iraq had tragically cost more than 4,200 American dead, along with hundreds of allied casualties, nearly a trillion dollars, and thousands more wounded—and seemingly had led to a relatively quiet and democratic Iraq whose beleaguered people were free, and elected a government as friendly to the United States as it was hostile to radical Islamic terrorists. Long after contemporary political furor over Iraq has quieted, history alone will judge in the modern instance, as it has in the ancient, whether such an expensive preemptive gamble ever justified the cost.[30]

FURTHER READING

What little we know about the career of Epaminondas and his preemptive attack in 370–369 on the Peloponnese is found in Xenophon's *Hellenica* and *Agesilaus*, the history of

Diodorus, and Plutarch's *Pelopidas* and *Agesilaus*, supplemented by information in Pausanias and Nepos (see the notes for the specific references). John Buckler in various works has serially discussed the rise of Boeotia under Epaminondas; see J. Buckler and H. Beck, *Central Greece and the Politics of Power in the Fourth Century BC* (Cambridge: Cambridge University Press, 2008); J. Buckler, *Aegean Greece in the Fourth Century* (Leiden: Brill, 2003), and idem, *The Theban Hegemony* (Cambridge, MA: Harvard University Press, 1980).

For the career of Epaminondas as a democratic liberator, see Victor Hanson, *The Soul of Battle* (New York: Anchor Paperbacks, 2001). There is a good description of Leuctra that has references to the major secondary and primary sources in J. K. Anderson, *Military Theory and Practice in the Age of Xenophon* (Berkeley and Los Angeles: University of California Press, 1993). Epaminondas is discussed at length from a Spartan perspective in P. Cartledge, *Agesilaos and the Crisis of Sparta* (Baltimore: Johns Hopkins University Press, 1987), and C. Hamilton, *Agesilaus and the Failure of Spartan Hegemony* (Ithaca, NY: Cornell University Press, 1991). For a larger narrative of events surrounding the decade of Theban hegemony, see also D. M. Lewis, J. Boardman, S. Hornblower, and M. Ostwald, *The Cambridge Ancient History: The Fourth Century B.C.*, vol. 6 (Cambridge: Cambridge University Press, 1994), 187–208 (J. Roy).

For specialists, almost all the ancient evidence concerning Epaminondas is collated (in Italian) by M. Fortina, *Epaminonda* (Turin: Società Editrice Internazional, 1958), and (in German) by H. Swoboda, s.v. "Epameinondas," in A. Pauly, G. Wissowa, W. Kroll, K. Witte, K. Mittelhaus, and K. Ziegler, eds. *Paulys Realencyclopädie der classischen Altertumswissenschaft: Neue Bearbeitung* (Stuttgart: J. B. Metzler, 1894–1980), 10:2674–707.

NOTES

[1] See Alfredo Bonadeo, "Montaigne on War," *Journal of the History of Ideas* 46, no. 3 (July–September 1985): 421–22. Cicero *Tusculanae Disputationes* 1.2.4; Ephorus (in Diodorus 15.88.2–4). It should be noted that young student Gen. George Patton admired Epaminondas as a model of military and ethical excellence: "Epaminondas was without doubt the best and one of the greatest Greeks who ever lived, without ambition, with great genius, great goodness, and great patriotism; he was for the age in which he lived almost a perfect man." See Victor Davis Hanson, *The Soul of Battle* (New York: Anchor Paperbacks, 2001), 283.

[2] There are still no biographies of Epaminondas in English, an understandable situation in light of the loss of the Plutarch's *Epaminondas*, the relative neglect of Boeotia in our sources, and our reliance for fourth-century Greek history on Xenophon's *Hellenica* and *Agesilaus*, which so often short Epaminondas. But two well-documented accounts that collate almost all the scattered ancient literary citations surrounding his life can be found in M. Fortina, *Epaminonda* (Turin: Società Editrice Internazional, 1958); and H. Swoboda, s.v. "Epameinondas," in *Paulys Realencyclopädie der classischen Altertumswissenschaft: Neue Bearbeitung*, ed. A. Pauly, G. Wissowa, W. Kroll, K. Witte, K. Mittelhaus, and K. Ziegler, vol. 10 (Stuttgart: J. B. Metzler, 1894–1980), 2674–707.

[3] On the nature of agrarian egalitarianism in rural classical Boeotia that predated the fourth-century establishment of the more radical democracy of Epaminondas and

Pelopidas, see Victor Hanson, *The Other Greeks* (Berkeley and Los Angeles: University of California Press, 1998), 207–10.

⁴ There are several accounts of the rise of the Theban hegemony after the Boeotians' break with Sparta following their successful alliance against Athens in the Peloponnesian War. A narrative of events is found in J. Buckler, *The Theban Hegemony*, (Cambridge, MA: Harvard University Press, 1980), especially his summation at 220–27. See also D. M. Lewis, J. Boardman, S. Hornblower, and M. Ostwald, *The Cambridge Ancient History: The Fourth Century B.C.*, vol. 4 (Cambridge: Cambridge University Press, 1994), 187–208 (J. Roy). We should remember that Thebes "medized" during the Persian War, fighting against the Greeks at the battle of Plataea. On the Athenian stage, a macabre mythology typically was associated with Thebes, as the incest, self-mutilation, fratricide, suicide, and sacrilege accorded the dead of the Oedipus cycle attest.

⁵ On some of the events of the period, see J. T. Hooker, *The Ancient Spartans* (London: Dent, 1980), 22–211. Thebes had demanded of Sparta autonomy for its Peloponnesian subservient allies, but it resisted reciprocal Spartan calls to allow the cities of Boeotia to be independent of Thebes, on the somewhat strained logic that they were already democratic and thus free, and as fellow Boeotians apparently needed group solidarity to resist oligarchic and foreign challenges.

⁶ For the Spartan invasions of Boeotia and the various responses to these serial Spartan attacks, see M. Munn, *The Defense of Attica* (Berkeley and Los Angeles: University of California Press, 1993), 129–83, and especially Paul Cartledge, *Agesilaos and the Crisis of Sparta* (Baltimore: Johns Hopkins University Press, 1987), 228–32.

⁷ For a good account of the battle of Leuctra and its strategic ramifications, see J. K. Anderson, *Military Theory and Practice in the Age of Xenophon* (Berkeley and Los Angeles: University of California Press, 1993), 193–202; C. Hamilton, *Agesilaus and the Failure of Spartan Hegemony* (Ithaca, NY: Cornell University Press, 1991), 211–14.

J. Buckler, *Aegean Greece in the Fourth Century* (Leiden: Brill, 2003), 293, n. 56, has a contentious note about my own criticisms of his earlier, and I still think mistaken, reconstructions of Leuctra (Victor Hanson, "Epameinondas, the Battle of Leuktra [371 BC], and the 'Revolution' in Greek Battle Tactics," *Classical Antiquity* 7 [1988]: 190–207). Buckler fails to grasp that demonstrating that none of Epaminondas's tactics at Leuctra per se (the combined use of cavalry and infantry, a supposed reserve force of hoplites, an oblique advance, putting the better contingents on the left, or the use of a deep phalanx) were in themselves novel is not the same as denying military insight and genius to Epaminondas in combining at Leuctra *previously known* military innovations.

⁸ For details of the invasion, see Buckler, *Theban Hegemony*, 71–90; Hanson, *Soul of Battle*, 72–94; and D. R. Shipley, *Plutarch's Life of Agesilaos: Response to Sources in the Presentation of Character* (Oxford: Clarendon Press, 1997), 336–49. The main ancient accounts of the invasion of 370–369 are found at Xenophon *Hellenica* 6.5.25–32; *Agesilaos* 2.24; Plutarch *Agesilaos* 31–32; *Pelopidas* 24; Diodorus 15.62–65; and Pausanias 4.26–7, 9.13–15. See Hamilton, *Agesilaus and the Failure of Spartan Hegemony*, 220–31.

⁹ The size of the Theban-led force and the length of the invasion are under dispute; see the discussions in Swoboda, *Epameinondas*, 2687, 40. Ancient estimates ranged from 50,000 to 70,000 troops, both heavy and light infantry along with auxiliaries—one of

the largest musters in the history of the Greek city-state. For the number of Messenian helots, see T. Figueira, "The Demography of the Spartan Helots," in *Helots and Their Masters in Laconia and Messenia: Histories, Ideologies, Structures*, ed. Nino Luraghi and Susan E. Alcock (Cambridge, MA: Harvard University Press, 2003), 193–239, and in the same volume, W. Scheidel, "Helot Numbers: A Simplified Model," 240–47. The problem is compounded by the existence of helots in both Messenia and Laconia, the paucity of historical references, and dispute over agricultural production models. Older estimates of about 250,000 Messenian helots may be too high.

[10] For B. H. Liddell Hart (*Strategy* [New York: Praeger, 1967], 34–37), Epaminondas's invasion of Messenia was one of the first examples in history of what he labeled the "indirect approach." For Hart, the favored way of conducting grand strategy was to avoid crippling losses in pitched and often serial battles through outflanking enemies' armies and attacking their infrastructure far to the rear.

[11] For a description of the liberation of the helots and the founding of the new fortified citadel at Messene, see most recently Nino Luraghi, *The Ancient Messenians: Constructions of Ethnicity and Memory* (Cambridge: Cambridge University Press 2008), 209–52. Luraghi points out that the Messenians may not have been ethnically or linguistically all that distinct from the Spartans, and most likely established the notion of a historically distinct Messenian identity right before and after their liberation by Epaminondas.

[12] For more ideas about the degree of planning and forethought involved in Epaminondas's decision to continue on to Messene after failing to cross the Eurotas and storm the Spartan acropolis, see H. Delbrück, *History of the Art of War* (English translation by Walter J. Renfroe of *Geschichte der Kriegskunst im Rahmen der politschen Geschichte*), 4 vols. (Lincoln: University of Nebraska Press, 1990), 1:165–70; G. Roloff, *Problem aus der griechischen Kriegsgeschichte* (Berlin: E. Ebering, 1903), 11–59; and Hanson, *Soul of Battle*, 72–94.

[13] For a good analysis of Xenophon's ambiguity about the genius of his contemporary Epaminondas, see H. D. Westlake, "Individuals in Xenophon's *Hellenica*," in *Essays on the Greek Historians and Greek History*, 213–16 (Manchester, UK: Manchester University Press, 1969).

[14] Thucydides 6.18.3, in *The Landmark Thucydides*, ed. R. Strassler, trans. Richard Crawley (New York: Touchstone, 1996). Note that the Syracusan democratic leader Athenagoras, in fear of rumors of an impending Athenian invasion of Sicily, tried in vain to rally the Syracusans themselves to preempt: "It is necessary to punish an enemy not only for what he does, but also beforehand for what he intends to do, if the first to relax precaution would not also be the first to suffer" (6.39.5).

[15] A preemptive attack is initiated by one side due to the perceived threat of imminent attack by another party. The initiator believes that there is an advantage in striking first, or at least that striking first is preferable to surrendering the initiative to the enemy. See D. Reiter, "Exploding the Powder Keg Myth: Preemptive Wars Almost Never Happen," *International Security* 20, no. 2 (Autumn 1995): 6–7. See also J. S. Levy, "Declining Power and the Preventive Motivation for War," *World Politics* 40, no. 1 (October 1987): 90; R. Schweller, "Domestic Structure and Preventive War: Are Democracies More Pacific?," *World Politics* 44, no. 2 (January 1992): 247; and G. H. Quester, "200 Years of Preemption," *Naval War College Review* 60, no. 4 (Autumn 2007): 16. There is

a good historical review of the strategies in S. van Evera, "Offense, Defense, and the Causes of War," *International Security* 22, no. 4 (Spring 1998): 9.

[16] Thucydides 1.118.2, 4.92.5. Again, preemptive wars are waged out of the expectation of an imminent attack; preventive wars hinge on the expectation of the relative decline in a state's position. Besides the question of the temporal proximity of the challenge, preemptive threats consist of an opponent's current capabilities; preventive threats lie in an opponent's future resources. And while the preventor is often the stronger state, the preemptor tends to be the weaker

[17] Thucydides 2.2 (Theban attack on Plataia), 4.92.5 (Pagondas's call to strike first). For the tragic history of Thespiae, see Victor Hanson, "Hoplite Obliteration: The Case of the Town of Thespiai," in *Ancient Warfare: Archaeological Perspectives*, ed. John Carmen and Anthony Harding (London: Stroud, 1999), 203–18.

[18] On the domestic debate whether to preempt, and the financial incentives offered by the Peloponnesians, see Buckler, *Theban Hegemony*, 70–76, and J. Roy, "Arcadia and Boeotia in Peloponnesian Affairs, 370–362 B.C.," *Historia* 20 (1971): 569–99; and in general, Xenophon *Hellenica* 6.5.9–20, and see 4.7.11; Diodorus 62–63; Plutarch *Agesilaus* 30.1; *Pelopidas* 24. 1–2; and Pausanias 9.14.2.

[19] We don't know at what particular point Epaminondas's arrival in winter 369 in Mantineia to help the Arcadians evolved into a subsequent campaign south to attack the homeland of Sparta, and then, after he failed to storm the Spartan acropolis, to enter Messenia to free the helots and found Messene. While our sources seems to suggest an ad hoc method of decision making, and a formal conference of allies at Mantineia (e.g., Xenophon *Hellenica* 6.5.22–23; Diodorus 15.62.4–5; Plutarch *Agesilaus* 31.1–2) at which the Thebans jettisoned their initial worries about the physical difficulties of entering Laconia, it is likely that the Thebans had some notion before they entered the Peloponnese that their stay would be a long one and would transcend the initial goal of guaranteeing the safety of the newly founded fortress at Mantineia.

[20] We have very little ancient information about the route, the nature of the march, or the number of allies who continued on into Messene. On the founding of the city in 369 B.C., see Carl A. Roebuck, *A History of Messenia from 369 to 146 B.C.* (Chicago: University of Chicago Press, 1941), 32–40; Christian Habicht, *Pausanias' Guide to Ancient Greece* (Berkeley and Los Angeles: University of California Press, 1985), 36–63.

[21] On the liberal attitude of Epaminondas of allowing some allied Peloponnesian states to maintain their oligarchies, and his preference not to create either garrisons or a formal league of pro-Theban democratic allies, see John Buckler and Hans Beck, *Central Greece and the Politics of Power in the Fourth Century BC* (Cambridge: Cambridge University Press, 2008), 137–39.

[22] Tearless battle: Plutarch *Agesilaus* 33.3–5. For the course of Spartan history, its steady decline after the liberation of the Messenian helots, and defections among the *perioikoi* and helots, see Cartledge, *Agesilaos*, 384–85, 395–431.

[23] See Xenophon *Hellenica* 7.5.27; Diodorus 15.88.4.

[24] While destruction of the Spartan acropolis or the Spartan army would have been advantageous to Thebes, it would probably only have accelerated a process well under way: started at Leuctra, enhanced by the invasions of Laconia and Mantineia, and capped by the defeat of the Spartan army again at Mantineia.

[25] There is great controversy over the degree of Theban involvement in both the creation of Mantineia and Megalopolis (though not Messene), involving both conflicts in our ancient sources and archaeological examination of the remains of the fortifications. See Hanson, *Soul of Battle*, 424–25, n. 3; and especially J. Roy, "Arcadia and Boeotia in Peloponnesian Affairs, 370–362 B.C.," *Historia* 20, nos. 5–6 (4th Quarter, 1971), 569–99.

[26] On the contemporary evocation of Iraq as Sicily, and Thucydides, see Victor Hanson, *A War Like None Other: How the Athenians and Spartans Fought the Peloponnesian War* (New York: Random House, 2005), 324, n. 1.

[27] Thucydides on the fault for the disaster on Sicily: "this failed not so much through a miscalculation of the power of those against whom it was sent, as through a fault in the senders in not taking the best measures afterwards to assist those who had gone out, but choosing rather to occupy themselves with private squabbles for the leadership of the people, by which they not only paralyzed operations in the field, but also first introduced civil discord at home" (Crawley translation); Pericles' rebuke of the Athenians for their fickle support of the war: "I am the same man and do not alter, it is you who change, since in fact you took my advice while unhurt, and waited for misfortune to repent of it" (2.61.2).

[28] On the influence of the Pythagoreans at Thebes and on Epaminondas in particular: Nepos *Epaminondas* 15.2.2; Diodorus 15.39.2; Plutarch *Pelopidas* 5.3; Xenophon *Agesilaus* 25 (internal opposition to the aggressive plans of Pelopidas and Epaminondas). And see Nancy H. Demand, *Thebes in the Fifth Century: Heracles Resurgent* (London: Routledge, 1982), 70–76, 132–35. It was the judgment of the historian Ephoros that the hegemony of Thebes was largely due to the careers of Epaminondas and Pelopidas (Diodorus 15.79.2, 15.88.4) and passed with their deaths. On the purported ties between "neocons" and President George W. Bush, see in general Jacob Heilbrunn, *They Knew They Were Right: The Rise of the Neocons* (New York: Doubleday, 2008).

[29] We should remember the supposed inscription on the statue of Epaminondas set up at Thebes that ended with "And all of Greece became independent and free" (Pausanias 9.15.6). There is an entire corpus of ancient passages attesting to the achievements, both moral and military, of Epaminondas, and the relationship of Theban hegemony to his singular leadership: e.g., Aelian *Varia Historia* 12.3; Nepos *Epaminondas* 15.10.3; Plutarch *Moralia* 194C; Strabo 9.2.2. For a review of the results of Epaminondas's invasions in the Peloponnese, see Hanson, *Soul of Battle*, 105–20. Controversy exists over Epaminondas's ultimate aims, which may well have been pan-Hellenic and transcended just Theban interests. See George L. Cawkwell, "Epaminondas and Thebes," *The Classical Quarterly*, n.s. 22, no. 2 (November 1972): 254–78.

[30] See the assessment of Buckler (*Theban Hegemony*, 227) on the campaigns of Epaminondas: "Even after Mantineia, Epameinondas and Pelopidas left Thebes the leading power in Greece, raised their homeland to heights which it had never before attained and would never see after them; and the history of the Theban hegemony is in no small measure the story of Epameinondas and Pelopidas."

5. Alexander the Great, Nation Building, and the Creation and Maintenance of Empire

IAN WORTHINGTON

ALEXANDER THE GREAT (356–23 BC) fought strategically brilliant battles and laid sieges against numerically superior foes to establish one of the greatest geographic empires of antiquity, from Greece in the west to what the Greeks called India (modern Pakistan) in the east. When he died he was ready to undertake an invasion of Arabia, and plausibly after that he would have moved against Carthage. He created his empire in a little over a decade, invading Asia in 334 and dying in Babylon in 323. Not even the Romans, who boasted the largest empire of antiquity, could attribute their empire to just one man, and it took centuries to reach the extent it did before it fell. Alexander's campaigns also facilitated the spread of Greek culture in the areas through which he and his army marched, and they opened new trading avenues and possibilities between West and East, which forever changed relations between Greece and Asia.

This chapter shows how Alexander established his empire, discusses the problems he faced in ruling a large, multicultural subject population, and examines the approaches and strategies he took to what might be called nation building. In doing so, it allows us also to praise and critique his actions. Alexander's experiences in Asia arguably can inform present makers of modern strategy and shed light on contemporary problems in this or any culturally different region of the world. At the same time, the argument can be made that Alexander's failings (sometimes his fault, at other times not) show how little the modern world learns from, or even ignores, the past.

~

Alexander succeeded to the Macedonian throne on the assassination of his father, Philip II, in 336. He had already proved himself on the battlefield. In 340, when he was sixteen, his father appointed him regent of Macedon, and during his tenure of power Alexander successfully marched against and defeated the Maedians on the upper Strymon River. Philip was impressed, for two years later, in 338, he gave his son the command of the Macedonian left flank, and of the Companion Cavalry, no less, at the Battle of Chaeronea. This was the battle by which the Greeks lost their autonomy and in the following year became members of the so-called League of Corinth, which was headed by the Macedonian king and used to enforce Macedonian hegemony. In fierce fighting at Chaeronea, Alexander distinguished himself by helping to annihilate the famous 300-strong Theban Sacred Band.

When Alexander became king, he immediately had to deal with a number of problems, not least a revolt of the Greeks from Macedonian rule, which he easily ended. Afterward he revived his father's League of Corinth, and with it his plan for a pan-Hellenic invasion of Asia to punish the Persians for the suffering of the Greeks, especially the Athenians, in the Greco-Persian Wars and to liberate the Greek cities of Asia Minor. However, it was not until the spring of 334 that Alexander led an army of some 48,000 infantry and 6,000 cavalry, supported by a fleet of 120 warships, from Greece to Asia. Before landing, the story goes, he threw a spear into Asian soil to indicate he regarded all of Asia as his spear-won territory.[1]

In three major battles against far numerically superior Persian armies (at the Granicus River in 334, Issus in 333, and Gaugamela in 331), Alexander defeated the Persians. He did so thanks to a better trained army, inherited from his father Philip II, than the Persian one, and by a combination of strategic brilliance, daring, and luck.[2] Darius III, the Great King, had not been present at Granicus (the Persian side was commanded by Arsites, the satrap of Hellespontine Phrygia), but he fought Alexander at Issus and Gaugamela, and on both occasions Alexander, the heart of his strategy being to kill or capture him, had forced him off the battlefield. The demoralizing effect this had on the Persian troops had turned the tide of battle in favor of Alexander both times. Also demoralizing, and taking place before both Issus and Gaugamela, must have been Alexander's visit to Gordium (close to the modern Ankara) in 333. Here was the wagon dedicated by Midas, son of Gordius, who allegedly left Macedon and became king of Gordium. The wagon was famous for the knot made of cornel wood on its yoke, and the accompanying prophecy that whoever untied it would rule Asia. Needless to say, the king undid it, either by slashing it with his sword or by unraveling it.[3] His visit to Gordium, then, was political: to show everyone he was the next ruler of Asia.

In between Granicus and Issus, Alexander had marched down the coastline of Asia Minor and Syria, in some cases receiving the immediate surrender of the cities, in other cases having to besiege them (his most famous sieges are probably at Halicarnassus, Tyre, and Gaza). In 332 he had entered Egypt, where the satrap, Mazaces, immediately surrendered the capital, Memphis, and hence all Egypt to him. Mazaces had no choice, for the Egyptians were tired of Persian rule and welcomed the Macedonian army as liberators; if Mazaces had resisted, the Egyptians would have risen up against him. While in Egypt, Alexander made his famous trek to consult the Oracle of Zeus Ammon at the Siwah oasis in the Libyan Desert to obtain confirmation that he was the son of Zeus.[4] His pretensions would, however, lead to his undoing later (see below).

Alexander's success at Gaugamela meant that the Persian Empire was to all intents and purposes no more. It would not be long before its more important and wealthier royal capitals were in Macedonian hands. These included Babylon, Ecbatana, Susa, and finally Persepolis, home of the palace of Darius and Xerxes, the "most hated city in Asia."[5] Shortly before the Macedonian army left Persepolis in spring 330, the palace burned to the ground. Whether this was accidental or deliberate is not known with certainty, but the symbolism of its burning, as with the Gordian knot, was exploited: the peoples of the Persian Empire no longer would pay homage to the Great King but to Alexander as Lord of Asia.

The burning of Persepolis meant, in effect, that the original aims of the invasion of Asia—punishment of the Persians and freeing of the

Greek cities of Asia Minor—had been achieved, and the men in the army evidently thought they would now be going home.[6] But Alexander did not turn westward. He needed to hunt down Darius once and for all, and so set off after him. He caught up with him at Hecatompylus, only to find him dead and that Bessus, satrap of Bactria, one of the men who had deposed Darius and had had a hand in his murder, had proclaimed himself Great King as Artaxerxes V. Again Alexander's men expected their king to give orders to start the long march home,[7] and again they were disappointed, as Alexander gave orders to pursue Bessus.

Although the army had wanted to return home at Persepolis and at Hecatompylus, Alexander was right to see the need to depose Bessus in order to maintain stability in his new Asian empire. Nevertheless, the Macedonian invasion had entered a different phase, one of conquest for the sake of conquest. Also different was how Alexander treated those people who defied him as he marched eastward, with mass slaughter and even genocide becoming something of a norm.

Bessus was quickly joined by Satibarzanes, satrap of Areia, and Bactrian chieftains such as Oxyartes (the father of Roxane) and Spitamanes, who commanded substantial numbers of men, and especially first class cavalry. To counter this threat, Alexander invaded Bactria and Sogdiana. The speed with which he moved caused these leaders to fall back beyond the Oxus, and not long after Alexander crossed this river, Oxyartes and Spitamanes betrayed Bessus to Alexander, who ordered his execution. Again, the removal of one leader meant nothing, for Spitamenes came to the fore, and the Macedonians were now faced with fierce guerrilla warfare in this different and hostile part of Central Asia. By 327, though, the resistance was over, Spitamenes was dead, and Alexander added cavalry contingents from the two areas to his army.

During the Bactrian campaigns, two potentially major conspiracies against Alexander were revealed. The first, the so-called Philotas affair, was in 330 at Phrada, capital of Drangiana. Although Philotas, commander of the companion cavalry and son of Parmenion, had nothing to do with the affair, his criticisms of Alexander's orientalism and pandering to Persian nobility led to his undoing. He was accused of complicity in the conspiracy and put to death. Alexander then gave orders for the killing of the equally critical Parmenion, who was at Ecbatana at the time and had no knowledge of any conspiracy. Then in 327 at Bactria a conspiracy involving some of the royal pages was discovered. Callisthenes, the court historian, who had defied Alexander's attempt to introduce *proskynesis* (the Asian custom of prostration before the Great King), was implicated and put to death, yet no evidence existed against him. If Alexander's likely manipulation of these conspiracies to rid himself of critics were not bad enough, Alexander also murdered his general Cleitus at Maracanda (Samarkand) in 328 after the two men got into a furious drunken row. There is no question that the Bactrian campaign was a turning point in Alexander's deterioration as a king and as a man.

After pacifying Bactria (or so he thought), Alexander pushed eastward into India. Here he fought only one major battle, against the Indian prince Porus at the Hydaspes River in 326. It was another Macedonian victory, but it was the high point militarily of Alexander's campaign in India. The men had expected to be returning home as early as 330 following the burning of Persepolis, but Alexander was showing no signs of that, and the campaign in India was the final straw. After seventy days of marching through drenching monsoon rains toward the Ganges, the army mutinied at the Hyphasis (Beas) River, forcing Alexander to turn back. One of Alexander's ambitions in India was to sail down the Indus River and out into the Southern (Indian) Ocean. He would achieve this (along the way almost losing his life at the siege of Malli), and his voyage was one of the highlights of his time in India.

Leaving India, Alexander led a contingent of his troops westward through the Gedrosian Desert. His reason was personal: Dionysus, with whom Alexander was by then identifying himself, had traveled through the desert, while Cyrus the Great of Persia had tried but failed. Alexander's ill-fated march saw about a third of the men with him die because of the hostile natural conditions. This mattered less to the king than the personal glory of marching through the desert.[8]

In the meantime, Bactria and Sogdiana revolted, and India followed suit. Alexander had mistakenly believed that defeated in battle meant conquered, but the Afghans were (and are) not conquered by anyone. The Pashtun tribes of the present northwest frontier of Afghanistan are constantly fighting each other, and there is a saying today that they are only united when they face a common enemy. That is exactly what Alexander was in the 320s, just as the British in the nineteenth century and the Russians in the twentieth were, and the same holds true today. This time there was little that Alexander could do.

Two years later, in 324, at Opis, a second mutiny occurred over Alexander's policy to discharge his veterans, although his plans to invade Arabia did not help—nor did his adoption of a combination of Persian and Macedonian clothing[9] or his belief in his own divinity, as the men's mocking "you and your father Zeus can go to Arabia if you want" indicates His powers of persuasion were unable to end this mutiny, and after three days he was successful only when he shamed the men into giving in by transferring Macedonian commands to Persians. In other words, he played on the men's racial hatred of the Persians to end the mutiny. A year later, in Babylon, in June 323, on the eve of his Arabian expedition, Alexander the Great died, a few months shy of his thirty-third birthday. He left behind no heir (his wife Roxane, a Bactrian princess, was pregnant when he died), and when asked to whom he left his empire, he enigmatically replied, "to the best." Thus began a thirty-year round of bloody wars between his generals that saw the carving up of the Macedonian Empire and the emergence of the great kingdoms of the Hellenistic period.

∿

It is important to remember that Alexander's empire was never static but continually shifting its frontiers and absorbing new peoples. There was never an instance when Alexander fought that one final battle; there was never a time when he ruled his empire peacefully, and he was faced with opposition all the time he was in Asia, from the Persian Great King to the chieftains of Central Asia and the princes of India to the aristocratic families, all of whom naturally saw Alexander as a threat to their power and prestige. After the Granicus River battle in 334, a goodly number of the survivors fled to Miletus to defy Alexander. When Miletus fell after a short siege, many from there fled to Halicarnassus, forcing Alexander to wage yet another siege. And so the years and resistance wore on. Against the background of the unabating opposition, the undoing of the Gordian knot makes even more sense, as Alexander strove to show everyone he was the new ruler of Asia, not merely by conquest but according to prophecy.

We might expect the political exploitation of this religious symbolism to be effective, and Alexander probably thought it would be, given the religious nature of the people. However, he was a conqueror, and despite attempts to endear himself to the aristocracy by involving them in his administration (see below), no one likes to be conquered. Even after the turning-point defeat of Darius at Issus, the Great King was able to regroup and bring Alexander to battle at Gaugamela. Alexander's victories were hard-won, the enemy always outnumbered him, and Darius, in addition to his enormous resources (far greater than those of Alexander), was a skilled strategist and commander.[10] And he never said die: after Issus, he gathered together another army, and after Gaugamela he was determined to fight Alexander again, this time with an army principally made up of his easternmost subjects. His failures in battle proved too much, though, and he was deposed and murdered.

Even then the resistance to Alexander did not fall apart but continued in the leadership of Bessus, forcing Alexander into Bactria and Sogdiana. Bessus was quickly joined by Satibarzanes, whom Alexander had appointed the satrap of Areia but who now sided with Bessus against the invader. This type of disloyalty was something Alexander would encounter time and again.

At first Alexander gained the upper hand in Bactria, as seen in the betrayal of Bessus to him, but Spitamenes, who succeeded Bessus, was far more dangerous and tactically cunning. Using the barren, desolate, and rocky topography that he and his people knew so well but the invading army did not, he forced Alexander into more than two years of intense guerrilla fighting and bloody siege warfare. Alexander was forced to deal with all this and with growing opposition from his senior staff as well as from the rank and file of his army, opposition that exploded in 326 at the Hyphasis, forcing him to turn back. If the army had not revolted, he would have reached the Ganges, and if he had not died in Babylon, he would have invaded Arabia.

Thus at no time did Alexander rule a fixed geographic area, at no time did he appear to want to rule an empire with fixed borders, as his continual campaigning shows, and at no time were all his subjects passive and supportive of his presence among them. All these factors made administering his empire in some longer-term uniform and efficient fashion and persuading his men to continue marching and fighting doubly difficult.[11]

~

The Persian kings had realized the impossibility of one man trying to rule the large and diverse kingdom they had created. That was why Darius I (522–486) divided his empire into twenty satrapies (administrative regions), personally appointing a satrap (governor) over each one. Apart from paying annual taxes to the Great King and furnishing troops for the Persian army, the satraps wielded all the power in their satrapies, although the Great King was at the top of the administrative hierarchy, and he ruled absolutely.

The satrapal system remained in existence because of the relative autonomy of the satraps and their acceptance of the Great King. While Alexander might call himself Lord of Asia, that was very different from being the Great King, and many of the satraps had fought in battle against him. Alexander as invader would have cause to question their loyalty, but he recognized the value of the satrapal system, so he kept it, with some changes.[12] In the earliest stages of his Asian campaign he placed his own men in charge of the western satrapies—for example, Calas was made satrap of Hellespontine Phrygia, Antigonus of Phrygia, Asander of Lycia, and Balacrus was made satrap of Cilicia. However, as Alexander's territories increased eastward, especially after Gaugamela, Alexander began to involve the aristocratic Persian families in his administration and appoint some as satraps. The first of these was really Mazaeus, who was appointed satrap of Babylonia in 331. Others included Abulites, satrap of Susa, Phrasaortes, satrap of Persis, and Artabazus, satrap of Bactria and Sogdiana. Alexander's action would help smooth the path of a new, "transition" regime (so he hoped) by nullifying opposition from these influential families whose power he was eroding. Besides, he needed these people for their knowledge of the language and customs of their people. The last point is important, because by being part of the administrative hierarchy, they would help to reconcile the mass of the people to his rule, the plan being to help him maintain a peaceful occupation.

The danger, of course, was that a conquered people could not be left to its own devices. Alexander could not afford an insurrection, so he made some important modifications to the satrapal system. Native satraps continued to have some civil authority and to levy taxes in their satrapies. However, they were little more than titular figureheads, for Alexander appointed Macedonians to be in charge of the treasury and the military forces of each satrapy. Thus, real power in the satrapies now lay with his men. The change extended the precedent he had set, for example, in Caria, where Ada continued as its satrap but Ptolemy was in charge of military affairs,[13] or in Egypt, where a Persian Doloaspis was governor of sorts but was dominated by Cleomenes, a Greek from Naucratis, who used his position as collector of taxes and overseer of the construction of Alexandria to seize the reins of power. The new system continued throughout the reign, although in 325, when Alexander returned from India, he punished many disloyal satraps (and generals of mercenary armies) with death and appointed as their successors both Persians and Macedonians; for example, Peucestas was made satrap of Persis (he was the only Macedonian who learned Persian and immersed himself in Persian customs, which pleased the people greatly, according to Arrian).[14]

While Alexander allowed the satraps to continue collecting taxes, he created the post of imperial treasurer at some point before (or in) 331. His boyhood friend Harpalus oversaw all imperial finances (first from Ecbatana and eventually from his headquarters in Babylon). Alexander seems to have put the Greek cities of his empire in a special category, for taxes from those in Asia Minor were to be collected by Philoxenus and those in Phoenicia by Coeranus.[15]

Alexander's men did not expect the enemy to retain any positions of influence, and needless to say, the satraps would have resented losing control of their armies and treasuries. The military might of the Macedonians held them in check, but it is no surprise that native satraps were disloyal when Alexander was in India, and that in Central Asia the satrapies of Bactria and Sogdiana revolted twice. Bactria proved to be such a problem area that when Artabazus resigned his post in 328, Alexander appointed Cleitus, co-commander of the Companion Cavalry, as its satrap, although Alexander killed him before he could take up this position. In his place he appointed another Macedonian, Amyntas, who would head the largest contingent of troops in any one satrapy.[16]

Such disloyalty is also part and parcel of imperial power being held by one man, and an invader at that. When Alexander was present with his superior army, resistance was not an option, but when he left it was a different matter. Bactria shows this, as does India. Here, Alexander confirmed the power of many of the local princes who submitted to him, for example Taxiles east of the Indus, and after the battle of the Hydaspes, Porus was allowed to retain his power (although he became a vassal of Alexander); however, once the king left India, the rulers reverted to their old ways and paid him only lip service.

Diodorus tells us another way that Alexander intended to manage his empire. In his account of Alexander's so-called last plans, he says that Alexander planned to found cities and to transplant people from Asia to Europe and vice versa, to bring "the biggest continents into a common unity and to friendship by intermarriages and family ties."[17] Alexander did not embark on any transpopulation policy, but he did found a large number of settlements, apparently as many as seventy. However, the majority of these were not actual poleis with developed constitutions, gymnasia, theaters, and all the attributes of a city but instead were more garrison posts, often inhabited by veteran soldiers and local peoples to keep a particular area in check.[18] Alexander probably founded only a dozen actual cities, the most famous being Alexandria in Egypt.[19]

Founding cities for strategic reasons was not novel. Philip II had done the same thing along his northwest frontier with the troublesome Illyrian tribes in 345, and Alexander's borrowing this leaf out of his father's book shows us he realized that using native satraps would not be enough to placate his subject peoples. Philip had conquered the various Illyrian tribes, unified Macedon as a result, and then incorporated them into the new Macedonian army. Even so, he was forced to monitor them continuously throughout his reign.[20] So Alexander also could not afford to assume his satrapal arrangements would be enough. Hence he took care to pepper the garrison settlements throughout the areas of his empire where he expected the most resistance—unsurprisingly, the greatest concentration was in the eastern half of the empire. Even so, these would not prove to be enough in Bactria and Sogdiana.[21]

The new settlements also facilitated trade and communications, although they rose to economic prominence only after Alexander. Thus, Alexandria (in Egypt) became the cultural center and an economic power in the Hellenistic period after Ptolemy I made it the capital.[22] The real advantage of using cities to help maintain rule over huge empires is shown by the later Seleucid rulers of Syria. It is no coincidence that Seleucus, the first of these rulers, and the first to make city foundations deliberate policy, was one of Alexander's generals. He had learned well by example.

Diodorus also talks about a "common unity" between the western and eastern halves of Alexander's empire and intermarriages. This sort of line, compounded by Plutarch's presentation of Alexander as a philosopher and idealist in his rhetorical treatise *On the Fortune or the Virtue of Alexander*, has led to a belief that Alexander wanted to create a brotherhood of mankind as a means of ruling his empire. There is, of course, merit to a policy that tries to make foreign rule acceptable not by enforcing it but by promoting equality and commonality among everyone, and some of Alexander's actions throughout his reign seem to support the belief that he was striving to achieve such an equality. Prominent among his actions here were the integration of foreigners into his army and administration, his marriage in spring 327 to the Bactrian princess Roxane, his attempt to enforce *proskynesis* at his court, the mass wedding at Susa in 324, at which he and ninety members of his senior staff married Persian noblewomen, and finally a reconciliation banquet at Opis in 324, at which he prayed for harmony between everyone.

Yet there was no such thing as a unity-of-mankind "policy" on Alexander's part.[23] None of the above actions was ideological in purpose, but, like Alexander himself, all were pragmatic and no different from, say, founding cities to maintain Macedonian control. For example, foreigners in his army, such as specialist troops from Iran or the Bactrian cavalry, were kept apart in their own ethnic units until 324, when Alexander incorporated them into the army for tactical reasons before the Arabian expedition.[24] Native satraps, as already noted, were merely figureheads, the powerful families being given some semblance of their former station to secure their support.

For Alexander, Roxane may well have been "the only woman he ever loved," but the marriage was political.[25] Her father Oxyartes had been one of Alexander's toughest opponents; the marriage, Alexander would have hoped, was to secure his support, and hence Bactria's passivity, and in return Alexander made him satrap of Parapamisadae. Hence, Alexander's marriage was no different from his father's first six marriages, undertaken to help consolidate Macedon's borders—and provide an heir. Roxane had a child who died in 326 at the Hydaspes,[26] thus giving us a motive for Alexander's marriages in 324 to two Persian princesses: to solidify his rule and to produce heirs on the eve of his Arabian campaign (Roxanne became pregnant soon after).

Proskynesis set Persians apart from Greeks, who thought the act was akin to worship. Alexander's attempt to enforce it on his own men looks like he was trying to fashion some common social protocol between the races, to get West to meet East. Yet he was brought up to believe in the traditional gods and still performed the traditional sacrifices as king in the last days of his life, so he must have known his men saw the act as sacrilegious. Even the posture was unacceptable, as Greeks commonly prayed standing up with their arms upraised, whereas slaves lay on the ground. More likely, then, is that Alexander now thought of himself as divine, and *proskynesis* reflected that.

The symbolism of the interracial mass marriage at Susa seems obvious, but it is important to note that no Greek women were brought out from the mainland to marry Asian noblemen, which we would expect if Alexander was sincere about fusing the races by intermarriage. What Alexander was doing was polluting the bloodline to ensure that children from these marriages would never have a claim to the Persian throne. Moreover, his men were against the marriages, and after Alexander's death, they all, apart from Seleucus, divorced their wives.

Finally, the prayer to harmony after the Opis mutiny: Alexander ended the mutiny by playing on his men's hatred of the Persians. At a reconciliation banquet the same evening the seating order sought to emphasize the superiority of the invaders: Macedonians sat next to Alexander, then came the Greeks, and then all others. Moreover, the prayer to concord was about unity in the army, not unity of mankind, because Alexander planned to invade Arabia, and so dissension in the ranks was the last thing he needed.

Aristotle, his personal tutor from the age of fourteen to sixteen, had advised Alexander "to treat the Greeks as if he were their leader and other people as if he were their master; to have regard for the Greeks as for friends and family, but to conduct himself towards other peoples as though they were plants or animals."[27] Aristotle may well have influenced Alexander's scientific curiosity to find out about the natural resources of the areas through which he traveled,[28] but Alexander did not follow Aristotle's advice about his Asian subjects. At the same time, Alexander knew he had to regard the conquered populations with suspicion; hence everything he did was for a political reason.

Another area that might throw light on Alexander's relationship with the conquered people, and hence the maintenance of his empire, is the spread of Greek culture. Hellenization became something of a staple in Alexander's nation building. To a large extent, the spread of Greek civilization was inevitable simply as an effect of Alexander's army marching through new areas and exposing the people there to things Greek. Alexander was an avid reader of Homer (especially the *Iliad*) and of Greek tragedy (Euripides was his favorite), and his men would have shared his tastes. Thus, when the army returned to Tyre from Egypt in the summer of 331, Alexander held a celebratory festival to Heracles, complete with games and dramatic performances. Among the performers were the celebrated actors Thessalus (a personal friend of Alexander) and Athenodorus, who reneged on a contract to perform at the culturally important festival of the city Dionysia in Athens to be at Tyre. For this he was fined, but Alexander paid the fine for him.

These sorts of cultural events would have been lost on his men if they did not appreciate them, and they must have had an effect on local peoples. Indeed, his fostering of Greek culture led later authors such as Plutarch to speak of him as the bringer of civilization to foreign peoples.[29] However, one might argue that the spread of Greek culture was not simply an offshoot of his campaigns but that he saw the political benefits to be gained from cultural change. The problem was, he made little attempt to tolerate local customs and religious practices, and he would end customs that Greeks condemned or that he personally disliked.

For example, Greeks were appalled that in Persia, brothers would marry sisters and sons married their mothers.[30] On the other hand, these practices might be overlooked because the Macedonians had marital customs that other Greeks condemned, specifically polygamy (later in Ptolemaic Egypt the practice of ruling brothers marrying sisters began with Ptolemy II Philadelphus and his sister, Arsinoë). However, the Scythians' practices of sacrificing their elderly parents, drinking the blood of their first human kill, and using as much of a corpse as possible in their everyday lives were another thing.[31] So too was the Bactrians' custom in regard to their elderly: "those who became infirm because of old age or sickness are thrown out alive as prey to dogs, which they keep specifically for this purpose, and in their native tongue they are called 'undertakers'. While the land outside the walls of the city of the Bactrians looks clean, most of the land inside the walls is full of human bones."[32]

We, like the Greeks back then, find this custom shocking, but nevertheless it was a traditional local custom. However, that did not stop Alexander ending it, and he had no business to do so. It was this type of disruption to established social practices that could only fuel discontent in the affected areas and encourage locals to resist the Macedonians, and it gave rise to an anti-Greek sentiment. This is very much in evidence with the Ptolemaic kings of Egypt, for example, who segregated the native Egyptians in society and precluded them from taking part in state administration. The feelings of exploitation had grown to explosive levels by the reign of Ptolemy IV (221–203), and Egypt was split by civil war that tested Ptolemaic rule to its utmost.

On the other hand, Alexander was more tolerant of religious beliefs, but then the equivalents of Greek gods were everywhere. For example, Alexander identified the local god Melqart at Tyre with Heracles; at Siwah there was an oracle of Zeus-Ammon, and at Nysa in India the local god Indra or Shiva was deemed the equivalent of Dionysus. Religion is a powerful tool for bringing about unity, and the king used it as and when he saw fit, though not always properly understanding what religion meant to different people. Thus, in Egypt he took care to sacrifice to Apis at Memphis and in Babylon he gave orders to re-build the temple to Bel, which Xerxes had destroyed. He spared the lives of the people of Nysa in 326 (a deviation from what had by then become his modus operandi of wholesale slaughter of native tribes) because they claimed descent from those who had traveled with Dio-nysus through the region, Nysa was the name of Dionysus's nurse, and Alexander was convinced a local plant was ivy, Dionysus's symbol.

However, Alexander could be far more myopic. In 332, after the peo-ple of Tyre had surrendered to him, Alexander expressed his wish to worship in their temple. The temple was to Melqart, the local equiva-lent of Heracles, who was one of Alexander's ancestors. The temple, then, was not to Heracles but to Melqart, and for Alexander to worship there was sacrilegious to the Tyrians, who refused, asking him to wor-ship on the mainland opposite (in antiquity, Tyre was an island). Rather than recognizing the political advantage he had just gained from the Tyrians' surrendering to him (it was essential for him to control Tyre to prevent the Phoenician navy using it as a base) and accepting the compromise because of its religious nature, Alexander took the rebuff as a personal affront. Furious, he gave orders for Tyre to be besieged. When it fell to him after a difficult and lengthy siege, he put many of its citizens to death and sold the rest into slavery. As an example to other places that might defy him, he ordered the crucified bodies of 2,000 Tyrians to be set up along the coastline. This act merely stiffened resis-tance to him, for the next town he approached, Gaza, refused to open its gates to him. After a short siege Gaza fell, and Alexander punished the people harshly, including dragging the garrison commander Batis behind a chariot around the walls of Gaza until he died.

~

As a king and at times even as a general, Alexander had flaws, but he was impossible to beat. He was, then, "his own greatest achieve-ment."[33] However, it is common to transfer his failings as a king and a man to his plans for the building of a single empire. He did not have a conscious economic policy, if such a term is not too modern, for the empire as a whole, although he recognized the economic potential of the areas through which he traveled and which he next targeted—one of the reasons for invading Arabia had to have been its lucrative spice trade. His continual marching east until his men forced him back leads one to conclude he knew nothing else but fighting.[34] Yet Alexander did give thought to how he could deal with the problems that faced him and manage his empire so as to maintain Macedonian rule over it. He introduced administrative measures to this end, such as streamlining the satrapal system and creating the office of imperial treasurer. He involved the powerful Persian aristocratic families, whose support he needed, in his administration, and he started wearing Persian dress and the upright tiara (in 330 after Darius III was killed) to endear himself to the Persians and to offset the threat from Bessus and Artaxerxes V.[35]

These factors help us to see how Alexander's exploits more than two millennia ago highlight the dilemma of modern nation building. It is easy for us to think of ways he could have endeared himself to his subject peoples more. For example, he could have worked to understand different customs, religious beliefs, and even cultures and maintain them on an equal basis with his own. While it was perfectly fine to expose the Asians to Greek culture, their own culture should not have been ignored, condemned, or reduced because the Greeks thought theirs was better (whatever that means). Then again, perhaps to achieve this "equality" was impossible in the real world. What Alexander did (or did not do) shows us that the dilemma of Western nation building was as alive in antiquity as it is now—or conversely, that Alexander's inherent problems in nation building set a trend for the centuries that followed and into the modern era that has not yet been reversed.

Thus, to persuade his men to keep marching, to keep conquering, and thus to keep expanding his empire, Alexander was forced to argue the benefits that hellenization would bring to the peoples of the former Persian Empire, as well as the advantages (economic and otherwise) that the conquest and maintenance of Asia would bring to Macedon. These benefits were worth fighting for—and dying for—although the material benefits of booty would not have been lost on the army. At the same time, he had to reconcile his rule with the native peoples and so rule his empire with minimum opposition. These peoples, however, might be attracted to aspects of his brand of Hellenism, but not at the expense of their own culture and, even more important, their freedom. Using powerful families in his administration, allowing natives to be satraps, involving natives in his army, and adopting Asian dress were some of the ways in which Alexander might have appealed to his subjects.

His methods, however, alienated his own men and were transparent to the locals: no native satrap could have thought for a moment that nothing had changed from the days of the Great King. The fact that Macedonians were in charge of the army and treasury in his satrapy was a daily reminder that a new regime existed. Thanks to the Macedonian army's continued victories, Alexander's position as Lord of Asia was as secure as it ever could be. However, the problems increased as he marched farther eastward, intent on expanding his empire. The intense fighting in Bactria and Sogdiana was a turning point in Alexander's relations with his own men, who up to that point had loyally followed their king. The fighting in these regions and then in India, together with Alexander's orientalism, proved too much, as seen in the mutiny at the Hyphasis. This event marked a decline in Alexander's control of Asia as a whole. That military success was the basis of his power, and not hellenization or empire building, is proved by the revolts of India, Bactria, and Sogdiana as he left, and by the activities in the west of the satraps, generals, and imperial treasurer in his absence. And it is significant that before the burning of Persepolis, the story goes, Parmenion warned Alexander about the possible native backlash from the palace's destruction. None came, a testimony not so much to the acceptance of Alexander's rule as to the military might of the conquering army.

No one wants to be conquered, and in the end, only military power, not idealism, can maintain a conqueror's power. Alexander's empire did not survive him, but that was probably its fate anyway. He established an empire that was for a time without parallel, but its very size and cultural diversity made it impossible for one man or one regime to govern it effectively. These factors alone led to the failure of his attempts to maintain it. At the same time, without Alexander, there would not have been the great Hellenistic kingdoms and the cultural capitals at Alexandria, Antioch, and Pergamum. These great centers arose from the spread of Greek civilization that began with Alexander and continued with the Hellenistic kings, as shown by the ease with which the Ptolemaic kings in Egypt and the Seleucid kings in Syria, whose dynasties were founded by Alexander's generals in the disintegration of his empire, were able to attract Greeks from the west to live and work in their empires.

FURTHER READING

Dozens of accounts of Alexander's reign were written during and shortly after his life-time (the so-called primary sources), but only fragments of these survive. The extant narrative histories of Alexander's reign that we have (the secondary sources) were written centuries after his death, beginning with Diodorus Siculus in the first century BC, Quintus Curtius Rufus sometime in the mid- to later first century AD, Arrian in the second century AD, and Justin's epitome of an earlier work by Pompeius Trogus (now lost), which he copied in either the second or the third century AD. Of these, Arrian is commonly accepted as the most reliable source, principally because of his critical and balanced approach to the primary sources and his reliance on the eyewitness account of Ptolemy. To these later sources may be added the biography of Alexander by Plutarch (second century AD) and his treatise *On the Fortune or the Virtue of Alexander*, though this is a rhetorical, not historical, work. Ian Worthington, *Alexander the Great: A Reader* (London: Routledge, 2003), includes a wide selection of translated primary sources, and Waldemar Heckel and J. Yardley, *Alexander the Great: Historical Sources in Translation* (Malden, MA: Blackwell, 2003), contains a selection of mostly secondary sources in translation.

There is an abundance of modern books about Alexander, from scholarly biographies to glossy coffee-table ones. Michael Wood's *In the Footsteps of Alexander* (Berkeley and Los Angeles: University of California Press, 1997) is recommended as a general introduction to Alexander and especially for its photographs of the areas through which he marched since Wood himself followed his route. More recent biographies that can be singled out include Peter Green, *Alexander of Macedon 356–323 B.C.: A Historical Biography* (Harmondsworth, UK: Penguin, 1974); Robin Lane Fox, *Alexander the Great* (London: Penguin, 1973); A. B. Bosworth's *Conquest and Empire: The Reign of Alexander the Great* (Cambridge: Cambridge University Press, 1988), the best scholarly biography, together with his *Alexander and the East* (Oxford: Oxford University Press, 1996); Major General J.F.C. Fuller, *The Generalship of Alexander the Great* (New Brunswick, NJ: Rutgers University Press, 1960); N.G.L. Hammond, *Alexander the Great: King, Commander and Statesman* (Bristol: Bristol Press, 1989), to be preferred over his later *The Genius of Alexander the Great* (London: Duckworth, 1997); Paul Cartledge, *Alexander the Great: The Hunt for a New Past* (London: Routledge, 2003); and Ian Worthington, *Alexander the Great: Man and God*, rev. ed. (London: Pearson, 2004). Some collections of scholarly articles that deal with different aspects of Alexander's reign are A. B. Bosworth and E. J. Baynham, eds., *Alexander the Great in Fact and Fiction* (Oxford: Oxford University Press, 2000); Guy T. Griffith, ed., *Alexander the Great: The Main Problems* (Cambridge: Cambridge University Press, 1966); Joseph Roisman, ed., *Brill's Companion to Alexander the Great* (Leiden: Brill, 2003); Waldemar Heckel and Lawrence A. Tritle, eds., *Crossroads of History: The Age of Alexander* (Claremont, CA: Regina Books, 2003); and Worthington,

Alexander the Great: A Reader. For the Persian Empire, the best book is still Pierre Briant, *From Cyrus to Alexander: A History of the Persian Empire,* trans. Peter D. Daniels (Winona Lake, IN: Eisenbrauns, 2002).

NOTES

[1] Diodorus 17.17.2; Justin 11.5.10.

[2] On Philip's army reforms, see Ian Worthington, *Philip II of Macedonia* (New Haven, CT: Yale University Press, 2008), 26–32; on Alexander's army, see A .B. Bosworth, *Conquest and Empire: The Reign of Alexander the Great* (Cambridge: Cambridge University Press, 1988), 266–77.

[3] Aristobulus, *FGrH* 139 F7 (Arrian 2.3.7); Plutarch *Alexander* 18.4.

[4] Cf. Plutarch *Alexander* 27.3–6.

[5] Diodorus 17.70.

[6] Plutarch *Alexander* 38.6–7.

[7] Q. Curtius Rufus 6.2.15–16.

[8] Note Arrian 3.3.2 implies that Alexander made the long and arduous trek to Siwah in Egypt to emulate his ancestors Perseus and Heracles.

[9] Diodorus 17.77.7; Q. Curtius Rufus 6.6.9–12.

[10] For a reappraisal of Darius, see Ernst Badian, "Darius III," *HSCP* 100 (2000): 241–68.

[11] See Ernst Badian, "The Administration of the Empire," *G&R2* 12 (1965): 166–82, and W. E. Higgins, "Aspects of Alexander's Imperial Administration: Some Modern Methods and Views Reviewed," *Athenaeum* 58 (1980): 29–52.

[12] On Alexander's satrapal appointments and arrangements, see in more detail Bosworth, *Conquest and Empire,* 229–41, and Badian, "Administration of the Empire," 166–82. On the Indian arrangements, see A. B. Bosworth, "The Indian Satrapies under Alexander the Great," *Antichthon* 17 (1983): 37–46.

[13] Arrian 1.23.6.

[14] Arrian 6.30.2–3.

[15] On Alexander's financial administration, see in more detail Bosworth, *Conquest and Empire,* 241–45.

[16] Arrian 4.22.3.

[17] Diodorus 18.4.4.

[18] Cf. Diodorus 17.111.6.

[19] On Alexander's cities, see P. M. Fraser, *Cities of Alexander the Great* (Oxford: Oxford University Press, 1996), who argues that excluding Alexandria in Egypt, Alexander founded only eight cities.

[20] See further A. B. Bosworth, "Philip II and Upper Macedonia," *CQ2* 21 (1971): 93–105.

[21] Justin 12.5.13 says that Alexander founded twelve cities in Bactria and Sogdiana, but he does not name them.

[22] See Arrian 4.1.3–4 on the potential of Alexander Eschate (Alexandria-on-the-Jaxartes, the modern Leninabad) as security against future Scythian attacks.

[23] Much has been written on this topic, but for excellent arguments against the unity of mankind, see Ernst Badian, "Alexander the Great and the Unity of Mankind,"

Historia 7 (1958): 425–44, and A. B. Bosworth, "Alexander and the Iranians," *JHS* 100 (1980): 1–21, citing previous bibliography.

[24] See Bosworth, *Conquest and Empire*, 271–73.

[25] Plutarch *On the Fortune or the Virtue of Alexander* 338d.

[26] *Metz Epitome* 70.

[27] Plutarch *On the Fortune or the Virtue of Alexander* 329b. On what Hellenism constituted, bound up with speaking Greek, see Herodotus 8.1442 and Thucydides 2.68.5, with J. M. Hall, *Hellenicity: Between Ethnicity and Culture* (Chicago: University of Chicago Press, 2002), 189–98.

[28] See Ernst Badian, "Alexander the Great and the Scientific Exploration of the Oriental Part of His Empire," *Ancient Society* 22 (1991): 127–38.

[29] Plutarch *On the Fortune or the Virtue of Alexander* 328b.

[30] See, e.g., Herodotus 3.32.4 on Cambyses marrying his sister; Strabo 15.3.20 on sons marrying their mothers. See A. M. Schwarts, "The Old Eastern Iranian World View According to the Avesta," in *Cambridge History of Iran*, ed. I. Gershevitch, vol. 2 (Cambridge: Cambridge University Press, 1985), 656.

[31] Sacrificing elderly parents: Herodotus 1.126; using corpses: Herodotus 4.64.1–65.

[32] Onesicritus, *FGrH* 134 F 5 (Strabo 11.11.3)

[33] See C. B. Welles, "Alexander's Historical Achievement," *G&R*2 12 (1965): 216–28; quotation at 228.

[34] Cf. Arrian 7.19.6.

[35] Cf. Bosworth, "Alexander and the Iranians," 6.

6.   Urban Warfare in the Classical Greek World

JOHN W. I. LEE

O N A RAINY, almost moonless night in early summer 431 BC, a Theban assault force of three hundred men entered the small town
of Plataea in central Greece. They were let in by a Plataean, part of an
oligarchic faction hoping to seize power with Theban support. In the
sodden darkness the Thebans hurried to Plataea's marketplace. There
they issued a proclamation: Plataea was occupied, and the sensible
thing to do was to accept the fact. Plataea and Thebes, after all, had
once been allies; they could be so again. At first the Plataeans, panicked
at the enemy presence in the heart of town, agreed to terms. Soon,
though, they realized how few Thebans there were. Digging passages
through the earthen walls of their houses and placing wagons in the
streets as barricades, the Plataeans surrounded the invaders. In the pre-
dawn twilight, they struck. Plataean soldiers rushed down the streets,
while women and slaves threw stones and tiles from the rooftops. The
surprised Thebans withstood several onslaughts but at last broke and
fled, with the Plataeans in pursuit. Unfamiliar with the twisting streets
of the town, hindered by mud and darkness, the Thebans scattered in
desperation. One group, thinking it had found an exit, stumbled into
a warehouse by the city wall, only to be trapped there. A few men
made it to the gates; others were cut down in the streets. By daybreak
it was all over. One hundred twenty Theban corpses lay scattered in the
streets and houses of Plataea. The Plataeans took 180 prisoners; fearing
further Theban treachery, they executed all of them.

Thanks to the Athenian writer Thucydides, the vicious fight at Plataea has passed into history as the opening act of the Peloponnesian War

(431–404 BC) between the rival alliances of Athens and Sparta.[1] Thucydides' narrative skill has made the assault on Plataea one of the most famous episodes of the war. Yet the larger phenomenon Plataea represents— pitched battle within city walls—remains relatively neglected in classical Greek warfare studies.[2] Instead, scholars have tended to focus on set-piece battles fought on open fields between armies of heavily armored spearmen, or hoplites. As well, studies of Greek fortifications and sieges have concentrated on siege engineering and on the struggle for city walls, rather than on fighting within cities themselves.

Urban combat, however, was hardly uncommon in classical Greece. Indeed, during the period from about 500 to 300 BC, the preeminent cities of Hellas, including Argos, Athens, Corinth, Sparta, and Thebes, all witnessed major battles within their city limits. Some of the most desperate and most decisive clashes of classical antiquity were urban ones. Athenian democracy was born out of a popular urban revolution against oligarchs and their Spartan supporters in 508–507 BC. After the Peloponnesian War, when a junta of Thirty Tyrants usurped power, democracy was restored only after a civil war that saw intense combat in Athens's port of Piraeus. It was through an urban uprising in 379 BC that the Thebans broke free of Spartan domination and embarked on their short-lived hegemony over Greece. During that period, Theban forces would attack Sparta twice, in 370–369 and 362, the second time penetrating almost to the center of town. Alexander of Macedon, in turn, would subdue the Thebans in brutal street fighting before razing their city in 335 BC.

The western and eastern regions of the classical world also experienced intra-urban war. The opening clash of the Ionian Rebellion of 499–494, which would ultimately lead to the Greco-Persian Wars and the battles of Marathon, Thermopylae, and Salamis, saw Ionian Greeks and their Athenian allies sack the Persian provincial capital of Sardis.[3] The mercenaries of Cyrus, whose story Xenophon tells in his *Anabasis*, engaged in urban combat during their retreat from Mesopotamia to Byzantium in 401–400 BC.[4] In Sicily, Syracuse and other cities witnessed repeated episodes of urban warfare from the 460s down to the 350s.[5]

In the twenty-five centuries since Plataea, the urban battleground has always to some extent remained on the minds of strategists and field commanders.[6] Despite the carnage of modern city fights in places such as Stalingrad, Berlin, Hue, Mogadishu, and Grozny, however, urban war in the past few decades has often faded into the background of military consciousness. Just as the ancient Greeks privileged the decisive hoplite clash, many modern soldiers have preferred to think about and prepare for conventional battle between massed armies on open ground. At the end of the first decade of the twenty-first century, though, urban warfare has again become a pressing concern. The ongoing U.S. involvement in Iraq, where Western armed forces trained and equipped for open battle were slow to adapt to the challenges of fighting in and occupying urban terrain, has been a decisive factor in a renewed appreciation of urban warfare. In a world of instantaneous televised communications, insurgents and terrorists have come to realize not only the tactical advantages but also the propaganda value of drawing Western conventional armies into cities, where they inevitably kill innocent civilians. But it is not only a question of Iraq. About half the world's population lives in cities, and the pace of global urbanization shows no sign of letting up.[7] The problems of fighting in built-up areas will continue to exercise military thinkers as the century progresses.

Armies and cities, of course, have changed radically between Plataea and Fallujah. Yet despite the many differences in topography, technology, and culture that separate antiquity and the twenty-first century, studying classical Greek city fighting not only sheds light on the history of war in antiquity, it also offers a fresh perspective on the present. This chapter provides an introduction to the practices and ideologies of urban warfare in the classical Greek world. We start by looking at the various types of classical urban clashes. From there we move to investigate the ancient city as a battleground, and to evaluate the capabilities of classical armies for urban operations. Putting terrain and troops together will permit us to understand the nature of ancient city fighting and to assess the place of urban warfare in classical Greek military thought. Finally, we put the classical experience into broader historical context to see what lessons it may hold for today's strategists and battlefield commanders.

Classical literary sources preserve numerous episodes of sieges and assaults on city walls. They also describe assassinations, riots, and low-level gang warfare inside cities. These phenomena merit study in their own right, but here we will focus on large-scale armed clashes inside city walls, where the combatants' behavior was shaped by settlement topography, not by fortifications. Within these limits, ancient texts furnish dozens of accounts of city combat. Many of these accounts are quite brief, but they permit us to distinguish several basic patterns of urban struggle.

First, an attacking army might breach a city's walls by assault, siege engineering, or treachery, only to face continued resistance in streets, houses, and public spaces. These were among the bitterest sorts of city fight, often resulting in the complete annihilation of the defending force. Plataea in 431 and Thebes in 335 are just two examples of this pattern. Not every successful siege or assault progressed to intra-urban fighting. Sometimes, especially when surprised, defending forces simply collapsed.[8] Even so, urban combat during the capture of cities likely occurred more often than classical texts might suggest. The city of Olynthos in northern Greece, taken by Philip II of Macedon in summer 348, provides an instructive case in point. Although the literary sources record only that certain wealthy Olynthians betrayed their fellow citizens to Philip, excavations in the ruins of Olynthos have uncovered hundreds of lead sling bullets, arrowheads, and other weapons. The distribution and context of these artifacts indicate that the Macedonians had to subdue Olynthos house by house.[9] Future archaeological investigation may someday reveal further instances of otherwise unrecorded urban fighting of the classical period.

A second cause of urban combat was *stasis*, or civil strife, between factions in a city.[10] Such strife could spring from competition between powerful families, from class-based hostility, or from the involvement of outside interests. During the Peloponnesian War, antagonism between pro-Athenian and pro-Spartan factions was responsible for internecine bloodshed in cities throughout the Greek world. Corcyra in northwestern Greece, site of the most notorious of these *staseis*, underwent two years of civil strife that began with intensive urban combat and culminated in the total annihilation of the losers and their families.[11] In other cities, factional clashes began with massacres in the marketplace.[12] Defeated factions that managed to escape often returned to try their luck again, leading to renewed urban war.

Urban combat could also result when rebels or insurgents attempted to eject foreign occupiers from their city. In 335 BC, for example, the Thebans rose up against a Macedonian garrison stationed in their city.[13] At other times the presence of a foreign garrison in support of a city's ruling faction could lead to an urban revolt intended to expel both the foreigners and those who collaborated with them. The Athenian revolution of 508–507 and the Theban uprising of 379 exemplify this sort of situation. In both these cases, victorious insurgents allowed enemy garrisons to leave under a truce. Urban insurrections of this sort, although not unknown in the classical world, would become more common in the Hellenistic period (323–30 BC), when foreign garrisons were more widely employed.

Invasion or civil strife occasionally resulted in opposing armies or factions, neither in complete control of a city, confronting each other within its bounds. So it was in the opening stages of the civil war at Corcyra, where oligarchs and democrats held separate districts of town and spent several days engaged in running street battles.[14] While the length of most urban clashes could be measured in hours or days, this sort of struggle could devolve into chronic conflict, with a city semi-permanently divided between warring sides, which might even construct internal fortifications against each other. One such division occurred at Notium in Asia Minor during the early years of the Peloponnesian War, when hostile pro-Athenian and pro-Persian factions entrenched themselves in separate quarters of the city.[15] Likewise, Syracuse in the late 460s was split between native-born citizens and rebellious foreign mercenaries, who for several years battled in and around the city.[16]

These rough categories by no means exactly describe every single classical urban clash. Indeed, some urban battles featured combinations of situations. At Sparta in 369, for example, King Agesilaus had simultaneously to defend against a Theban assault and to squelch an uprising by a group of disaffected Spartans.[17] The Thebans in 335 had just succeeded in regaining their city from its Macedonian garrison when they faced an external attack from Alexander's main army. No matter how they began, though, all urban clashes were shaped by the characteristics of the ancient Greek city.

THE URBAN BATTLEGROUND

The *polis*, sometimes translated as "city-state," was the characteristic political form of classical Greece.[18] In physical terms the typical polis consisted of a walled urban settlement surrounded by a rural hinterland. The urban center was built around its acropolis, a defensible high point. Within the city walls could be found temples, public buildings, a marketplace, and private dwellings. In the fourth century, Mantineia, Megalopolis, and Messene incorporated open fields and croplands within their fortifications, but such vast circuits were exceptional. Elsewhere, suburbs sometimes extended beyond the walls.[19] Larger *poleis* featured small towns or villages in their hinterlands; poleis near but not directly on the sea often developed harbor towns. With the exception of Piraeus, which grew into a sizable town, none of these subordinate settlements ever came close to approaching the urban center in size or significance.

By modern standards, most poleis were tiny. The acropolis of Halai in central Greece, for example, measured a mere 160 by 70 meters, and the city's entire walled area may have been only 0.85 ha (2.1 acres).[20] Classical Halai probably had a total population of perhaps a few thousand. Athens, with its hundreds of thousands of native Athenians plus foreigners and slaves all living within several miles of walls, was exceptional. Whether their polis was large or small, most Greeks lived in the countryside, not in the city.

The circuit wall of a city defined its urban space.[21] Greeks had begun constructing fortified enceintes in earnest during the sixth century BC, and by the end of classical times only a handful of major sites, notably Sparta, remained unfortified. Most walls were built of massive stone blocks, though bricks, clay, and rubble were also employed. Gates with flanking towers and sometimes with elaborate entryways regulated access to the city. Additional towers and bastions along the walls provided positions for defenders.

The urban battleground proper began just inside a city's walls, but that did not render walls superfluous. Even if they could not forestall entry into a city, walls in urban combat could become inverse barriers, as at Plataea, where the circuit wall kept numerous Theban attackers from escaping.[22] The inside edges of city walls also furnished a secure backstop against which troops involved in urban combat could regroup. City gates, too, remained important as access points for reinforcements. At Tegea in 370–369 BC, for example, the factions contesting the city retreated to opposite sides of town after their initial clash. The pan-Arcadian faction fell back under the city wall, near the gates leading east to Mantineia, whence they expected to receive additional troops. Their opponents clustered on the other side of town, near the gates leading to Pallantion. When the pan-Arcadians were reinforced, their opponents quickly fled west out the gates.[23]

Fortified citadels inside cities could also shape the course of urban battle. Most cities had only one acropolis, but larger ones could contain multiple strong points. Athens, for instance, had the Mouseion hill near the Acropolis and the Mounichia hill in Piraeus, in addition to its famous Acropolis.[24] Defenders who retained an acropolis or other fortress could use it as a base for counterattacks. At Syracuse in the 350s, for example, the mercenaries of Dionysus II launched assaults from the fortified island of Ortygia against the rest of the city.[25] Holding the acropolis, however, did not guarantee control of a city. The popular revolutionaries at Athens in 508–507 BC successfully trapped the oligarchs and their Spartan supporters on the Acropolis.[26] At Sardis in 499, the Persians held the acropolis, but could not prevent the Athenians and Ionians from ravaging the town below.[27] When the Thebans in 335 BC regained control of their city, they left the Macedonian garrison bottled up on the Cadmea, Thebes's acropolis.[28] In chronic intraurban conflict, as we have seen, rival factions or communities might rely on internal cross walls to bolster their positions.[29] Such walls could pen urban combatants into a narrow slaughter pen with no room for maneuver, as happened at Syracuse in 357–356.[30]

The real nerve center of the classical city was the marketplace or *agora*. Located at the junction of major streets and often containing major administrative buildings, the agora was the largest open area within the city walls. Foreign attackers entering a city usually headed straight for the agora, and defenders typically fell back toward it.[31] If the defenders could hold on to the agora and reform their troops, they stood a chance of pushing the attackers out of the city. The Athenians and Ionians at Sardis in 499 BC, for example, were forced to fall back after they encountered Persian troops massed in the agora.[32] Conversely, the loss of the agora could be the final blow that crushed defenders' morale.[33] Even so, overconfident or outnumbered forces, like the Thebans at Plataea, might find that taking the agora alone was insufficient.

Many civil wars began with coups or massacres in the agora.[34] Again, winning the agora did not guarantee victory, as the oligarchic party discovered at Elis in 397 BC. Having seized the agora, the oligarchs declared victory, only to find that Thrasydaios, leader of the popular faction, was not dead but just at home sleeping off his midday wine. Shaking off a hangover, Thrasydaios led a counterattack that routed the oligarchs.[35]

In addition to being communication centers and rallying points, marketplaces could contain vital arms supplies for urban combatants.[36] The conspirators who allegedly sought to seize power at Sparta in 400–399 BC, for example, had planned to use Sparta's tool market, with its abundance of axes, hatchets, and sickles, as their arsenal.[37] At least one other city was taken by insurgents employing weapons that had been smuggled into the agora inside baskets of fruit and boxes of clothing.[38] Forgetting the dangers of an urban armed mass, the Spartan officer commanding the defense of Mytilene in 427 made the mistake of arming the city's populace, which promptly rebelled against him.[39]

Beyond the agora, any spacious and defensible location where combatants could form up or find refuge was tactically important. These places included theaters, temples, gymnasia, and other large buildings.[40] During the Athenian civil war of 404–403, oligarchic horsemen used the Odeion of Pericles, a meeting hall just below the Acropolis, as their base, while the democratic light infantry gathered at the theater in Piraeus.[41] Like marketplaces, temples and public buildings could furnish arsenals for urban combat. At Thebes in 379, the anti-Spartan forces equipped themselves with weapons, probably religious dedications, taken from a portico.[42] Given enough time, defenders might dig trenches across open areas, or sow them with obstacles to impede an enemy advance.[43]

Large buildings promised security but could become death traps. During the final stages of the Corcyrean civil war, members of the oligarchic faction, knowing they were about to be executed, tried to hold out in what may have been a warehouse. Their enemies climbed atop the building, broke open the roof, and rained down tiles and arrows; the defenders who survived the barrage killed themselves rather than surrender.[44] Something similar happened at Tegea in 370–369, when members of a defeated faction took refuge in the temple of Artemis. Their opponents surrounded the temple, climbed up, dismantled its roof, and hurled down tiles. The men inside gave up, only to be put to death.[45]

Urban war also meant street fighting. The oldest Greek towns had grown up organically over the centuries and so did not have regular layouts. The irregular web of narrow streets and alleys that crisscrossed these cities could confuse and disorient foreign invaders—think again of the Thebans at Plataea—while defenders who knew the shortcuts could move quickly from one neighborhood to another. Irregular street networks forced commanders to split forces into small detachments, making communications and mutual support nigh impossible. With attackers and defenders split into uncoordinated small groups, a street battle could last all night, with troops slaying each other at random in the darkness, as happened at Syracuse in 355.[46]

By the mid-fifth century, regular street grids became popular for new cities and for expansions to old ones.[47] Street widths in these grids could range from 3–5 meters (9.8–16.4 feet) for residential byways to 13–15 meters (42.6–49.2 feet) for main thoroughfares.[48] As Aristotle noted, cities built in this new "Hippodamian" style made for more convenient and pleasant living but for less security in war.[49] To keep a city defensible, Aristotle recommended that planners use grids only in certain neighborhoods, or lay out blocks with a few wide avenues connecting to smaller streets.[50] A regular street plan made matters easier for attackers, who could send mutually supporting detachments up parallel avenues with less risk of getting lost. In response, defenders could dig pits or trenches in streets and set up barricades. They might also burrow through house walls to outflank enemy forces.[51]

Even in grid-planned cities, narrow streets compelled commanders to draw up troops in unwieldy formations. In Piraeus in 404–403, for example, the oligarchs had to form their hoplites fifty ranks deep.[52] A regular street grid also provided missile troops better fields of fire. The oligarchs at Piraeus were able to take the agora, but when they advanced up a main avenue toward the Mounichia hill, the democrats threw them back with a volley of stones, javelins, and arrows.[53]

In grid-planned cities, houses were built in blocks sharing common walls, sometimes with a narrow alley running down the center of the block. As in modern subdivisions, houses in each block often shared a similar design. Houses in planned districts could be spacious. Plots on the North Hill of Olynthos, for example, average about 17 meters on a side.[54] In older cities, houses were often smaller and house layouts less regular. New or old, houses were perhaps the most difficult of classical Greek urban terrain. From Sicily to Ionia, the typical house was of mud brick on stone foundations.[55] It faced inward, with a narrow entry giving access to a central courtyard around which rooms were arranged. Exterior-facing windows were high off the ground and generally inaccessible. Some houses had second stories, often used for women's quarters. Houses generally had pitched, tiled roofs, although in some regions flat roofs were preferred.

Unlike pitched field battle, urban warfare took place in three dimensions. In city fights, house roofs provided a vital height advantage. Roof tiles, which could weigh from 10 to 30 kg, provided ready-made projectiles for defenders to hurl down upon invaders. Even women and slaves ascended the roofs of their homes to assail advancing enemies with such missiles.[56] Sometimes other structures gave a height advantage. A Theban attempt on Corinth in 369 BC was repelled by light troops who mounted burial monuments and grave markers to hurl stones and javelins.[57] Attackers too used roofs as firing platforms, as the Thebans did when taking Oeum from the Spartans in 370–369.[58] Rooftop positions were not invulnerable. Boeotian troops defending Corinth in 393, for example, climbed to the roofs of ship sheds and warehouses, only to be trapped and killed there.[59]

With their narrow doorways and solid construction, private homes could become fortresses of last resort for a defending population. A city might be declared secure once the agora and public buildings were taken, but inhabitants determined to resist could still force an attacker to root them out house by house. If neighbors cut through shared walls to link up with each other, they could convert an entire block into a final redoubt. House-to-house combat was dangerous and difficult. Beyond every darkened doorway and around every blind corner might lurk a desperate enemy ready to fight to the last. At Olynthos, the distribution of excavated sling bullets and arrowheads suggests that Macedonian attackers had to force their way into house courtyards, only to be shot at from the surrounding rooms. The Macedonians apparently responded with volleys of their own missiles before moving in to clear each room.[60] Thirteen years later, the Macedonians probably faced a similar situation at Thebes. After Alexander's forces seized the city's key points, some Theban infantry fled to their houses, where they and their families fought and died.[61]

In addition to posing tactical difficulties, combat in houses threatened an invading army's discipline and cohesion. Soldiers who turned aside from the fight to loot, rape, and pillage were useless for further combat. Worse, they might be surprised by a counterattack. At Syracuse in 355 BC, for instance, Dion and the Syracusans caught enemy mercenaries in the act of plundering and utterly routed them.[62]

Houses had such defensive potential that they were sometimes incorporated into fortification architecture. Motya in Sicily, for example, featured multiple-story houses near its northern gate. During the Greek capture of the city in 397 BC, Carthaginian defenders employed these houses as a second line of defense.[63] When Philip of Macedon tried to force his way into Perinthos in 341–340, the defenders turned their homes into impromptu fortresses, blocking streets and alleys to stymie the Macedonian advance.[64] Plato advocated that houses "be arranged in such a way that the whole city will form a single wall; all the houses must have good walls . . . facing the roads so that the whole city will have the form of a single house, which will render its appearance not unpleasing, besides being far and away the best plan for ensuring safety and ease of defense."[65] Plato's suggestion is reflected at Olynthos, where the backs of the first row of houses along the west edge of the North Hill are built into the northwestern fortifications of the city.[66]

Sparta's unusual topography turned the two Theban attacks on it into hybrids of open battle and city fight. Classical Sparta was unwalled and spread out along the banks of the Eurotas River. At its outer neighborhoods, houses were interspersed with groves and fields. The central area of town, where the Spartiates or full Spartan citizens lived, seems to have been densely built up, without a regular plan. Even so, the center of town contained walls, fences, and open spaces. Around the town center were a number of religious sanctuaries and public buildings.[67]

In 370–369, the Thebans under Epaminondas initially confined themselves to plundering the suburbs. There they felled trees to build field fortifications wherever they camped, just as they did in rural terrain. Eventually the Thebans took a stab at the heart of the city, advancing toward the open racecourse in the sanctuary of Poseidon. In response, the Spartans used the urban topography to their advantage, by setting an ambush in the Temple of the Tyndaridae.[68] The ambush, combined with a conventional cavalry charge across the racecourse, halted the Thebans. In 362 BC, fearing a direct assault, the Spartans prepared by demolishing houses in the central part of town and using the rubble to block up entrances, alleys, and open spaces. Some even alleged that the Spartans used large bronze tripods taken from religious sanctuaries to build barricades.[69] Epaminondas, however, did not attempt a head-on attack, fearing that his troops would be exposed to missile attack from rooftops.[70] Instead, he took an indirect approach, as if maneuvering on an open battlefield, which allowed his forces to advance on the inhabited area without coming under missile fire. Only a desperate counterattack of fewer than a hundred Spartans under King Archidamus threw the Thebans back.

THE COMBATANTS

The equipment, formations, and command structures of classical Greek armies were ill-suited for built-up terrain. Hoplites, the mainstay of all polis armies, were armored militia infantry who carried large round shields and long thrusting spears. Although the hoplite shield has been judged heavy and unwieldy, there are some indications it could be handled effectively in individual combat, even in cities; fourth-century tomb reliefs from Asia Minor even show shield-carrying hoplites climbing assault ladders. Although there is no certain evidence, possibly hoplites fighting house to house discarded their shields for greater maneuverability. The more serious problem for hoplites in cities was weaponry. While they carried swords as secondary weapons, hoplites were primarily spearmen; their 2.5-meter-long spears would have been awkward at close quarters or inside houses. Matters would have been even worse for Macedonian troopers equipped with the 12- to 16-foot-long *sarissa*, or pike. Some Greeks did study swordsmanship, but systematic weapons training remained the province of a wealthy few. Indeed, outside of Sparta, most hoplites underwent no formal training until the end of the classical period.

A greater challenge for hoplites in cities was battle formation. Hoplites typically employed a deep infantry array called the phalanx. The ideal phalanx, an unbroken mass eight ranks deep, could extend a mile or more across an open battlefield. Needless to say, a phalanx could not be maintained on city streets or in houses. Only in an agora could hoplites employ their customary formation. Splitting a phalanx into smaller detachments to cope with urban topography was complicated by the general lack of subordinate units and officers. With the exception of the Spartans, who had a complex tactical hierarchy and an almost religious devotion to good order, most Greek armies had a very low proportion of officers and no tactical units below the company level. What officers there were could be rendered impotent by the laxness of classical military discipline.[71]

The amateur ethos of most polis armies had other important consequences for urban war. For one thing, the Greeks never developed units of specialists such as pioneers, sappers, or combat engineers. Hoplites could and did build improvised field works, but their engineering skills and equipment never came close to matching those of the Roman legions. At the same time, because hoplite militias equipped themselves, a wide proportion of citizens owned arms. Fighting in a city, whether as a result of invasion or civil war, typically involved the whole populace, not just regular armed forces.

Light infantry, including archers, slingers, and javelineers, was much more effective in urban fighting. Light troops could hurl missiles from rooftops or sweep the streets with volleys of projectiles.[72] The archaeological evidence from Olynthos indicates that slingers and archers could wield their weapons even inside the confines of houses.[73] Light troops proved their value during the fighting at Piraeus in 404–403. The oligarchic forces, with hoplites enough to mass fifty shields deep, advanced up the Mounichia hill toward the democrats, who were able to muster only ten ranks of hoplites. Behind these ten ranks, though, were the democratic light infantry. The hilly topography of Mounichia gave the defenders a height advantage, allowing the light infantry to shoot over the heads of their own hoplites. With their opponents packed fifty deep into the street below them, the light troops could hardly miss.[74]

The role of cavalry in urban battle is difficult to determine. The Athenian Thirty Tyrants apparently brought a sizable cavalry force to Piraeus in 404–403, but the horsemen played no role in the battle.[75] They may have deployed in Piraeus's agora to guard the rear of the oligarchic hoplite force. Theban cavalry participated in the fighting at Thebes in 335, although they were hampered by the narrow streets, and quickly fled once the Macedonians captured the agora.[76] The Roman writer Pausanias saw a trophy near the Painted Stoa at Athens, just outside the agora, that commemorated an Athenian cavalry victory there against Macedonian cavalry, probably in 304 BC.[77] At least the classical Greeks did not deploy elephants in urban fighting. Pyrrhus of Epiros would later try to do so at Argos in 272, only to discover that his troops had to remove the fighting platforms from the elephants in order to pass through the city gates.[78]

URBAN WARFARE AND CLASSICAL MILITARY THOUGHT

Assessing the place of urban warfare in classical military thought requires understanding the centrality of walls in the polis mind-set. Building a circuit wall was the largest and most expensive communal task that the citizens of most poleis would ever undertake.[79] Once built, walls marked polis identity and autonomy. Plato might advocate "walls of bronze and iron" rather than earth, but when it came to defending their cities, Greeks never ignored the practical value of fortifications.[80] Indeed, while classical warfare has been portrayed as an agonal affair that valorized open battle over sieges and stratagems, by the mid-fifth century BC the idea of a defensive strategy based on impregnable city walls was well established at Athens.[81] Athens was exceptionally well prepared for such a strategy because it could draw supplies from its overseas empire. Nonetheless, the citizens of smaller poleis considered staying behind the walls a perfectly normal defensive move, especially when faced with a numerically superior invader. They would choose open battle only if the numbers were even. In fact, close analysis of the Peloponnesian War reveals that sieges and city assaults were twice as common as pitched battles.[82]

The stock that classical Greeks placed in their walls is reflected in the absolute panic that sometimes overcame defenders when they realized enemy forces had penetrated the bounds of their city. Not even the Spartans, who prided themselves on their lack of city walls, were immune to this reaction: in 370–369, both men and women panicked at the appearance of Thebans in the suburbs.[83] Given the expense involved in building a city wall, and the psychological value attached to maintaining its integrity, it is no surprise that fighting inside city walls was almost always undertaken out of necessity rather than as a strategic choice. Tellingly, our ancient sources preserve only a single reference to troops deliberately abandoning their walls in order to fight inside their city. This was at Pharcedon in Thessaly during the mid-fourth century BC, where the defenders unsuccessfully attempted to draw Philip's Macedonians into an urban ambush.[84]

Greek military thinkers were probably also disinclined to adopt urban battle as a preferred mode of warfare, because it upset accepted gender and status hierarchies. The classical citizen ideal emphasized warfare as the exclusive realm of free males. Women and slaves were supposed to stay indoors, secure within the walls of the household. Combat inside cities, however, upset the masculine dominance over war, not to mention the notion of the household as an inviolable private space. It is notable that accounts of urban battle prominently mention the active participation of women and slaves.[85] As well, city fights favored the poor and unarmored over middle-class hoplites, challenging hoplite dominance of the battlefield.

Furthermore, Greek commanders understood that urban warfare was particularly vicious and uncertain, even by ancient standards. Women and children, along with combatants, were fair game. Treachery, massacres, and fights to the death were commonplace. Urban topography made battle more desperate, as troops confined in streets and houses could not easily flee. Even soldiers inclined to grant quarter to surrendering foes might hesitate to do so if they feared surprise attack from another direction. The lack of communications and control in urban fighting meant that commanders had less opportunity to appeal to the limiting rituals, such as truces, that moderated field battles. Fighting at night or in bad weather exacerbated the effects of topography and poor control. The nature of the combatants as much as the nature of the terrain contributed to the brutality of city fighting. Opposing factions in civil strife were implacably hostile; at Corcyra, infamously, citizens set fire to their own city in an attempt to drive out rivals.[86] Troops defending a city against external invasion, too, knew they were fighting not just for their own lives but also for their families and for the very existence of their home. For their part, attackers who gained access to a city after a long siege or a bloody assault were primed to inflict as much revenge or "payback" as possible on any inhabitant, armed or not.[87] All these factors made Greeks wary of fighting in cities.

There are nonetheless a few indications that Greek commanders understood how to conduct urban warfare when they had to. The Plataeans certainly were quick to take advantage of their city's topography to entrap the Theban invaders. In Piraeus during 404–403, since the democrats did not have enough men to hold the entire circuit wall surrounding the harbor, they deliberately concentrated on the Mounichia hill, a strong point that could be approached only through the town's street grid. By deploying on Mounichia's slopes, the democratic leader Thrasyboulos maximized the defensive potential of the urban landscape and exploited his preponderance in light troops to offset the oligarchs' strength in hoplites.[88] Epaminondas, one of the masterminds of the Theban uprising of 379, was likewise well aware of the complexities of street fighting. Recognizing that the urban terrain of central Sparta was not good for pitched battle between phalanxes, he avoided direct assaults on the city center in both 370–369 and 362.[89] At Syracuse in the 350s, the general Dion made attempts to overcome the fragmentation of urban fighting. He divided his troops into separate commands and grouped them in columns, so that he could attack at several places at once.[90]

In the later classical era, urban warfare did receive some attention in the writings of Aeneas Tacticus. Aeneas, who perhaps hailed from the town of Stymphalos in the Peloponnesus and possibly served as a general of the Arcadian League, was active in the first half of the fourth century BC. Although today his work is largely unknown outside the specialist circles of Greek history, Aeneas might be called the world's first strategist of urban war.[91]

Aeneas penned several treatises, of which only one has survived, the *Poliorkêtika*, composed around 355–350 BC.[92] Though its title is often rendered as *Siegecraft*, the *Poliorkêtika* is in fact a guide to protecting a threatened city from internal treachery, surprise assaults, and fickle mercenaries. It is an extraordinary collection of advice, anecdotes, and observations, containing everything from practical tips ("when sawing through a cross-bar pour oil on it, to make the task quicker and quieter") to astute psychological insight ("In parts of the city which the enemy can easily . . . attack . . . [station] those with the largest stake in the community and thus the greatest incentive not to succumb to self-indulgence").[93]

Aeneas stresses many of the same aspects of the urban battleground that we have already examined. He underlines the importance of the agora and other strategic spots.[94] He offers procedures to help cities guard against surprise assaults and internal plots. A city's troops, he writes, must be well organized and forcefully led; the hiring and discipline of mercenaries must be carefully regulated. Moreover, Aeneas advocates all sorts of remarkably modern-sounding methods for keeping an urban population under control: registering or confiscating weapons, issuing identity tokens, interrogating merchants and hotel guests, forbidding communal dinners, and so on. Even processions and religious festivals must be watched, he adds, lest they become occasions for violent revolution. Mutual scrutiny of everyone's actions, he emphasizes, will deprive plotters of any opportunity to carry out their plans.

Now, Aeneas was clearly familiar with classical Greece's long history of city fights. He refers to the clashes at Plataea, Sparta, and Argos as examples of how to defend urban terrain. And he does offer some techniques for fighting inside the walls, including a stratagem to lure enemy troops into open gates and then entrap them.[95] Even so, Aeneas's true goal was not to describe how to win a city fight but to forestall urban warfare before it broke out, through tight security at the gates and in the marketplace, active defense of city walls, and strict supervision of potentially rebellious elements. In a sense, he simply perpetuated the traditional classical emphasis on a wall-based defensive strategy.

There was irony to Aeneas's stance, for just as he was completing his handbook, a new era of Greek military technology was arising. Large torsion-powered bolt-shooters and stone throwers would give new dominance to the attackers of cities. Within a few years of the appearance of the *Poliorkêtika*, Philip of Macedon would use his siege engines to take the once impregnable city of Amphipolis. By sticking to the old emphasis on city walls, Aeneas and his fellow Greeks played right into the offensive capabilities of the powerful new siege machinery. Perhaps if he had written a few years later, Aeneas might have offered a different approach, one that did not try to meet attackers at the walls but instead drew them into the city, where they could be surrounded and destroyed, just as the Plataeans had annihilated the Thebans in 431.

LESSONS LEARNED

Spears and swords, mud brick houses, women with roof tiles. At first glance it seems hard to imagine how stories from twenty-five centuries ago could shed any light on modern urban warfare, in which high-tech Western armies confront RPG-armed irregulars in sprawling concrete conurbations. Outside the experiences of divided cities such as Notium and Syracuse, there is little in the history of classical city fighting directly comparable with modern urban counterinsurgency. Yet place Plataea side by side with Mogadishu in 1993, where an outnumbered American assault force was bewildered by a maze of unfamiliar streets, and it is clear some things have not changed.[96]

Perhaps the first lesson that emerges from examining Greek urban war is the importance of good intelligence and local knowledge. Without understanding urban topography—not only in the physical sense, but also in the wider sense of the economic and social relationships that link neighborhoods and people—modern soldiers will remain as lost in the mud and darkness as were the Thebans at Plataea. For Western armies operating abroad in cities, low-tech, low-cost solutions, such as having sufficient interpreters or providing all troops with basic foreign language training, will enable better access to local knowledge than expensive jet fighters or other high-tech gadgetry can ever provide.

Furthermore, the classical experience helps contextualize the vengeance and factionalism that mark modern urban war. The sectarian hostility that characterizes many of today's urban conflicts does not seem so aberrational when placed against the backdrop of civil strife in places like Corcyra. The classical Greek city was very much a family and tribal affair. Civil strife was the vessel into which all its antagonisms—class, politics, personal differences—could pour.[97] Bitter factional hatreds, mass slaughter, choosing suicide over surrender—these were the inevitable corollaries of *stasis*, not the property of one ideology, place, or time. As Thucydides recognized long ago, the details may change, but people's responses will remain similar.[98]

Too, the ability of Greek cities to mobilize the entirety of the population for urban war presents a lesson for modern Western armies used to assuming a strong distinction between military and civilian personnel. From the classical perspective, an armed populace looks like a more normal state of affairs than does a professional volunteer military isolated from the rest of a society. The Greeks, it is true, preferred to think of hoplite battle as strictly for male citizens. In urban combat, though, this ideology broke down, and every male and female inhabitant could take part in the fight. Women's use of roof tiles in ancient city fights reminds us how successfully irregular combatants can employ urban terrain to neutralize the technological advantages of conventional forces.

The histories of urban combat at Athens and Thebes, moreover, show that foreign troops and garrisons, however useful they may be for propping up a sympathetic regime, provide a focal point for local opposition. Sometimes military forces in a city cause more harm than benefit. One wonders, for example, what would have happened in Athens in 508–507 if the oligarchic party had not called in Spartan assistance. Perhaps they would have held on to power, and Athenian radical democracy would have been stillborn. Here Aeneas Tacticus's warnings about the dangers of mercenaries provide additional food for thought. While classical authors sometimes overstated the evils of hired soldiery, there was truth to their complaints. Arrogant, violent, or careless mercenaries could inflame popular resentment and cause uprisings. These days, unregulated and overaggressive private military contractors such as Blackwater threaten the success of Western armies and hinder the accomplishment of strategic goals.

If a city is to be taken or retained, the Greek experience shows that holding just one central point, whether acropolis or Green Zone, is insufficient. Urban war requires controlling markets, streets, and houses. Even better, as Aeneas Tacticus recognized, is to achieve victory by using repression, surveillance, and mutual responsibility to forestall rebellion or invasion before it occurs. Aeneas, of course, did not have to deal with world opinion, but in that difference lies perhaps the greatest lesson that Greek urban combat has to teach us. The excesses and atrocities of Corcyra, Thebes, and Syracuse underline the dangers of letting troops get out of control, of succumbing to the psychology of "payback," and of fighting with no higher purpose than the seizure or maintenance of power. Modern Western democratic armies are not just military forces. They embody the public reputation and values of their nations, and are sustainable abroad only to the degree that they retain majority support back home. As deceptive and dishonorable as the enemy may be, the officers and soldiers of modern democracies must always remember their moral and ethical obligations, whether on the urban battlefield or anywhere else.

FURTHER READING

Readers wanting to learn more about ancient urban war might start with Aeneas Tacticus; for a translation and commentary see Whitehead, *Aineias the Tactician* (1990). For Thucydides and Herodotus, the excellent Landmark editions of Strassler, *The Landmark*

Thucydides (1996) and *The Landmark Herodotus* (2007), may be consulted. Ober, "Hoplites and Obstacles" (1991), and Lee, "Urban Combat at Olynthos" (2001), analyze the mechanics of ancient city fighting. Lintott (1982) offers an overview of civil strife (*stasis*) in the classical city. For more about classical Greek armies, see Sabin, van Wees, and Whitby, *The Cambridge History of Greek and Roman Warfare* (2007). Ashworth, *War and the City* (1991), Desch, *Soldiers in Cities* (2001), and Dufour, *La guerre, la ville et le soldat* (2002), provide long-term perspectives on the history of urban warfare. For urban combat in the modern global context, see Kaldor, "New and Old Wars" (2007), and Thornton, *Asymmetric Warfare* (2007).

BIBLIOGRAPHY

Antal, John, and Bradley Gericke, eds. *City Fights: Selected Histories of Urban Combat from World War II to Vietnam.* New York: Presidio Press, 2003.

Ashworth, J. G. *War and the City.* London: Routledge, 1991.

Barry, W. D. "Roof Tiles and Urban Violence in the Ancient World." *Greek, Roman, and Byzantine Studies* 37, no. 1 (1996): 55–74.

Bowden, Mark. *Black Hawk Down: A Story of Modern War.* New York: Penguin, 1999.

Cahill, Nicholas. *Household and City Organization at Olynthus.* New Haven, CT: Yale University Press, 2002.

Camp, John. "Walls and the *polis,*" in *Polis and Politics: Studies in Ancient Greek History Presented to M. H. Hansen,* ed. P. Flensted-Jensen, Thomas Heine Nielsen, and Lene Rubinstein, 41–57. Copenhagen: Museum Tusculanum Press, 2000.

———. *The Archaeology of Athens.* New Haven, CT: Yale University Press, 2001.

Desch, Michael C., ed. *Soldiers in Cities: Military Operations on Urban Terrain.* Carlisle, PA: Strategic Studies Institute, U.S. Army War College Command, 2001.

Dufour, Jean-Louis. *La guerre, la ville et le soldat.* Paris: Odile Jacob, 2002.

Garlan, Yvon. *Recherches de poliorcétique grecque.* Paris: E. de Boccard, 1974.

Garland, Robert. *The Piraeus from the Fifth to the First Century BC,* 2nd ed. London: Duckworth, 2001.

Gehrke, Hans-Joachim. *Stasis: Untersuchungen zu den inneren Kriegen in den griechischen Staaten des 5. und 4. Jahrhunderts v. Chr.* Munich: Beck, 1985.

Gill, David. "Hippodamus and the Piraeus." *Historia* 55, no. 1 (2006): 1–15.

Glenn, Russell, Christopher Paul, Todd Helmus, and Paul Steinberg. *"People Make the City," Executive Summary: Joint Urban Operations Observations and Insights from Afghanistan and Iraq.* Santa Monica, CA: RAND Corporation, 2007.

Habicht, Christian. *Athens from Alexander to Antony,* trans. Deborah Lucas Schneider. Cambridge, MA: Harvard University Press, 1997.

Hansen, Mogens, and Thomas Heine Nielsen, eds. *An Inventory of Archaic and Classical Poleis.* Oxford: Oxford: Oxford University Press, 2004.

Hoepfner, Wolfram, and Ernst-Ludwig Schwandner. *Haus und Stadt im klassischen Griechenland.* Munich: Deutscher Kunstverlag, 1994.

Isserlin, B.S.J., and J. du Plat Taylor. *Motya: A Phoenician and Carthaginian City in Sicily.* Leiden: Brill, 1974.

Joes, Anthony James. *Urban Guerrilla Warfare*. Lexington: University Press of Kentucky, 2007.

Kaldor, Mary. *New and Old Wars: Organized Violence in a Global Era*, 2nd ed. Stanford: Stanford University Press, 2007.

Krentz, Peter. *The Thirty at Athens*. Ithaca, NY: Cornell University Press, 1982.

———. "The Strategic Culture of Periclean Athens." In *Polis and Polemos: Essays on Politics, War, and History in Ancient Greece in Honor of Donald Kagan*, ed. Charles Hamilton and Peter Krentz, 55–72. Claremont, CA: Regina Books, 1997.

Lawrence, A. W. *Greek Aims in Fortification*. Oxford: Oxford University Press, 1979.

Lee, John W. I. "Urban Combat at Olynthos, 348 BC." In *Fields of Conflict: Progress and Prospect in Battlefield Archaeology*, ed. P.W.M. Freeman and A. Pollard, 11–22. B.A.R. International Series 958. Oxford, 2001.

Lintott, Andrew. *Violence, Civil Strife, and Revolution in the Classical City*. London: Croom Helm, 1982.

Martin, Roland. *L'urbanisme dans la Grèce antique*, 2nd ed. Paris: A. & J. Picard, 1974.

McNicoll, A. W., and N. P. Milner. *Hellenistic Fortifications from the Aegean to the Euphrates*. Oxford: Oxford University Press, 1997.

Ober, Josiah. "Hoplites and Obstacles." In *Hoplites: The Classical Greek Battle Experience*, ed. Victor Davis Hanson, 173–96. Berkeley and Los Angeles: University of California Press, 1991.

Raftopoulou, S. "New Finds from Sparta." In *Sparta in Laconia: Proceedings of the 19th British Museum Classical Colloquium held with the British School at Athens and Kings' and University Colleges, London (6–8 December, 1995)*, ed. W. G. Cavanagh and S.E.C. Walker. London: British School at Athens, 1998.

Rawlings, Louis. "Alternative Agonies: Hoplite Martial and Combat Experiences Beyond the Phalanx." In *War and Violence in Ancient Greece*, ed. Hans van Wees, 233–59. London: Duckworth and the Classical Press of Wales, 2000.

Roy, James. "The Threat from the Piraeus." In *Kosmos: Essays in Order, Conflict and Community in Classical Athens*, ed. Paul Cartledge, Paul Millett, and Sitta von Reden, 191–202. Cambridge: Cambridge University Press, 1998.

Rusch, Scott Michael. "Poliorcetic Assault in the Peloponnesian War." PhD dissertation, University of Pennsylvania, 1997.

Sabin, Philip, Hans van Wees, and Michael Whitby, eds. *The Cambridge History of Greek and Roman Warfare*. Cambridge: Cambridge University Press, 2007.

Shipley, Graham. "Lakedaimon." In *An Inventory of Archaic and Classical Poleis*, ed. Mogens Hansen and Thomas Nielsen, 569–98. Oxford: Oxford University Press, 2004.

Sokolicek, Alexander. "Zum Phänomen des Diateichisma im griechischen Städtebau." *Forum Archaeologiae* 27/VI/2003 (http://farch.net).

Strassler, Robert. *The Landmark Thucydides*. New York: Free Press, 1996.

———. *The Landmark Herodotus*. New York: Pantheon, 2007.

Thornton, Rod. *Asymmetric Warfare: Threat and Response in the Twenty-First Century*. Malden, MA: Polity Press, 2007.

Tritle, Lawrence. *From Melos to My Lai: War and Survival*. London: Routledge, 2000.

van Wees, Hans. *Greek Warfare: Myths and Realities*. London: Duckworth, 2004.

Waywell, Geoffrey. "Sparta and Its Topography." *BICS* 43 (1999): 1–26.

Whitehead, David. *Aineias the Tactician: How to Survive Under Siege*. Oxford: Clarendon Press, 1990.

Winter, F. E. *Greek Fortifications*. Toronto: University of Toronto Press, 1971.

NOTES

[1] The story of Plataea is told in Thucydides 2.1–5.

[2] For an overview of the latest scholarship on Greek warfare, see Sabin, van Wees, and Whitby, *The Cambridge History of Greek and Roman Warfare*.

[3] Herodotus 5.100–101.

[4] Xenophon *Anabasis* 5.2.7–27.

[5] Diodorus Siculus 11.67.5–11.68.5, 11.73, 11.76, etc.

[6] For useful overviews of the history of urban warfare, see Ashworth, *War and the City*; Dufour, *La guerre*; Antal and Gericke, *City Fights*.

[7] On urbanization and the future of urban war, see Desch, *Soldiers in Cities*, 3–5; Glenn et al., "People Make the City," xiii; Joes, *Urban Guerrilla Warfare*, 2–3.

[8] For surprise in city assaults, see Rusch, "Poliorcetic Assault," 824–32.

[9] For the battlefield archaeology of Olynthos see Lee, "Urban Combat at Olynthos."

[10] On *stasis*, see Lintott, *Violence, Civil Strife, and Revolution*, Gehrke, *Stasis*.

[11] Thucydides 3.70–85, 4.46–48.

[12] Diodorus Siculus 13.104, 15.57; *Hellenica Oxyrhynchia* 15.2.

[13] Arrian 1.7.1.

[14] Thucydides 3.72–76.

[15] Thucydides 3.34.

[16] Diodorus Siculus 11.73–76.

[17] Plutarch *Agesilaus* 32.

[18] Hansen and Nielsen, *Inventory of Archaic and Classical Poleis*, 4–153, offer an excellent overview of the polis and its characteristics.

[19] Thucydides 4.69; Xenophon *Hellenica* 5.3.1.

[20] Hansen and Nielsen, *Inventory*, 667–8.

[21] On Greek walls and the *polis*, see Camp, "Walls and the *Polis*"; Hansen and Nielsen, *Inventory*, 135–37.

[22] Thucydides 2.4.5.

[23] Xenophon *Hellenica* 6.5.9.

[24] On Mounichia, see Aristotle *Athenaion Politeia* 19.2, and Garland, *Piraeus*, 35–36; on the Mouseion, see Camp, *Archaeology of Athens*, 166–67, 265. For cities with multiple strong places, see Aristotle *Politics* 1330b5.

[25] Plutarch *Dion* 41.

[26] Herodotus 5.72.

[27] Herodotus 5.101.

[28] Arrian 1.7.1, 1.7.10.

[29] On cross walls (*diateichismata*), see Lawrence, *Greek Aims*, 148–55; Sokolicek, "Zum Phänomen."

[30] Diodorus Siculus 16.11.2.

[31] For the agora as the key to a city, see Aeneas Tacticus 2.1, 3.5, 22.2; Arrian 1.8.6–7; Polyaenus. 5.5.1.

[32] Herodotus 5.100–101.

[33] Arrian 1.8.7.

[34] Diodorus Siculus 13.104; *Hellenica Oxyrhynchia* 15.2.

[35] Xenophon *Hellenica* 3.2.27–29.

[36] Aeneas Tacticus 30.1–2.

[37] Xenophon *Hellenica* 3.3.7.

[38] Aeneas Tacticus 29.6.

[39] Thucydides 3.27.

[40] Aeneas Tacticus 3.5.

[41] Xenophon *Hellenica* 2.4.24, 2.4.33.

[42] Xenophon *Hellenica* 5.4.8.

[43] Xenophon *Hellenica* 2.4.27.

[44] Thucydides 4.48.

[45] Xenophon *Hellenica* 6.5.9.

[46] Diodorus Siculus 16.19.4.

[47] On Greek city planning, see Martin, *L'urbanisme*; Hoepfner and Schwandner, *Haus und Stadt*.

[48] Hoepfner and Schwandner, *Haus und Stadt*, 19–20; Cahill, *Household and City Organization*, 21–2; Gill, "Hippodamus," 7–8.

[49] Aristotle *Politics* 1330b6.

[50] Aristotle *Politics* 1330b7. For more on Hippodamian planning and Aristotle's recommendations, see Cahill, *Household and City Organization*, 15–18.

[51] Thucydides 2.3; Aeneas Tacticus 2.1–6.

[52] Xenophon *Hellenica* 2.4.11.

[53] Xenophon *Hellenica* 2.4.12–19.

[54] Cahill, *Household and City Organization*, 75.

[55] For overviews of Greek domestic architecture, see Hoepfner and Schwandner, *Haus und Stadt*; Cahill, *Household and City Organization*.

[56] Barry, "Roof Tiles," provides a thorough discussion of the use of roof tiles in urban combat.

[57] Xenophon *Hellenica* 7.1.19.

[58] Xenophon *Anabasis* 6.5.26–27.

[59] Xenophon *Hellenica* 4.4.12.

[60] Lee, "Urban Combat at Olynthos," 19–20.

[61] Arrian 1.8.7–8; Diodorus Siculus 17.13.

[62] Diodorus Siculus 16.20.3–4.

[63] Isserlin and du Plat Taylor, *Motya*, 91–92.

[64] Diodorus Siculus 16.76.2–3.

[65] Plato *Laws* 779B.

[66] Cahill, *Household and City Organization*, 29.

[67] On the topography of Sparta, see Raftopoulou, "New Finds from Sparta," 127; Shipley, "Lakedaimon," 592; Waywell, "Sparta." For the attack of 370–369, see Xenophon

Hellenica 6.5.27–31. On the center of town, see Aeneas Tacticus 2.2. Plutarch *Agesilaus* 31 mistakenly describes Sparta as having city walls in the fourth century BC.

[68] On these Spartan buildings, see Pausanias 3.14.6, 3.16.2, 3.20.2.

[69] Aeneas Tacticus 2.2.

[70] Xenophon *Hellenica* 7.5.11.

[71] On discipline, see van Wees, *Greek Warfare*, 108–13. On hoplites in cities, see also Ober, "Hoplites and Obstacles."

[72] Plutarch *Cleomenes* 21.

[73] Lee, "Urban Combat at Olynthos," 15–16.

[74] Xenophon 2.4.10–20. On this battle, see also Diodorus Siculus 14.33.1–4; Krentz, *Thirty at Athens*, 90–92, 99–100.

[75] Xenophon *Hellenica* 2.4.10.

[76] Arrian 1.8.7.

[77] Athenian cavalry action: Pausanias 1.15.1. See also Habicht, *Athens from Alexander to Antony*, 74–75.

[78] Plutarch *Pyrrhus* 32.

[79] Camp, "Walls and the Polis," 47.

[80] "Walls of bronze and iron": Plato *Laws* 779b. Aristotle (*Politics* 1330b10) wrote, "to claim that cities do not merit having walls around them . . . is like not having walls for private houses on the grounds that the inhabitants will become unmanly."

[81] Krentz, "Strategic Culture," 62–65.

[82] Krentz, "Strategic Culture," 168–70; Rusch, "Poliorcetic Assault."

[83] Plutarch *Agesilaus* 31.

[84] Polyaenus 4.2.18.

[85] Gehrke, *Stasis*, 243–44; Polyaenus 8.68–70.

[86] Thucydides 3.74.

[87] On the idea of payback, see Tritle, *From Melos to My Lai*, 121–2, 131.

[88] Xenophon *Hellenica* 2.4.11.

[89] Xenophon *Hellenica* 7.5.11.

[90] Plutarch *Dion* 45.

[91] For Aeneas's work in wider historical perspective, see Dufour, *La guerre*, 63–64.

[92] For a translation and commentary, see Whitehead, *Aineias the Tactician: How to Survive Under Siege*.

[93] Aeneas Tacticus 19.1, 22.15.

[94] Aeneas Tacticus 1.9, 2.1, 3.5, 22.2–4.

[95] Aeneas Tacticus 39.1–2.

[96] On Mogadishu, see Bowden, *Black Hawk Down*.

[97] Lintott, *Violence*, 261.

[98] Thuc. 1.22.

7. Counterinsurgency and the Enemies of Rome

SUSAN P. MATTERN

THE ROMANS, like every other imperial power in history, lacked the resources to rule by overwhelming force. The Roman economy was by some measures advanced—population density, urbanization, monetization, and mining activity all reached levels in the Mediterranean world of the second century CE that remained unequaled until modern times. But scholars agree that the imperial government collected taxes amounting to less (perhaps much less) than 10 percent of GDP, this tax burden being unevenly distributed in an economy in which much of the population produced or earned barely enough to survive. With this income the Roman state supported an army of less than one-half million men, charged with the occupation, expansion, and defense of an empire of 60–70 million inhabitants, with an area of 4 million km².[1] As the only large public labor force available, the army also performed nonmilitary or paramilitary functions such as manning tollbooths and guard posts, escorting VIPs, collecting taxes, guarding prisons and work gangs, and construction.[2] Italy, the empire's center of power and the homeland of the Roman people, did not export a large number of emigrants, either as colonists or as soldiers. The exception is a brief period under Julius Caesar and Augustus, when perhaps 200,000 cashiered soldiers—mainly Italians, veterans of the civil wars who could not safely or practically be kept under arms—received land in overseas colonies because Italian land was in short supply. While they were instrumental to the cultural transformation of the western empire, they were a single generation, catalysts only; these colonies never formed an ethnically distinct population or a ruling class. That label belongs, in the west, to a Romanized native aristocracy, and in the east and on Sicily, to the Hellenic or hellenized local aristocracy that predated the arrival of the Romans.[3] Nor did Rome export a large bureaucracy; the governor of any given province, his civilian staff, and officials of equestrian rank might number in the dozens, though they also brought an entourage of friends, slaves, and freedmen.[4] The Romans were aware of these limitations.

Modern scholars have identified forces that made the empire feel like a compelling entity to its inhabitants. Taxation unified, monetized, and urbanized the economy; the allure of civilization led to profound cultural change, especially in the west; certain imperial ideals and forms—Roman law and legal procedures, the image of the emperor, the imperial cult—emanated everywhere and generated a sense of shared participation in a vast project.[5] But the Romans accomplished all of this with a rudimentary state and a vanishingly small senatorial ruling class, mainly through social mechanisms.

To prevent and respond to insurgency, the Romans relied on a complicated network of relationships that reached into almost every stratum of society, plus intensive military occupation of the most volatile areas, a reputation for horrific brutality when challenged, and the ability to muster, although with difficulty and at great cost to themselves, an overwhelming force when the military resources of the empire were concentrated in one place. A rhetoric that distinguished the Romans from their less civilized, less virtuous, and less disciplined enemies and subjects masked a reality in which elements of the subject population worked together with the Romans, and in which it was difficult to distinguish Romans from their subjects. None of the means the Romans used against rebellion and insurgency worked in the sense of eradicating the problem. The Romans managed insurgency but did not eliminate it; innumerable major and minor uprisings are attested throughout the imperial period, and banditry was endemic in all periods and areas of the empire. There was never a time when the Roman army's size could safely be reduced—its task of occupation having come to an end—or freed for major new conquests. On the contrary, the Roman army grew gradually as the empire's territorial size also grew gradually.[6]

Major rebellions and minor acts of insurgency are documented throughout the imperial period. One scholar has counted references to more than 120 separate instances of insurgency from the reign of Augustus, the first emperor, through 190 CE; this counts only the events documented in ancient sources, but it is safe to assume that many episodes escaped mention by contemporary historians.[7] Shifting areas within the empire remained mostly free from Roman domination, under the control of local "bandits" or strongmen.[8] Two major rebellions are documented in detail by eyewitness sources: the revolt of Vercingetorix in 52 BCE, which Caesar described in his *Commmentaries on the Gallic War*, and the Jewish revolt of 66–73 CE, chronicled by Josephus. Josephus commanded rebel troops in the revolt, was taken prisoner by the future emperor Vespasian, and wrote an account of the war in Aramaic (this version has been lost) and later in Greek (this version survives).[9]

These were not the only violent rebellions against Rome. In an infamous episode of 9 CE, the German chief Arminius defeated the Roman legionary army under its commander Quintilius Varus in the Teutoburg Forest, with the stunning result that Rome never claimed dominion over "Free Germany" again. Other famous incidents include the revolt of Boudicca in Britain under Nero, the revolt of the Batavians under Civilis during the Roman civil war of 69 CE, and the revolt of the Jews under Simon Bar-Kokhba in 132–35 CE.[10]

Some scholars have described a traumatic and humiliating process of consolidation immediately following conquest in which new taxes and the drafting of troops were especially resented, the population was volatile, and the danger of rebellion was high. The Romans shared this view. Roman writers (the views of native rebels do not survive) emphasized the idea of liberty, the threat to ancestral values and lifestyle, and the corruption of Roman administrators when they described the motives for these early revolts.[11] Examples of this type of revolt—led by native leaders soon after conquest, in response to the hardships of consolidation—are those of Vercingetorix in Gaul, Arminius in Germany, and Boudicca in Britain.

But insurgency and revolt also occurred in provinces long incorporated into the empire, for different reasons. In provinces with open frontiers—unpacified regions beyond them, or inaccessible regions within them—a zone of long-term or permanent instability could develop as locals switched loyalties among different power brokers in response to shifting circumstances (such regions included northern Spain, northern and eastern Britain, the African provinces, and other areas with endemic banditry; see below).

Also, local aristocrats in "Romanized" provinces of long standing might lead revolts when they perceived an opportunity; the best examples are from Gaul (the revolt of Julius Florus and Julius Sacrovir in 21 CE and the revolt of Julius Civilis in 69 CE). Gaul had rapidly become urbanized and Romanized; in the first century CE many families had Roman citizenship, and an act of Claudius in 48 CE allowed some Gallic Romans into the empire's ruling class, the Senate. But these leaders could call on a sense of native identity, one perhaps newly developed or more highly developed as a result of Roman conquest ("Gauls" didn't know they were Gauls until Julius Caesar labeled them as such). Finally, would-be kings or emperors of high rank and great influence might invoke local alliances in the civil wars with which they bid for the throne (for example, Sertorius in Spain, Vindex in Gaul, and Avidius Cassius in the East; the civil wars that ended the republic drew on a myriad of such alliances).[12]

This scheme oversimplifies; but the point that hardly any province was reliably peaceful is valid, although the nature and intensity of insurgency changed over time. At least three uprisings in Asia and Achaea were led by men claiming to be the emperor Nero, who had committed suicide when deposed in 68 CE. In the province of Bithynia, now northern Turkey, the emperor Trajan banned organizations of any kind (*collegia*) because of the region's reputation for insurgency; although we have little further evidence to shed light on Trajan's concerns, the emperor would not even allow a fire brigade, and his edict was part of the basis for the persecution of Christians.[13] By the time the Bar-Kokhba revolt broke out, Judaea had been a Roman protectorate or a Roman province for nearly 100 years. During the political and military crisis of the third century CE, huge parts of the empire in the East and West—Syria and Egypt under Queen Zenobia of Palmyra, and Gaul under its own line of emperors—revolted and operated independently for decades before they were eventually subdued, but for the most part

I shall leave this turbulent period out of my discussion and focus on the better-documented era from about 100 BCE through 200 CE.

To keep the peace, the Romans relied partly on their perceived ability to punish, an idea they articulated using value terms rather than more abstract, strategic language. Roman historians write as though revolt were an insult and a challenge to which the appropriate response was vengeance extreme enough to reinstill awe and fear in their rebellious subjects. In some cases they attempted genocide, the extermination of a tribe or people, a concept well attested in Roman literature. They used terror as a policy tool, in the sense that they inflicted extreme brutality on a mass scale to frighten their subjects. Although Rome never reoccupied territory across the Rhine after Arminius's revolt, campaigns under the future emperor Tiberius, and eventually under the latter's nephew and adopted son Germanicus, laid waste to territory, slaughtered noncombatants, and aimed for the annihilation of the Germans.[14] The Romans also used mutilation, mass deportation, mass destruction, and mass slaughter short of genocide to punish, avenge, and deter. After the Bar-Kokhba revolt, the emperor Hadrian, who led the expedition to repress the revolt in person, expelled the Jews from Jerusalem and refounded it as a Roman colony. One ancient source tells us that over half a million souls perished in the war and that few survived. Other evidence attests to a rich rabbinic culture in the region after the revolt—depopulation and extermination are difficult policies to carry out thoroughly and successfully—but the Roman intent to inflict extreme brutality is documented here and in many other examples. This is the meaning behind the saying Tacitus attributes to the British rebel Calgacus, "when they have made a desert, they call it peace." Famous passages from Polybius and Josephus, historians who described the conquest of their own people, reflect the reputation for brutality and invincibility that the Romans wished to cultivate.[15]

Rome's investment of resources in some of these campaigns was very high. The revolt of Illyricum in 6 CE occupied ten of the empire's twenty-eight legions under the command of the future emperor Tiberius. A few years later, after Arminius's revolt, the same commander invaded Germany with eight legions—the entire army of the Rhine, some 40,000 men, plus an auxiliary army of unknown strength but probably equal or greater in number. The Jewish revolt of 66 tied up four legions and a total of about 50,000 troops for several years.[16]

But this analysis oversimplifies. Insurgency under the Roman Empire was not a series of discrete events and responses; insurgency is attested in all periods of Roman history and in many locations. Armed revolt and conventional warfare were only two of its aspects. How and with what permanent institutions did the Romans prevent, manage, and respond to resistance day by day?

Some insurgents used terror as a tactic. The example most historians point to is a group that Josephus calls the *sicarii*. According to him, they arose in Jerusalem in the 50s CE; they assassinated their targets in daytime, often under cover of a crowded festival; and they took their name from the type of sickled dagger they used. Like some modern terrorists, the *sicarii* chose symbolic targets; their first victim was the high priest Jonathan, "symbol of the sacerdotal aristocracy's collaboration with the alien Roman rulers and its exploitation of the people."[17] They also attacked wealthy landowners in the countryside and destroyed their property, again apparently as a warning and deterrent to collaboration with the Romans. According to Josephus, the *sicarii* were ideologically motivated adherents of the "fourth philosophy," which advocated rebellion from the Romans on religious grounds.[18]

Josephus calls the *sicarii* "bandits" (*lestai*), and he uses the same derogatory term to refer to other insurgents besides the *sicarii*. Banditry was a very widespread phenomenon in the empire, and even when it lacked ideological aspects it can fairly be described as insurgency because of the Roman government's oft-stated interest in eliminating it. Although some generals and emperors claimed in their propaganda that they had eradicated banditry from the territory under their rule, in fact references to banditry pervade literary and documentary evidence from all periods of the Roman Empire and from every provenance, including Rome's most ancient provinces and especially including Italy.[19] The Greek and Roman terms for banditry usually signified predatory rural violence, which might include raiding, rustling, kidnap, extortion, highway robbery, and murder; because of banditry, travel was very dangerous in the Roman world, even over short distances. Bandits often came from the margins of society; they might be slave shepherds, pastoralists who lived on the margins of civilization (this is especially well attested in Sicily and southern Italy), retired soldiers, or deserters from the army.

Large groups living within the Roman Empire, including certain tribes and certain ethnic units, were also classified as bandits by ancient sources. Among the most notable of the latter were the *Boukoloi* of the swamps around the Nile Delta. In Cilicia, in southeast Asia Minor, the Isaurians of the highlands never were incorporated into the Roman Empire but maintained their own language, tribal organization around strongmen, and predatory conflict with the more urbanized lowlands throughout the Roman period and throughout history; the Romans negotiated and fought small-scale wars with them as against a foreign enemy.

In Judaea, which is the only area for which a large body of literary evidence exists over several centuries, banditry was endemic in all periods of Roman rule. Much banditry in that province had an ideological element: locals perceived bandits as champions of Jewish freedom from Rome. The distinction between banditry and guerrilla warfare in this region is difficult to draw. Networks of rock-cut caves in some settlements in Judaea could be headquarters for bandits or hiding places for guerrilla rebels, perhaps in connection with the Bar-Kokhba revolt, or these populations might have overlapped substantially. They are difficult to date and may have functioned over decades or centuries.[20]

The difference between a bandit, a tribal chief, a petty king, or the leader of a rebellion could be open to interpretation; many individuals are located in more than one of these categories by the ancient sources. Thus, large geographic areas within the Roman Empire were independent of Roman authority, mostly highlands with mobile populations and inaccessible terrain. There were pockets of Rome's empire where its writ did not run.

The analogy between ancient banditry and modern terrorism is loose. Ideology might or might not figure in ancient banditry, which was largely economic in nature, and even where resistance was ethnic or ideological, terror (in the sense of random, unpredictable violence designed to create instability and fear) is poorly attested as a tactic, except for the *sicarii*. Again with the exception of the *sicarii*, those labeled bandits in antiquity operated in the countryside, often based in inaccessible highlands, and not in the crowded cities that are the preferred targets for modern terrorists. However, there are also significant parallels. Bandits were not perceived as common criminals; they were enemies of the state, against whom the Romans waged war. This was not, as they thought, war in its truest sense, as against a legitimate state; instead, they conceived the war against bandits as guerrilla, bush, or (as we now say) "asymmetrical" warfare, though they did not use those terms. Bandits were not imagined as working alone. They commanded the loyalty and resources of a local community that would aid and abet them, or else they enjoyed the protection of powerful landowners, who employed them for their own purposes: to rob and rustle from, kidnap, and bully their neighbors, and as shock troops in the continual competition for land and power in which they were all engaged. Some landlords amassed what amounted to private armies of bandits, more than a match for anything the Roman state could muster locally.

Bandits with connections to the local community or to a landlord were best apprehended by stealth, information, and betrayal. One caught them by "hunting" them; our sources describe posses of soldiers, hired hit men, and local vigilantes.[21] Professional or semiprofessional experts in bandit hunting are attested; some of these were not easily distinguished from bandits themselves.[22] The law encouraged or required communities and individuals to hunt and surrender bandits, and individuals could kill bandits with legal impunity.[23] Roman law also took aim at those who abetted, protected, or received stolen goods from bandits, probably with little effect.[24] Some of the empire's wealthiest and most powerful individuals benefited the most from banditry, perhaps including many members of the Roman senatorial class. The simplistic rhetoric that opposed banditry to legitimate power masked a situation in which a rudimentary Roman state operated in the shadow of, or as part of, a much more complex and highly developed system of personal power that included bandits and their protectors.

The army policed for bandits. Augustus and Tiberius maintained military detachments or *stationes* throughout Italy to control the banditry, which had escalated during the civil wars that ended the republic.[25] In some areas roads were militarized for protection against banditry, and some structures perceived as frontier systems were constructed and staffed to control banditry. In Cilicia, the Romans eventually (in the third and fourth centuries) fortified an inner frontier against the Isaurian bandits of the highlands.[26]

Against large groups of bandits or outlaw peoples, Roman governors and their subordinates waged small wars. Cicero led brutal punitive expeditions against bandits during his term as governor of Cilicia, during which he razed villages and exterminated their inhabitants, and took hostages from one settlement after a long siege, but without long-term success. Tacitus describes further campaigns in the region under delegates of the governor of Syria in the 30s CE and in 51.[27]

Roman governors and emperors sometimes tried to neutralize bandit gangs by hiring them to enforce order, or by recruiting bandits into the army individually or en masse.[28] More often, Roman commanders negotiated diplomatically with bandits. Cicero established a tie of *hospitium* or hospitality with one Isaurian strongman (Cicero calls him a "tyrant"); this and other types of "ritualized friendship" were the main instruments of Roman foreign and internal relations in the late republic and throughout much of Roman history generally. Cicero, Pompey, and Mark Antony all successively recognized another Isaurian leader, Tarkontidmotos, as a "friend" of Rome or of themselves.[29]

In the tiny mountainous province of Mauretania Tingitana in extreme northwestern Morocco, Roman provincial governors negotiated peace with highland chiefs; records of their ritualized agreements, inscribed on stone, are almost the only written evidence of Rome's experience in the area. Outside the heavily militarized zone in the lowlands, Roman cultural influence did not extend, though this was a region surrounded by Roman provinces of long standing. While no surviving sources refer to the highland population of Mauretania as bandits, the analogy with Isauria is very striking.[30]

As with banditry, so with insurgency in general: the military factor is important to the equation, but the army operated parallel to, and to some extent within, a wider set of social relationships. The Roman army was an army of occupation as well as of external aggression and defense. This was especially true of the provinces of Spain, Britain, Mauretania (modern Morocco), Syria, Palestine after the Jewish revolt of 66, and Egypt. In these provinces the army was stationed in urban centers or dispersed throughout, rather than heavily concentrated on frontiers (the province of Spain had no frontier, and Britain's frontier was very short).[31] A few areas of the empire were intensively occupied, notably Judaea, a very small territory that housed perhaps 20,000 troops in the early second century CE, and Mauretania Tingitana was essentially an armed camp occupied by 10,000 troops, with little evidence of Roman influence outside the military zone.[32] In both cases, intensive occupation proved ineffective. Judaea's garrison failed to prevent the Bar-Kokhba revolt or to suppress endemic banditry in the province, and Mauretania Tingitana was abandoned in the third century.

A complicating factor is that the army was not deployed from center to periphery, as one people dominating many others, even though the emperor claimed ultimate authority over the whole apparatus. During the first century CE the Roman army rapidly changed from a force of Italian citizen-soldiers to one that was recruited from all over the empire, not mainly from Italy. Legionaries mainly came from citizen populations in the provinces, notably veteran colonies. But veteran colonies were not isolated, ethnically distinct communities; their citizen-inhabitants might be veteran settlers or their freedmen, or remote descendants of those settlers or of their freedmen, having mixed for many generations with the local population. The descendants of retired auxiliary soldiers were probably another important source of legionary recruits. The auxiliary army, recruited entirely from noncitizens, was much larger than the legionary army. Discharged after decades of service, these soldiers acquired Roman citizenship on retirement and usually settled in the regions in which they had been stationed. Thus Rome's army was recruited from among its subjects.[33]

Consider the situation in Judaea before the revolt of 66: when Herod the Great ruled with Roman support (until his death in 4 BCE), he commanded a typical Hellenistic army of troops from local military settlements.[34] These troops were mainly Sarmatians, Idumaeans, Babylonian Jewish archers, and ethnic Palestinian Jews, although Herod also had a famous bodyguard of Germans, Thracians, and Gauls. The indigenous settlements continued to supply the army that supported all of Herod's successors and formed the garrison of Judaea after 6 CE. Much of this army remained loyal to the Romans and fought with them to suppress the revolt of 66 CE, under the command of Herod's great-grandson, King Agrippa II. Conversely, Herod probably modeled his army on the Roman army and used some ethnic Roman officers, and it is likely that many Jews were recruited into the Roman legionary or auxiliary army both in his reign and later. But Mel Gibson's portrait of Latin-speaking soldiers in *The Passion* is inaccurate. The soldiers in the "Roman" garrison of Judaea spoke Aramaic.

The army that the Romans initially sent against the rebels in 66, under the command of Cestius Gallus, governor of Syria, included legionary (i.e., Roman citizen) soldiers, auxiliary (i.e., noncitizen) soldiers, contingents from the armies of two local allied ("client") kings, and local Syrian militia. At the same time, the royal Jewish forces loyal to Agrippa II moved against the rebels in three separate locations. Later, the larger Roman army under the command of Vespasian numbered 55,000–60,000 legionary and auxiliary troops and 15,000 allied troops, and included at least one Jewish high officer, Tiberius Julius Alexander of Egypt.

In this example and in others that could be discussed from around the empire, it is difficult to distinguish the Romans from their subjects, a procedure made even more complicated because natives, when enfranchised, took Roman names, and many cannot be distinguished in the historical record from ethnic Italians. For example, while several of Herod's military officers had Roman names, we do not know if they were enfranchised Jews or soldiers imported or borrowed from Rome's legionary armies. Should we count all Roman citizens as "Roman," including King Herod and his successors and Josephus himself, and all retired auxiliary soldiers, their freedmen, their descendants, and the descendants of their freedmen? Should Paul of Tarsus, whose family had acquired Roman citizenship from an unknown patron, therefore count as Roman, along with any freedmen in his family? Should we rather count only the staff sent from Italy, the procurator and his entourage? Should we count only legionary soldiers—but there were no legions deployed in Judaea before the revolt of 66? One scholar, writing on Gaul, has described the term "Roman" as a social status, not an ethnicity, and as such it was fluid: one could be more or less Roman, more or less enmeshed in the web of Roman culture and influence, and there was no sharp line between ruler and subject.[35]

What most historians refer to simplistically as the conquest of Judaea by Pompey in 66 BCE and its subjection to Rome through a series of puppet kings, Josephus describes as a bafflingly complex process entwining Jewish dynastic intrigue, Roman civil war, a triangular set of international relations and conflicts among Romans and Parthians, Romans and Jews, and Jews and Parthians, as well as a more local sphere of relationships, especially between Judaea and Arabia. Every withdrawal of Roman troops from the region saw a new uprising under a new candidate for leadership and a reassertion of local power bases until finally a period of relative stability followed Herod's defeat of Aristobulus in 37 BCE. Rome's incorporation of the Greek East or Caesar's conquest of Gaul could be described in a similar way: only close attention to tensions and conflicts indigenous to the area can adequately explain Roman intervention and describe its results.[36] The story of Roman imperialism is not the story of an invincible army deployed from the empire's center against a surrounding ring of hapless, less sophisticated future subjects, nor did it govern its empire as a militarized ruling class controlling ethnically and culturally distinct populations.

Modern studies of any aspect of how the Roman Empire worked go badly astray when they underestimate the role of personal power as compared to the power of the state. One scholar notes that in his exhaustively detailed history of Judaea under Roman rule, Josephus hardly discusses the Roman state and does not seem to understand the concept of state power.[37] The army was by far the largest institution of the Roman state; but it was social relationships, and not mainly the army, that knit the empire together. Much of "Roman" rule was done by local aristocracies, petty kings, chiefs, "big men," and large landowners acting out their own agendas and bringing in the Roman army or the Roman government when it suited them. Taxes were collected by local agents, and many local governing institutions continued to operate. Parties to local feuds and rivalries turned to their Roman governors to settle disputes—this was the essence of Roman law and of Roman provincial government, not edicts and occupation. Even in places where indigenous institutions were transformed by their contact with the Roman Empire, many people never saw an official representative of Rome apart from the occasional soldier, and in some provinces even these were rare. The traffic in favors and injuries that governed Roman social relations governed the empire as well.

One could go even further and say that to describe Rome's provinces as distinct territorial regions is to oversimplify. Although Roman law and policy recognized the province as an administrative unit, each under a governor of senior senatorial rank, areas like Sicily, Gaul, or Judaea did not have a single uniform relationship with Rome. Rather, each was a network of communities and individuals with a unique set of relationships to the Roman state, represented by the Senate and the emperor (or, in the republic, the "Senate and the People of Rome"), and to individual Roman aristocrats. That is true even where Rome ruled provinces directly; but at all times we hear of a bewildering array of petty kings and local chiefs allied to Rome and considered part of its empire. These are complicated points, which I illustrate with two examples.

It would raise few eyebrows among scholars of Roman history to say that in Judaea, the Romans supported a friendly king, Herod the Great, for several decades until his death in 4 BCE. However, it would be more accurate to say that first Julius Caesar, then the tyrannicide Cassius, then Mark Antony, and eventually the emperor Octavian supported Herod and that Herod supported each of these men in turn.[38] In the turmoil that followed the assassination of Julius Caesar in 44 BCE, even though Herod's father owed his Roman citizenship and status as king to Caesar, Herod accepted troops from Cassius in return for a presumed alliance. When Mark Antony defeated Cassius, Herod switched allegiances and offered his support to Antony. When the Parthians invaded Syria and Judaea and deposed its high priest and set up their own nominee, Antony supported Herod in his efforts to get them out and had the Senate formally declare him king of Judaea. Herod and his army also took part in Antony's unsuccessful campaigns against Parthia that occurred at the same time. Finally, when Octavian defeated Antony at Actium in 31 BCE, Herod made a famous pilgrimage to Octavian to switch sides once again. After he convinced the emperor that he would be as loyal to him as he had been to Antony, Octavian acknowledged his friendship. He also gave Herod possession of certain cities in Palestine that the Romans at the time considered subject to them or to the deceased queen of Egypt.

Herod supported his Roman friends with troops when they asked him to, and he was a promoter of their interests in other ways. But in return, Herod received the means with which to defeat his dynastic rivals and enlarge his kingdom. His story inextricably entwines Jewish politics and Roman civil war with regional and international politics. It is largely through these complex relationships that the Roman Empire managed foreign and internal threats, which in this system are not always easily separable; and the system worked better to the extent that all parties benefited.

After Herod's death, his kingdom was divided among his four surviving sons until 6 CE.[39] At that time, amid civil unrest, the Romans deposed Archelaus and established as the prefecture of Judaea a part of Herod's kingdom that included Jerusalem. But Herod's sons continued to rule the rest. In 41 the emperor Claudius gave Herod's grandson, Agrippa I, sovereignty over the whole kingdom once ruled by Herod. After Agrippa I died in 44 CE, Claudius made most of that territory subject to a Roman procurator of equestrian rank, except that Agrippa I's son, Agrippa II, continued to rule part of Galilee. This is the situation in the province we know most about; whether its history was more complicated than that of other provinces is not known. But clearly a definition of empire that mainly relies on direct military or bureaucratic control fails to capture the essence of the situation. Only one that takes account of dynamic relationships among Rome the state, individual Romans, and local elites can capture it.

The most accessible window onto a province long under direct Roman rule—that is, subject to a Roman governor—are the speeches that record Cicero's prosecution of its corrupt governor Gaius Verres in 70 BCE. At that time Sicily had been part of the Roman Empire for nearly two centuries. Cicero's orations *Against Verres* reveal the complexity of Rome's relationship with Sicily and of the social ties that connected the Roman ruling class to its indigenous, hellenized urban ruling class.

Most of the province paid one-tenth of the grain crop as tax. The contract to collect the tax was sold in Sicily, to local corporations; this was, or was at least perceived to be, the same system that prevailed under the last king of Syracuse, Hiero II, who ruled during the first two Punic Wars. Throughout his long speeches Cicero refers to the "law of Hiero" with reverence, as an institution for which disrespect amounted to gross misrule. Besides this, five cities were exempt from taxation; two paid on their own without contracts; and the contracts to collect taxes from some cities were sold at Rome, an arrangement less advantageous to them.[40] The terms of each community's relationship to Rome reflected the circumstances of its participation in the First Punic War or in subsequent conflicts, or its relationship to individual Roman patrons. The Claudii Marcelli and Cicero himself considered themselves patrons of the province as a whole; Cicero calls the Sicilians "allies and friends of the Roman people and close connections of myself." Some individual cities, such as Segesta, Syracuse, and Messana, had relationships with specific aristocratic families.[41] And individuals from among Sicily's hellenized elite also enjoyed special relationships with Roman senators that continually surface in the course of the trial; the one most commonly mentioned is *hospitium*. It is an especially damning sign that evidence against Verres can be extracted, on cross-examination, from his own *hospes*, Heius of Messana, or that he presided over the unjust conviction of another of his *hospites*, Sthenius of Thermae.[42]

There was no Roman army in Sicily. When Verres needed shock troops to carry out his extortionist schemes, he called on the slave guards of the local Temple of Aphrodite at Eryx, whose normal job was to protect the temple treasury.[43] He took kickbacks from local tax corporations and from feuding aristocrats prosecuting their enemies in his court.[44] Seeking redress, Sicilian individuals went to Rome and cities sent delegations pleading their cases to their patrons and connections in the Senate, before whom he would be tried.[45] Verres's rule was corrupt and rapacious, but it was only his social connections inside and outside Sicily that allowed him to get away with it. Cicero makes no references to insurgency in this period and characterizes the Sicilians in paternalistic terms as a docile, childlike people.[46] A more plausible explanation for the low level of insurgency in Sicily in Cicero's time— if this characterization is accurate—is the density of the connections between the local ruling class and the Roman aristocracy, which Cicero's speeches illustrate very well.

What, then, is insurgency, and what is counterinsurgency? One way to view insurgency, resistance, and banditry is as attenuated areas or holes in the network of social relationships that linked the empire together and bound it to the senatorial aristocracy and to the emperor. In other cases one of the nodes in the network—a petty king, a Roman aristocrat, an auxiliary commander—might yank its strings in a new direction, activating a new set of connections at cross-purposes with the dominant ones. Foreign relations, local politics, and rivalries internal to the Roman ruling class worked inextricably together or against one another.

The Romans negotiated diplomatically with petty kings, tribal chiefs, bandits, and nomads.[47] They paid subsidies and made treaties. They granted citizenship, titles, or military support. They formed an infinite variety of personal connections that linked the Roman ruling class to local aristocrats and strongmen. When this social network failed, as it often did, they ruled by force. They occupied territory, in a few cases very densely. They waged major wars against rebels and took pride in defeating them with their superior discipline, tenacity, and military engineering. They fought bandits with patrols, posses, and occasional military campaigns. They terrorized rebellious subjects with harsh reprisals. Whether these latter measures worked is difficult to say. The Roman Empire endured a long time, but no era was free of insurgency and banditry. My argument, however, is not about the efficacy or inefficacy of the Roman army; it is that the military aspect of insurgency and counterinsurgency, and of empire itself, is only the tip of the iceberg. The Romans ruled because their social relationships reached everywhere—or at least, they reached far. Those relationships could be manipulated by anyone. Postulating a tense and dynamic network of relationships in which all actors vigorously pursue what they believe to be their own interests—a network that may have gaps and holes, and in which alternative networks only loosely connected to the dominant one also operate—might be the most effective way to envision empire.

In its foreign policy, the United States faces problems similar to those of all ancient and modern empires. In particular, the occupation of overseas territory is always expensive and difficult, and the "ruling" power always governs as a tiny minority. It has become fashionable in the last decade to look to the Roman Empire for lessons applicable to modern times. Some of this has seeped outside the universities and the Beltway and into popular culture.[48] Fundamental economic, technological (imagine the Romans with nuclear weapons), demographic, and social differences between the modern and premodern worlds make this lesson-seeking a very challenging activity, and not everyone agrees that the analogy is appropriate or the scholarly endeavor justified. I myself have expressed skepticism on this question.[49] But when I am asked to comment on the practical lessons of Roman history, my response, with these caveats, focuses on the critical role of social institutions in holding the Roman Empire together. The Romans ruled because, as a collective "state" and as individuals, the ruling class's network of dependencies, favors owed, and negotiated relationships extended everywhere. Where the Roman social network did not extend, or where part of the ruling class chose to deploy its own network against the interests of another part, there trouble arose. Rome succeeded because it drew on, or built, a common social and cultural language with the elites of the territories subject to it, and because many powerful elements of its subjects' populations found it in their best interest to recognize Roman authority. The nearest modern parallel may be the "global village" created by telecommunications technology, financial institutions, free trade, and the consumer tastes and interests that link international communities today. A focus on shared economic and cultural interests rather than on ideology is a promising direction for foreign policy in the future.

FURTHER READING

The subject of revolt and insurgency has received inadequate attention from scholars. Two articles by Stephen Dyson, "Native Revolts in the Roman Empire" (*Historia* 20 [1971]: 239–74) and "Native Revolt Patterns in the Roman Empire" (*Aufstieg und Niedergang der römischen Welt* [Berlin: Walter de Gruyter, 1975], 2, 3:138–75), are still important. On banditry, the work of Brent D. Shaw, especially his classic "Bandits in the Roman Empire" (*Past and Present* 105 [1984]: 3–52), has been most influential. Benjamin Isaac has done much to call attention to the function of Rome's army as an occupying force, controlling the population and policing for banditry and other small-scale threats: *The Limits of Empire: The Roman Army in the East*, 2nd ed. (Oxford: Clarendon, 1992). On the Jewish revolt, the most influential study is by Martin Goodman, *The Ruling Class of Judaea: The Origins of the Jewish Revolt against Rome, A.D. 66–70* (New York: Cambridge University Press, 1987); and now see his more general work, *Rome and Jerusalem: The Clash of Ancient Civilizations* (New York: Knopf, 2007). On personal power in the Roman Empire, important works are Richard P. Saller, *Personal Patronage under the Early Empire* (Cambridge: Cambridge University Press, 1982); Brent D. Shaw, "Tyrants, Bandits and Kings: Personal Power in Josephus" (*Journal of Jewish Studies* 49 [1993]: 176–204); the essays collected in *Patronage in Ancient Society*, ed. Andrew Wallace-Hadrill (London: Routledge, 1989); and Fergus Millar's *The Emperor in the Roman World*, 2nd ed. (Ithaca, NY: Cornell University Press, 1992). J. E. Lendon, *Empire of Honour: The Art of Government in the Roman World* (Oxford: Clarendon, 1997), is critical to understanding how personal power operated.

Erich S. Gruen's *The Hellenistic World and the Coming of Rome*, 2 vols. (Berkeley and Los Angeles: University of California Press, 1984) revolutionized our understanding of Roman imperialism by refocusing attention on the institutions and political struggles of its future subjects, showing how only a thorough understanding of these can explain how Rome became involved in a region and the shape that its domination took. Other important works on nonmilitary aspects of Roman imperial control are Greg Woolf, *Becoming Roman: The Origins of Provincial Civilization in Gaul* (Cambridge: Cambridge University Press, 1998), and Clifford Ando, *Imperial Ideology and Provincial Loyalty in the Roman Empire* (Berkeley and Los Angeles: University of California Press, 2000).

NOTES

[1] On population, see most recently Walter Scheidel, "Demography," in *The Cambridge Economic History of the Greco-Roman World*, ed. Walter Scheidel, Ian Morris, and Richard Saller (Cambridge: Cambridge University Press, 2007), 45–49. On the size of the army, for a summary of arguments, see Susan P. Mattern, *Rome and the Enemy: Imperial Strategy in the Principate* (Berkeley and Los Angeles: University of California Press, 1999), 82–83. On taxes as a fraction of GDP, for a summary of arguments see Elio Lo Cascio, "The Early Roman Empire: The State and the Economy," in Scheidel et al., *The Cambridge Economic History*, 622–25. On subsistence levels and per capita income, Jongman argues that overall per capita income was relatively high for antiquity, though very low by modern standards (Willem M. Jongman, "The Early Roman Empire: Consumption," in Scheidel et al., *The Cambridge Economic History*, 592–619), but wages for unskilled workers still barely exceeded, or failed to meet, subsistence levels for a family, even if women and children also worked (Walter Scheidel, "Real Wages in Early Economies: Evidence for Living Standards from 2000 BCE to 1300 CE," Version 1.0, March 2008, Princeton/Stanford Working Papers in Classics).

[2] The classic study of Ramsay MacMullen, *Soldier and Civilian in the Later Roman Empire* (Cambridge, MA: Harvard University Press, 1963), is still important. See also Benjamin Isaac, *The Limits of Empire: The Roman Army in the East*, 2nd ed. (Oxford: Clarendon, 1992), chaps. 3 and 6; Richard Alston, *Soldier and Society in Roman Egypt: A Social History* (London: Routledge, 1995), chap. 5.

³ On the difficult topic of Romanization, see Greg Woolf, *Becoming Roman: The Origins of Provincial Civilization in Gaul* (Cambridge: Cambridge University Press, 1998); Ramsay MacMullen, *Romanization in the Time of Augustus* (New Haven, CT: Yale University Press, 2000) (for the figure 200,000, 132); and see Alston, *Soldier*, chap. 3.

⁴ On the size of the Roman government, see J. E. Lendon, *Empire of Honour: The Art of Government in the Roman World* (Oxford: Clarendon, 1997), 2–4.

⁵ Keith Hopkins, "Taxes and Trade in the Roman Empire (200 B.C.–A.D. 400)," *Journal of Roman Studies* 70 (1980): 101–25; Woolf, *Becoming Roman*; Clifford Ando, *Imperial Ideology and Provincial Loyalty in the Roman Empire* (Berkeley and Los Angeles: University of California Press, 2000).

⁶ On this last point, see Mattern, *Rome*, chap. 3.

⁷ Thomas Pekáry, "*Seditio*. Unruhen und Revolten im römischen Reich von Augustus bis Commodus," *Ancient Society* 18 (1987): 133–50.

⁸ Brent Shaw, "Bandits in the Roman Empire," *Past and Present* 105 (1984): 3–52, discussed further below.

⁹ The most influential study of the Jewish revolt is still Martin Goodman, *The Ruling Class of Judaea: The Origins of the Jewish Revolt against Rome, A.D. 66–70* (New York: Cambridge University Press, 1987).

¹⁰ On revolts, see Mattern, *Rome*, 100–104 and 191–94 with references. Scholarly consensus now places the Battle of Teutoburg at Kalkreise in Lower Saxony. On this much-studied event, see recently Adrian Murdoch, *Rome's Greatest Defeat: Massacre in the Teutoburg Forest* (Gloucestershire, UK: Sutton, 2006).

¹¹ Isaac, *Limits*, chap. 2; Stephen Dyson, "Native Revolts in the Roman Empire," *Historia* 20 (1971): 239–74; see also Woolf, *Becoming Roman*, 30–33. On Roman representations, see Greg Woolf, "Roman Peace," in *War and Society in the Roman World*, ed. J. Rich and G. Shipley, 171–94 (London: Routledge, 1993).

¹² Stephen Dyson, "Native Revolt Patterns in the Roman Empire," in *Aufstieg und Niedergang der römischen Welt*, II.3, 138–75.

¹³ False Neros: see Pekáry, "*Seditio*," under the years 69, 79–81, and 88–89 CE. Trajan's edict: Pliny the Younger *Letters* 10.34, and see 10.117. Christians: Pliny the Younger *Letters* 10.96.

¹⁴ On genocide, see Mattern, *Rome*, 120–21, 192–94 for references. On Tiberius's and Germanicus's wars of revenge, see ibid., 90, 120, 189.

¹⁵ Mutilation: Dio Cassius 53.29 (Spain). Deportation: Dio Cassius 53.29 (Spain). The Bar-Kokhba revolt: Dio Cassius 69.14.1, and see Mattern, *Rome*, 193–94, for further references. Calgacus's speech: Tacitus *Agricola* 30. Polybius on how Romans sacked cities: 10.15–17. Josephus on the invincibility of the Romans: *Jewish War*, 2.365–87.

¹⁶ On the size of the Roman army and the commitment of troops, see Mattern, *Rome*, 81–109.

¹⁷ See Richard A. Horsley, "The Sicarii: Ancient Jewish 'Terrorists,'" *Journal of Religion* 59 (1979): 435–58, quotation at 440.

¹⁸ Horsley, "Sicarii," 442–44; Josephus, *Jewish War*, 7.253–55.

¹⁹ For what follows, see Shaw, "Bandits," 3–52. This and other studies of Roman-era banditry have been deeply influenced by the classic work of Eric J. Hobsbawm, *Bandits*,

first published in 1969 (4th ed., New York: New Press, 2000), and his description of the "social bandit."

²⁰ On banditry in Judaea, see Isaac, *Limits*, 77–89, and idem, "Bandits in Judaea and Arabia," *Harvard Studies in Classical Philology* 88 (1984): 171–203. Isaac argues subtly from rabbinic evidence that most Judaean banditry had an ideological or political element of resistance to Rome. On the caves, see Isaac, *Limits*, 84–85. Also on banditry in Judaea, see Brent D. Shaw, "Tyrants, Bandits and Kings: Personal Power in Josephus," *Journal of Jewish Studies* 49 (1993): 176–204. On Isauria, see idem, "Bandit Highlands and Lowland Peace," *Journal of the Economic and Social History of the Orient* 33, no.2 (1990): 199–233, and 33, no.3 (1990): 237–70. On banditry in Egypt, including the *Boukoloi*, see Alston, *Soldier*, 81–86.

²¹ Hunting: e.g., Dio Cassius 75.2.4 (Shaw, "Bandits," 43), and see next note.

²² See Fronto *To Antoninus Pius* 8 (discussed in Shaw, "Bandits," 10–12) for Julius Sextus, a friend noteworthy for his "military zeal in hunting and suppressing bandits" whom Fronto will bring with him to his province of Asia; see also *Digest* 1.18.13 (discussed in Shaw, "Bandits," 14) on the duty of a governor to hunt bandits; on hired assassins, see Shaw, "Bandits," 16–18 with n. 35.

²³ Shaw, "Bandits," 19.

²⁴ Shaw, "Bandits," 37–38.

²⁵ Suetonius *Augustus* 32 and *Tiberius* 37; Shaw, "Bandits," 33–34.

²⁶ Roads: Isaac, *Limits*, 102–15; Alston, *Soldier*, 81–83. Frontier systems: Shaw, "Bandits," 12 with n. 26, and see Mattern, *Rome*, 113–14 for further references. Cilician inner frontier: Shaw, "Bandit Highlands," 237–38.

²⁷ Shaw, "Bandits," 12–14 and n. 26 for references to military commands against bandits. Cicero's campaigns are attested in his letters; for references and discussion, see Shaw, "Bandits," 14; idem, "Bandit Highlands," 223–26. Tacitus *Annals* 6.41, 12.55; Shaw, "Bandit Highlands," 230.

²⁸ On hiring, see Shaw, "Tyrants," 199–200, for a case attested in Josephus; on recruitment, see Shaw, "Bandits," 34–35.

²⁹ Tarkontidmotos: Shaw, "Bandit Highlands," 226 for references. On the term "ritualized friendship," the basis for much premodern diplomacy, see G. Herman, *Ritualized Friendship and the Greek City* (Cambridge: Cambridge University Press, 1987). Shaw, "Tyrants," demonstrates how various forms of ritualized friendship mediated relations among Romans, Herod, bandits, petty dynasts, and other power players in Judaea of the late first century BCE.

³⁰ On Mauretania, see Brent D. Shaw, "Autonomy and Tribute: Mountain and Plain in Mauretania Tingitana," in *Désert et montagne au Maghreb: Hommage à Jean Dresch* (*Revue de l'occident musulman et de la méditerranée* 41–42 [1986]: 66–89); idem, *At the Edge of the Corrupting Sea: The Twenty-Third J. L. Myres Memorial Lecture* (University of Oxford, 2006).

³¹ On the Roman army as occupying force, see Isaac, *Limits*, chap. 3; Mattern, *Rome*, 101–4. See also Alston, *Soldier*, chap. 5; he argues that the army was not very good at suppressing revolts and was mainly engaged in policing for banditry and other small-scale threats. Alston also suggests persuasively that the army in Egypt was a strategic balance to Syria's large force, intended to deter the revolt of the latter province. To my

knowledge he is the first scholar to argue that the possibility of revolt in heavily armed provinces determined the strategic disposition of the army in other provinces, which seems quite possible.

[32] On the army of Judaea, see Isaac, *Limits*, 105–7; on Mauretania, see Shaw, "Autonomy" and "On the Edge."

[33] On recruitment, for references see Mattern, *Rome*, 85; also Yann Le Bohec, *The Imperial Roman Army* (New York: Hippocrene, and London: Batsford, 1994) (= *L'Armée romaine sous le Haut-Empire* [Paris: Picard, 1989]), 68–102; Alston, *Soldier*, chap. 3, emphasizes that the garrison of Egypt was drawn from throughout the western provinces in all periods (though recruits from Africa predominated after the first century) and that Egyptian evidence contradicts the view of the army as a closed caste having little interaction with the native population. On the size of the auxiliary army, see P. A. Holder, *Studies in the Auxilia of the Roman Army from Augustus to Trajan*, British Archaeological Reports (Oxford, 1980); A. R. Birley, "The Economic Effects of Roman Frontier Policy," in *The Roman West in the Third Century*, ed. A. King and M. Henic, British Archaeological Reports (Oxford, 1981), 1:39–43.

[34] For what follows, see Jonathan Roth, "Jewish Military Forces in the Roman Service," paper delivered at the annual meeting of the Society for Biblical Literature, San Antonio, Texas, November 23, 2004 (www.josephus.yorku.ca/Roth%20Jewish%20 Forces.pdf, accessed August 15, 2008).

[35] Woolf, *Becoming Roman*, 240–41.

[36] On the Greek East, the foundational study is Erich S. Gruen's two-volume masterpiece *The Hellenistic World and the Coming of Rome* (Berkeley and Los Angeles: University of California Press, 1984). This may be the only scholarly work to date to give full consideration to the role of indigenous politics and institutions in Roman imperialism. I would argue that mechanisms similar to what Gruen describes operated in later periods.

[37] Shaw, "Tyrants," 196.

[38] For a subtle analysis of what follows and of the workings of personal power and "ritualized friendship," see Shaw, "Tyrants." On the mechanisms by which personal power worked, Lendon, *Empire*, is a key contribution.

[39] For a concise history of Roman rule over the Jews from Herod's death, see Martin Goodman, *Rome and Jerusalem: The Clash of Ancient Civilizations* (New York: Knopf, 2007), 379–423.

[40] A good introductory history of Sicily under the republic is R.J.A. Wilson, *Sicily under the Roman Empire: The Archaeology of a Roman Province, 36 B.C.–A.D. 535* (Warminster, UK: Aris and Phillips, 1990), 17–32. On taxation in Sicily, Cicero *Against Verres* 2.3.13–15; also see Christopher Schäfer, "Steuerpacht und Steuerpächter in Sizilien zur Zeit des Verres," *Münstersche Beiträge zur antiken Handelsgeschichte* 11 (1992): 23–38, with full bibliography. Cicero normally refers to local tax collectors as *decumani* (e.g., 2.3.21, 66, 75), so called because they collected the 10 percent grain tax of Hiero; he also calls them *publicani* (e.g., 2.3.77). Cicero refers to one representative of the Italian company that collected the pasture tax in Sicily, named Carpinatius (2.2.169ff., 2.3.167), but there is no evidence of a bureaucratic apparatus exported by the Italian corporations beyond this one individual.

[41] Claudii Marcelli and Cicero: Cicero *Againt Verres* 2.2.8, 2.1.16–17, 2.2.122. *Socii atque i amici populi Romani, mei autem necessarii:* 2.1.15. Segesta and the Scipiones: 2.4.79–80. Syracuse and the Marcelli: 2.2.36, 50–51. Messana and Verres: 2.4.17–26.

[42] *Hospitium* between Roman aristocrats and the Sicilian elite: Cicero *Against Verres*, 2.2.24, 83, 96, 2.3.18, 2.4.25, 49, and many more references throughout. On *hospitium*, see also Koenraad Verboven, *The Economy of Friends: Economic Aspects of Amicitia and Patronage in the Late Republic*, Collection Latomus 269 (Brussels: Éditions Latomus, 2002), 51, 58. Heius of Messana: Cicero *Against Verres* 2.4.18–19. Sthenius of Thermae: Cicero *Against Verres* 2.2.110; see also 2.2.113, where Sthenius is acquitted by Pompey, another former guest; Sthenius is Cicero's own *hospes* also, 2.2.227.

[43] Cicero calls them *Venerii*; e.g., *Against Verres* 2.3.61, 62, 65, and many more references. On the cult, see Wilson, *Sicily,* 282–84. While there was no "Roman" army in Sicily, there was a small Sicilian navy: Cicero *Against Verres* 1.13, 2.3.186.

[44] For aristocrats prosecuting their enemies, see the cases of Sopater (Cicero *Against Verres* 2.2.68–75) and Sthenis (2.2.83–118).

[45] For cities sending delegations to the senate or to a patron, see, e.g., Cicero *Against Verres* 2.2.10–11, 2.2.122.

[46] See, e.g., Cicero *Against Verres,* 2.2.8, 2.3.67.

[47] On nomadic tribes and their relations with the Roman Empire, a wide scholarship exists. See notably Isaac, *Limits,* 68–77; Brent D. Shaw, "Fear and Loathing: The Nomad Menace and Roman North Africa," in *L'Afrique romaine: Les Conférences Vanier 1980,* ed. C. M. Wells, 29–50 (Ottawa: University of Ottawa Press, 1982); D. Graf, "Rome and the Saracens: Reassessing the Nomad Menace," in *L'Arabie préislamique et son environment historique et culturel,* ed. T. Fahd, 341–400 (Strasbourg: Université des Sciences Humaines de Strasbourg, 1989).

[48] Note recently Cullen Murphy, *Are We Rome? The Fall of an Empire and the Fate of America* (New York: Houghton Mifflin, 2007); Thomas Madden, *Empires of Trust: How Rome Built—and America Is Building—a New World* (New York: Dutton, 2008).

[49] In a paper presented at the conference titled "Invasion: The Use and Abuse of Comparative History," University of Michigan, Ann Arbor, November 21, 2008.

8.   Slave Wars of Greece and Rome

BARRY STRAUSS

Butchery of civilians, charismatic religious leaders proclaiming reigns of terror, insurgents running circles around regular soldiers, legionaries chasing runaway slaves into the hills, rows of crosses lining the roads with the corpses of captured insurgents, shrines later springing up to the martyred memory of a chivalrous rebel: some of the images are familiar, some are not; some were popularized by Hollywood, others seemingly "ripped from the headlines," as the tabloid phrase goes. They are real images of ancient slave revolts. Except for a seventy-year period in the Late Roman Republic, however, from about 140 to 70 BC, slave revolts proved rare events in the ancient world.

That may seem odd, because slavery played a central role in the economy of Greece and Rome. Millions of men and women around the ancient Mediterranean lived and died in chains. Most of them made their peace with the banal truth of enslavement; some found an escape route in manumission, which was more common in ancient than in modern slave societies. Others responded to mistreatment and humiliation with daily acts of resistance. Slaves misbehaved, manipulated the master, or fled—or simply accepted their fates and made the necessary accommodations. Yet rebellion—that is, armed and collective uprisings in search of freedom—was exceptional.

Spartacus, the rebel gladiator whose revolt upended Italy between 73 and 71 BC, was as unusual as he is famous. Special conditions, as we shall see, made the Late Roman Republic the golden age of ancient slave wars. For the rest of antiquity, few slaves were willing to risk what little they had in a war against the Roman legions or Greek phalanx; fewer still had the know-how or the opportunity to fight in a rebel army, let alone to raise one. But masters worried nonetheless, and the relative scarcity of revolt reflects in inverse proportion the attention that masters devoted to security. Elite Greek and Roman opinion called for constant vigilance by free people against violence by slaves. A whole range of precautions by masters became common sense, from not buying strong-willed individuals as slaves to keeping slaves of the same nationality apart, lest they make common cause.

Still, revolts broke out, even in other periods than the late republic. Before describing them we need to define terms, because ancient slavery was not a monolithic institution. The ancient world knew various kinds of nonfree labor. The two main ones were chattel slavery and communal servitude.[1] Chattel slavery is the commonsense notion of slavery, familiar today from such places as the American South, the Caribbean, or Brazil, in which individuals are imported from abroad and bought and sold like objects. Communal servitude refers to the collective enslavement of whole groups, either within one community or across community lines. For the sake of clarity, many scholars refer to communal slaves as serfs, although the conditions of communal servitude were harsher than medieval serfdom. Serfs, for instance, could not be killed without cause, but the victims of communal servitude could. Yet the ancients tended to treat chattel slaves with greater contempt than those in communal servitude, so the distinction between serf and slave makes rough sense.

Chattel slavery was widespread in classical and Hellenistic Greece and in republican and imperial Rome. Athens and other city-states such as Aegina and Chios, along with various parts of Anatolia, were centers of Greek slavery, while Italy and Sicily and the Spanish mines were foci of Roman slavery. Before its destruction by Rome in 146 BC, Carthage also fostered large-scale slavery in North Africa. Communal servitude was primarily a Greek phenomenon, found in such places as Thessaly, Crete, and Argos, but the best-known example was the helots of Sparta. They consisted of two regional groups, each having been conquered separately by Sparta: the helots of (Spartan-controlled) Laconia, in the southeastern Peloponnesus, and the helots of (Spartan-controlled) Messenia, in the southwest.

A preliminary word about sources is also called for. Ancient warfare is relatively well documented, but the same is not true of ancient slave revolts. Relatively few records survive. In part, this represents bad luck, but it probably also reflects a lack of interest in the subject by the ancient elite. Slave wars offered little glory, less loot, and potentially a lot of embarrassment. Slaves were deemed contemptible. It was no honor to conquer them, a truth that the Romans recognized by refusing to allow a triumph to a general for merely winning a slave war. Nor was there much chance for booty, since commanders would not tolerate looting in friendly territory. A final problem was the paradox of war against slaves, in which killing the enemy was counterproductive, because it destroyed one's countrymen's property. Losing to slaves, of course, was insufferable.

Another point about the sources is that virtually all of them represent the masters' point of view. We can do little but make educated guesses about the plans or motives of the rebels. Much the same is true of the study of slavery even in more modern periods of history.

To turn to slave wars is to face two different phenomena: rebellions by chattel slaves and rebellions by communal serfs. Communal serfs in revolt had the advantage of common nationality and local roots going back generations. They were more likely than chattel slaves to have served in the masters' army or navy, usually only as servants or rowers but sometimes as soldiers.[2] Representing as they did a potential sword in the masters' side, serfs had a chance of attracting support from the masters' enemies abroad. As rebels, chattel slaves had all the corresponding disadvantages: heterogeneity, alienation, relative lack of military experience, and the unlikelihood of gaining foreign aid. They did, however, enjoy one big advantage over communal serfs: surprise. The rarity of revolts by chattel slaves sometimes lulled masters into letting down their guard. The lower status of chattel slaves probably tended to help them as well, because it left the masters unenthusiastic about waging war against so "unworthy" and ostensibly so weak an enemy.

Revolts by communal serfs were not unusual in classical Greece. According to Aristotle, the *penestai* (communal slaves) of Thessaly and Sparta's helots often revolted.[3] We know little about Thessaly and a fair amount about Sparta. Various ancient writers detail the security measures that Sparta took against helot revolt, from locking their doors (and taking off their shield straps while on campaign) to declaring war against the helots annually to unleashing eighteen- to twenty-year-old Spartan military trainees in helot country. It was Messenia's rather than Laconia's helots who represented the major threat. They rose around 670 BC in a shadowy revolt known as the Second Messenian War (the first Messenian War, ca. 735 BC, marks the Spartan conquest of Messenia) and in a slightly better documented uprising known as the Third Messenian War from around 464 to 455 BC.[4]

The Third Messenian War ended in ca. 455, when Sparta granted the rebels a safe-conduct to leave their stronghold; Athens, Sparta's rival, settled them in the city of Naupactus on the northern shore of the Corinthian Gulf, a strategic naval base. In 425 Athens established a fort at Pylos, on the coast of Messenia, and used Messenians from Naupactus to raid the territory and encourage helot escapees. In 424 and 413 Athens set up other bases in Spartan territory in order to encourage helot desertion. Full freedom for the Messenian helots awaited the invasion of the Peloponnesus by the Boeotian army in 369, which liberated Messenia and reestablished Messene as the capital of an independent city-state after roughly 350 years of Spartan control.

Compared to revolts by communal serfs, revolts by chattel slaves were rare. Greek history affords only three certain examples of such revolts: one on the island of Chios, led by a certain Drimacus, probably in the third century BC; another in Athens, Delos, and elsewhere around 135–134 BC; and a third in Athens around 104–100 BC. Much more common in Greek history was the phenomenon of states or rebels who offered freedom to chattel slaves in exchange for their support, much as Athens offered freedom to Spartan helots during the Peloponnesian War. During the last years of the Peloponnesian War (431–404 BC.), for instance, more than 20,000 Athenian slaves escaped to the Peloponnesian fort at Decelea in the hills on Athens's northern border.[5] The Spartans, who set up the fort, were only taking revenge for Athenian assistance to rebellion on the part of Sparta's Messenian helots. By the way, some of the Athenian runaways seem to have gone from the frying pan to the fire, since apparently some of them were "bought cheaply" by Thebans across the border from Athens.[6]

Other examples of rebels or states that promised to free slaves include what seems to have been an attempted coup d'état by one Sosistratus in Syracuse in 415–413 BC; offers of freedom to slaves in anti-Roman wars by Syracuse in 214, by the Achaean League in 146, and by Mithridates VI Eupator of Pontus in 86 and again in 65 BC; a nationalist revolt against Rome in Macedon by Andriscus in 149–148 BC that seems to have had some slave support; and a similar uprising in Anatolia by Aristonicus of Pergamum in 133–129 BC.

To turn to Roman history, the sources for revolts by chattel slaves are somewhat better, although still hardly rich. We hear of uprisings from the earliest days of the republic, but the first reliable report is of a slave rebellion in central Italy in 198 BC, a revolt of enslaved Carthaginian prisoners of war, captured during the recently ended Second Punic War (218–201 BC). Several other slave insurrections in southern Italy (and in one case, central Italy) in the 180s and around 104 BC are recorded. Several of these were revolts of herdsmen, in some cases possibly inspired by ecstatic religious rituals. Some of these incidents involved thousands of rebels, but they were dwarfed by what followed.

Huge slave insurrections, each involving many tens of thousands of rebels, broke out first in Sicily and then in Italy between 140 and 70 BC. They were the First and Second Sicilian Slave Wars (respectively 135–132 and 104–100 BC) and Spartacus's rebellion (73–71 BC). These were the greatest slave wars of the ancient world; indeed, they rank among the major slave revolts of history. They took place within a space of seventy years and within a relatively small geographic area—even smaller, if one considers that Spartacus tried to spread his revolt from southern Italy to Sicily. Spaced about twenty to thirty years apart, they represented roughly three generations of revolt.[7]

Exaggerated in their significance by Marxist scholars and dwarfed in most "bourgeois" accounts of the late republic by other events, the great Roman slave wars were genuinely important. Rome's failure to suppress the first Sicilian revolt contributed to the sense of military crisis that spurred the reforms of Tiberius Gracchus, which in turn began the Roman revolution.[8] Rome's inability to stop Spartacus advanced the careers of the career generals who represented the greatest threat to the republic. By rendering the countryside unsafe, rebel slaves contributed to the sense of insecurity that made Romans ready to turn the state over to the Caesars.

Neither the timing nor the location of the great slave wars was an accident. Between 300 and 100 BC, a new slave economy emerged in Roman Italy and Sicily. Fueled by its military conquests around the Mediterranean, Rome flooded Italy with nonfree labor. By the first century BC there were an estimated 1–1.5 million slaves on the peninsula, constituting perhaps about 20 percent of the people of Italy. A large percentage of those slaves had been taken from freedom. The sources of slaves were Roman commanders, local entrepreneurs and slave traders, and pirates. The last group proliferated in the eastern Mediterranean around 100 BC and entered slave trading in a big way. Just as criminal cartels today move drugs across international boundaries, pirates moved people—innocent victims of kidnapping who were sold as slaves.

Although some of Rome's slaves engaged in urban pursuits, most were employed in agriculture, where large-scale enterprises predominated. The two main units of agricultural production were farms and ranches, both staffed by slaves. Sicily and southern Italy, especially Campania, were the main centers of slave agriculture. The countryside in these regions teemed with slaves.

Rome inadvertently set the stage for rebellion by breaking all the rules. It combined mass exploitation with scant attention to security. Although ancient writers from Plato and Aristotle to Varro and Columella warned against concentrating slaves of the same nationality, the Romans dumped huge numbers of slaves from the eastern Mediterranean together. Although they came from various countries, most of them spoke a common language, Greek. The Romans also permitted large concentrations of Thracians and Celts, for example, in the gladiatorial barracks where Spartacus's revolt was hatched. Spartacus was Thracian and his two co-leaders, Crixus and Oenomaus, were Celts.

By the same token, the policing of slaves was inadequate. Public police forces were primitive or nonexistent. Farm slaves faced a fairly strict security regimen of chains and barracks, but things were different on the ranches. Herders of cattle, sheep, pigs, and goats were left free to drive their herds from pasture to pasture. They moved from the highlands in the summer to the plains in the winter. Their knowledge of the backcountry made them experts at hiding from the authorities. Because of the danger of bandits, bears, and boars, slave herdsmen were allowed to carry arms. Many slaves knew how to use weapons well, since many were prisoners of war who had been trained in foreign armies. Spartacus, for example, had served as an auxiliary in the Roman army (that is, he fought in an allied unit, probably as a cavalryman) before he somehow ran afoul of the law and ended up as a slave. No doubt other slaves had gained experience as speakers or organizers in public life during their experience of freedom. Slave bailiffs too had organizational skills, and some of them joined the rebels. Athenion, for example, one of the leaders of the Second Sicilian Revolt, was an ex-bailiff.

Left to find their own food for themselves, some Sicilian slave herdsmen formed gangs and turned to banditry. By concentrating slaves of the same nationality or language, many of them former soldiers, and giving them relative freedom and even weapons, as well as access to mountain hideaways, Rome was playing with fire.

Readers might anticipate finding antislavery ideology as fueling ancient slave revolts. Modern movements such as abolitionism and the earlier struggle to abolish the slave trade, as well as the American Civil War and, above all, the Marxist appropriation of Spartacus as a symbol of proletarian revolution, have all created this expectation. As several scholars have pointed out, however, that ideology is lacking in the case of almost all ancient slave revolts. We hear of a few people who opposed slavery in principle. They include Greek philosophers (only one of whom, the little-known Alcidamas, is named by the sources), perhaps two Jewish fringe groups, at least one Christian Church father, Gregory of Nyssa, and perhaps certain Christian heretical groups. Otherwise, we know of no doctrine of abolitionism, either among free citizens or among slaves.[9]

Naturally, rebel slaves sought their freedom. The slaves who rebelled in the First Sicilian War complained of harsh and humiliating treatment. The Louis XVI and Marie Antoinette of the revolt were the slaveowners Damophilus of Enna and his wife Metallis (or Megallis) of Enna, whose cruel punishments fueled the outbreak of slave violence.

Damophilus owned huge cattle ranches and was known for his vulgar display of his wealth; Metallis had a reputation for abusing her maids with great brutality. When once approached by naked slaves in need of clothes, Damophilus told them to steal cloaks from travelers, a "let-them-eat-cake" remark if there ever was one.[10] When the revolution came, husband and wife were captured in the countryside and dragged bound and chained to Enna, where they were displayed before a crowd in the theater. Damophilos was killed there, without trial; Metallis was tortured by her female slaves and thrown off a cliff. Their teenage daughter, however, was spared because she had always treated slaves humanely.

If the first war arose from excessive punishment, the Second Sicilian Slave War emerged from false hope incited by the Romans. In response to a complaint by an important ally in Anatolia, the Romans decided to offer freedom to kidnapped slaves. The first hearings by the governor in Sicily liberated several hundred slaves, but then rich Sicilian slave owners used their influence to stop the process. Inadvertently, they spurred another major servile insurrection.

To turn to another example, when Spartacus and his followers in 73 BC broke out of the gladiators' barracks where they were enslaved, they did so, according to one author, having decided "to run a risk for freedom instead of being on display for spectators."[11] Liberty and dignity motivated them, according to this account, but we hear nothing of a more general desire to free all slaves. Nor, it seems, did they try. Spartacus and his men, for example, freed mainly gladiators and rural slaves; few of their followers came from the softer and more elite group of urban slaves.

Occasionally there is a glimpse of what might have been a broader ideology. Aristonicus's revolt in Anatolia (133–129 BC) catches the eye because he mobilized poor people, non-Greeks, and slaves, whom he freed; he called them all Heliopolitae ("Sun citizens").[12] The Greek philosopher Iambulus (possibly third century BC) had written about a utopia called Heliopolis, "Sun City," a caste society that possibly was free of slavery; the few fragments of the work leave that unclear.[13] Perhaps Aristonicus himself had a utopia in mind, or perhaps he was simply mobilizing propaganda to drum up support.

It was also significant that Spartacus insisted on sharing loot equally among his followers rather than taking the lion's share. This might have represented smart politics rather than incipient communism. Egalitarianism was not present in the Sicilian slave rebellions, whose leaders declared themselves to be kings, complete with diadems and purple robes. Spartacus took no kingship, but he did allow such trappings of Roman republican high office as the fasces, symbol of the power to command, including capital punishment.

A generalized hostility toward slavery on the part of rebels ought not be ruled out entirely. Although it cannot be demonstrated in the sources, those sources are full of holes and written from the masters' perspective.[14] Yet such an ideology is unlikely, because the pre-Christian world of Greece and Rome tended to lack mobilizing ideologies of universal liberation. Nor did anything in antiquity combine, as Marxism later would, a secular utopian vision with an international ideology. Revolutions tended to be more local and parochial.

By the same token, they contained strong elements of messianism.[15] Religion had always played an important role in ancient politics, from Themistocles' use of oracles to mobilize the Athenians at Salamis to the Romans' deification of their emperors. The leaders of slave revolts went further, however, and made themselves the gods' representative on earth, if not gods themselves. When it came to ancient slave revolts, charismatic leadership stood front and center.

One slave rebel with the gods on his side was Drimacus (probably third century BC). He announced to the citizens of Chios that the slave uprising was no mere secular event but rather the outcome of a divine oracle. They agreed with him, at least posthumously. Drimacus's voluntary surrender to their demand for his execution brought only frustration to the masters because it led to an upswing in rebel attacks on their holdings. So they built a hero shrine to Drimacus in the countryside and dedicated it to the Kindly Hero. Four hundred years later, in the second century AD, runaway slaves still dedicated to him there a portion of whatever they stole. Meanwhile, Drimacus supposedly appeared to free Chians in their dreams and warned them of an impending slave revolt, after which they too made dedications at his holy place.[16]

The leaders of the First and Second Sicilian Slave Wars each claimed a direct, personal pipeline to the gods. In the First War (135–132 BC), Eunus, a Greek-speaking slave in the Sicilian city of Enna, encouraged discontented slaves to revolt. A native of Syrian Apamea, he maintained that he had divine visions in his dreams, from which he recited prophetic messages. His pièce de résistance was to go into a trancelike state, breathe flames from his mouth (using a trick involving a hollow shell and embers), and issue yet more prophecies. Chosen king by the rebels, he took the throne name Antiochus, like a Seleucid monarch, and had coins issued in that name. His coins display the image of a goddess, perhaps the Greek goddess Demeter or the immensely popular Mother Goddess of the East—or both.

The rebels in the Second Sicilian Slave War (104–100 BC) chose as their king one Salvius, known for playing ecstatic music on the flute at women's religious festivals and as a prophet. He took the throne name Tryphon, reminiscent of a Cilician adventurer who had claimed the throne of Syria around 140 BC, which no doubt appealed to the many Cilicians in the island's slave population. Another leader of that revolt, Athenion, was known for his skill as an astrologer.

Dionysus also loomed large in slave revolts. In addition to being the god of wine and theater, Dionysus was the god of liberation. He was unwelcome to the Romans. In 186 BC the Roman Senate claimed that Italy's widespread Dionysiac groups masked a conspiracy. In a frenzied atmosphere, the Senate drove Romans out of the cult and permitted only women, foreigners, and slaves to worship the god. Dionysus was left to the powerless of Italy, and they embraced him. In 185–184, the slave shepherds of Apulia, the heel of the Italian "boot," revolted, and the sources hint that they claimed Dionysus as their patron. Both Sicilian slave revolts invoked Dionysus.[17] Mithridates VI Eupator of Pontus, who rebelled against Rome in 88–63 BC, called himself the "new Dionysus" and minted coins showing Dionysus and his grapes on one side and the cap worn by a freed slave on the other.

Spartacus's revolt (73–71 BC) combined Dionysus and prophecy with an added touch of star power. As a gladiator, Spartacus cut an imposing figure. He was a man "of enormous strength and spirit," which was probably more than a boilerplate description: gladiators were selected for size and power and Spartacus was a *murmillo*, that is, a heavyweight.[18] He was also a Thracian, a people known for their intimidating size.

Thracians also had a reputation for religious fervor, and Spartacus did not disappoint. He had a Thracian "woman" (either his wife or girlfriend) who went into trances inspired by Dionysus.[19] A flexible deity, Dionysus was, in one of his many guises, the national god of Thrace. No doubt this added credibility to the prophecies that Spartacus's woman uttered. When Spartacus was first sold into slavery at Rome, a snake wrapped itself around his face while the man slept; or so it was said. Since snakes do not wrap themselves around sleeping men's faces, it was either a dream or a miracle. In either case, the Thracian woman announced it as "a sign of great and fearful power" and predicted that Spartacus would come to a lucky (or, in some manuscripts, unlucky) end.[20] There may be an echo of the Thracian woman's propaganda in the statement of a later Roman poet that Spartacus "raged through every part of Italy with sword and fire, like a worshipper of Dionysus."[21]

From Chios to Sicily to Italy, charisma inspired the rebel chief's followers. They needed inspiration indeed, because ancient slave rebellions always represented the triumph of hope over realism. Because the enemy had the resources of a state at its disposal, the insurgents had little chance of success in the long run against a determined foe. By employing surprise and unconventional tactics, however, they could score short-term victories, sometimes spectacular ones. Spartacus and his men, for example, sneaked down from their camp on Mt. Vesuvius by clinging to ropes that they wove from the local wild grapevines, then took a poorly guarded Roman army camp by storm.

It also came with the territory that the rebels went after soft targets— that is, civilians. Revenge was a powerful motive, leading to the sexual abuse, torture, mutilation, and murder of masters who had mistreated slaves. Greed was a motive, too, causing very widespread looting and destruction of property.

The rebels usually lacked weapons, food, and other supplies. The Sicilian slave leader Eunus, for example, armed his men with farming implements such as axes and sickles; Spartacus's followers began their revolt with kitchen knives and cooking spits. Both groups went on to make such homemade weapons as vine-woven shields and fire-hardened spears; later they looted weapons from Roman prisoners and corpses. They also melted down their chains and hammered them into arms and armor. Less poetically, Spartacus's men bought iron and bronze for weapons.

Although more than a few slaves had military experience, since many were ex-prisoners of war, rebel armies lacked the cohesion that comes of training together. They often represented linguistic or ethnic heterogeneity, which hampered communication, let alone solidarity. They also faced the problem of setting up camp in hostile territory without a walled, urban base.

Since the enemy usually mustered well-armed and well-trained men who were used to fighting together and ready to wage pitched battles, they represented a force that the rebels could not hope to defeat in regular combat. More accurately, they could not hope to defeat them in the long run. Rebel armies could in fact win victories in pitched battle at first, while they outnumbered the Romans and faced untrained legions. In Sicily, for example, the governor's two legions were more constabularies than fighting forces. It took reinforcements from the mainland, led by a consul, to stand up to the rebels. In Italy, Spartacus and his men faced scratch troops at first. They were even able to beat consular armies. No mean feat, this pays tribute to Spartacus's tactical skill, but it also reflects the absence of Rome's veteran troops, who were abroad fighting wars in Spain, the Balkans, and Anatolia.

The best tactic for the rebels, therefore, was usually raiding. Guerrilla warfare and unconventional tactics were the staples of slave revolts. That often presented a military problem to the masters, compounded by a political predicament and an economic paradox. Their heavy-armed infantry was ill-equipped to defeat hit-and-run raiders. They found it hard to counter the rebels' local knowledge of the hills and mountains that were the habitual terrain of slave rebellion.

For the masters, retooling themselves for counterinsurgency was frustrating and time-consuming, and besides, they rarely wanted to. There was little glory in suppressing a slave rebellion and little dignity in fighting in what they perceived as contemptible styles of combat. A slave war, says one Roman, "had a humble and unworthy name."[22] The ideal solution was getting most of the rebels to surrender, preferably after killing their leaders, so as to cut off the shoots of future rebellion. Laying siege to rebel strongholds was a preferred tactic. In the First Sicilian Slave War, for example, the Roman consul Publius Rupilius laid siege successfully in 132 BC to the two main rebel strongholds of Tauromenium and Enna.

Knowing as they did these realities, wise insurgent leaders had three possible strategic goals: (1) to tire out the enemy sufficiently that he let the rebels maintain a runaway settlement in the hills—what in later days was called a community of maroons (from a Spanish word meaning "living on mountaintops"), (2) to break out and escape abroad, or (3) to find allies among the free population, either from abroad or from discontented groups at home.

Drimacus, rebel slave leader in Chios, probably in the third century BC, applied the maroon strategy successfully. After fleeing to the hills and becoming leader of the fugitive slaves, Drimacus attacked Chian farms and beat back armed Chian attempts to defeat him. He offered a truce that promised to limit future looting and to return runaway slaves who could not demonstrate maltreatment by their masters. The Chians accepted these remarkably pragmatic terms, and supposedly they indeed led to a decline in the number of runaways. But the Chians found the situation intolerable in the end and put a reward on Drimacus's head. The story goes that in his old age, Drimacus had his lover kill him and decapitate the corpse in order to collect the reward money. It was only afterward that he became divine in Chian eyes.

Less realistic, no doubt, Sicily's slave leaders claimed to set up their own kingdoms, complete with monarchs, councils, and assemblies. Having driven Carthage from the island, Rome was not about to let a group of slaves take it over. Perhaps the insurgents took undue encouragement from the support of some of Sicily's population of free poor people. Now, the sources for the Sicilian Slave Revolts are so very inadequate and confused that one scholar argues they weren't slave revolts at all but rather nationalist uprisings.[23] This theory is more clever than convincing, but it is true that the slaves found allies among the free poor. When the First Sicilian revolt broke out, "the citizen masses . . . rejoiced because they were jealous at inequities of wealth and differences in lifestyle." Instead of helping suppress the insurgency, "the free masses, because of their jealousy, would go out into the countryside on the pretext of attacking the runaways and plunder the property there, and even burn down the farms."[24] In the Second Sicilian war, says one source, "Turmoil and an Iliad of woes possessed all Sicily. Not only slaves but impoverished freemen were guilty of rapine and lawlessness."[25]

Ever agile, Spartacus tried both strategies: he attempted to break out and escape abroad, but also sought allies. His original plan, once the revolt caught fire, was to march into northern Italy and then have his men split into separate groups and cross the Alps, where they would seek their respective homelands. The plan failed, however, because of division among his men. Spartacus was never able to impose his authority on the ethnically heterogeneous group of rebels who fought with him. They consisted of large numbers of Celts and Germans as well as Thracians and other groups, many of whom resisted his commands. Besides, success spoiled them: their many victories encouraged them to stay in Italy. A veteran soldier, Spartacus knew better: he understood that Rome would pull together a trained and experienced army that no ragtag insurgency could defeat, no matter how long they drilled.

So it happened. Marcus Licinius Crassus gained a special command and raised a big, new army. Many of the recruits were probably veterans who had fought for Sulla in Rome's civil wars a decade earlier; others were brought into line by the iron discipline that Crassus imposed. For good measure, the Roman army recalled its legions from Spain, where Pompey (Caius Pompeius Magnus) had just defeated the rebels. With the handwriting on the wall, Spartacus convinced his men to retreat south and to try to cross the Strait of Messina to Sicily. He hoped to renew his fortunes there, either by starting a third slave war or perhaps by using the island as a stepping-stone to escape across the sea. But first he had to cross the strait.

Not having any boats himself, Spartacus tried to hire pirates who, in those days, used Sicily as a base for raids. It was not his first experience in alliances with free men. The Thracian gladiator had found support in the early days of his rebellion from "many runaway slaves and certain free men from the fields."[26] He may have even gained some backing from southern Italian elites, either because of their simmering enmity to Roman rule or because Spartacus had bought them.

Returning to the pirates: they came from southern Anatolia or Crete, considered themselves enemies of Rome, and had a history of alliance with Rome's main enemy in the east, Mithridates. Hence, they represented a promising collaborator. After taking Spartacus's money, however, the pirates left him and his men on the Italian shore. It was either a case of simple dishonesty or fear of the Roman governor of Sicily, Caius Verres. Immortalized by Cicero for his corruption, Verres in fact seems to have taken energetic action to fortify Sicily's shoreline and arrest slave troublemakers around the island. He plausibly also negotiated with the pirates himself, and may simply have outbid Spartacus. Afterward, the Thracian tried to get across the strait another way, by having his men build rafts, but they foundered in the winter waves. It is also possible that Spartacus made contact with Mithridates, as the Roman rebel Sertorius had done a few years earlier, from Spain. Mithridates later used his knowledge of Spartacus's rebellion as a rhetorical device to try to stir up a Celtic invasion of Italy (it didn't materialize). In any case, Spartacus found no new allies. The slaves were stuck in Italy.

The endgame differed little in essentials when it came to each of the two Sicilian slave wars and Spartacus. The rebels of the First Sicilian Slave War managed to defeat in pitched battle several Roman armies, whose forces they greatly outnumbered, and to take several cities. After Rome's humiliating defeats, the consul Publius Rupilius laid siege to the two main rebel cities and each time found a traitor to open the gates. Then he engaged in mopping-up operations around the island. After a series of incompetent generals failed to put down the second rebellion, the consul Manius Aquilius rose to the occasion. He killed the rebel king in single combat, which would have won him Rome's highest military honor had his opponent been a free man and not a slave.

Spartacus had defeated nine Roman armies, but he could not stand up to Crassus's revitalized forces. First Crassus tried to blockade him in the mountains of the toe of the Italian boot, in winter 72–71 BC, which the Romans sealed with a massive project of walls and trenches. Spartacus fought his way out, but at great cost. Pressed on his march northward by the enemy, Spartacus finally gave battle, probably in the upper valley of the Silarus (modern Sele) River, not far from the modern city of Salerno. The Romans defeated the enemy army and killed Spartacus.

as the route to freedom. Greek and Roman slavery always offered manumission on far more generous terms than did modern slave societies. To say so is not to detract from the brutality of ancient slavery, but it may help explain why men like Spartacus eventually became monsters to frighten children with rather than real figures of Roman society.

In modern times, Spartacus's reputation has generally boomed. Except for Arthur Koestler, the disillusioned ex-communist who saw Spartacus as a kind of post-revolution Lenin, corrupted by power, most moderns praise Spartacus. They see him as a liberator or an early socialist; the nineteenth century made him into a nationalist like Garibaldi.

If, however, we were to subject Spartacus or Drimacus, Salvius or Eunus, to the cold light of a military staff-college seminar, a different picture would emerge. From a military point of view, they demonstrate the unlikelihood of insurrections defeating regular armies. The ragtag rebel slaves of Greece and Rome could not match the logistical advantages and institutional advantages of an established state. They could march their men in mock legions and defeat frightened local militia; they could put out feelers for allies overseas. Once the state bore down on them with all its might, however, they faced ruin.

Nor could slaves attract much voluntary support from local populations of free people, who could figure out that in the end, most rebels would end up in chains or hanging from crosses. After their initial escape, and after making enough raids to get loot and revenge, rebel slaves were well advised to flee, either to the hills or abroad.

There is a lesson for today. Insurgents can crash onto the scene as loudly as Spartacus and his rebel gladiators did. They can rally religious support and terrorize local populations. They can draw other discontented people into their ranks at first. They can even come out of the hills and try to establish their authority over a city or a province. Once the state responds in all its armed might, however, the rebels are usually doomed.

Modern insurgencies will usually face a similar fate. In Iraq, for example, once the allied states found the political will and the military tactics to apply force effectively, they broke the back of the insurgency (2003–9). Still, success is not completely out of reach for insurgents. They can change the equation through one of several means, all unlikely but not impossible. For instance, they can buy time and space to turn themselves from a raiding force into a regular army. Having an isolated location, far from the center of power, helps this process greatly. The experience of the Chinese communist Red Army after the Long March of 1934 is an example. A second possibility is acquiring a state as an ally. The mujahideen of Afghanistan leveraged support from such states as China, Iran, Pakistan, and the United States into victory over the Soviet Red Army in the 1980s.

Today's insurgents, finally, have one advantage that antiquity's rebel slaves did not: they can target domestic opinion in the enemy's state. In the Algerian War of Independence (1954–62), for example, the insurgents lost the military battle but won the war by wearing out French public opinion.

The Haitian Revolution (1791–1804) was history's only successful slave revolt, and it incorporated these various advantages. The rebels fought a prolonged struggle, far from metropolitan France. The British fleet provided help via a blockade. The French Revolution gave the rebels the moral high ground. After years of difficult fighting and disease, the French gave up.

Successful insurgencies are the exception, however. Ancient slave rebellions remind us that, when it comes to war, states usually hold all the cards.

FURTHER READING

An excellent starting point is Brent D. Shaw, *Spartacus and the Slave Wars: A Brief History with Documents* (Boston: Bedford/St. Martins, 2001). Theresa Urbainczyk, *Slave Revolts in Antiquity* (Stocksfield, UK: Acumen Publishing, 2008), offers a very good overview. For slave rebellions in ancient Greece, see Yvon Garlan, *Slavery in Ancient Greece*, rev. ed., trans. Janet Lloyd (Ithaca, NY: Cornell University Press, 1988), 176–200; for those in ancient Rome, see Keith Bradley, *Slavery and Rebellion in the Roman World, 140 B.C.–70 B.C.* (Bloomington: Indiana University Press, 1989).

Important books on ancient slavery include M. I. Finley, *Ancient Slavery and Modern Ideology* (Princeton, NJ: Markus Wiener Publishers, 1998); Joseph Vogt, *Ancient Slavery and the Ideal of Man*, trans. Thomas Wiedemann (Cambridge, MA: Harvard University Press, 1975); Keith Hopkins, *Conquerors and Slaves* (Cambridge: Cambridge University Press, 1978); Peter Garnsey, *Ideas of Slavery from Aristotle to Augustine* (Cambridge: Cambridge University Press, 1996); F. H. Thompson, *The Archaeology of Greek and Roman Slavery* (London: Duckworth, 2003); Thomas Grünewald, *Bandits in the Roman Empire: Myth* and Reality, trans. John Drinkwater (London: Routledge, 2004); Niall McKeown, *The Invention of Ancient Slavery?* (London: Duckworth, 2007); and the collection of documents edited by Thomas Wiedemann, *Greek and Roman Slavery* (London: Routledge, 1981).

Studies of individual subjects include Karl-WilhemWelwei, *Unfreie in antiken Kriegsdienst*, 3 vols. (Wiesbaden, Germany: Steiner, 1974–88); Peter Hunt, *Slaves, Warfare, and Ideology in the Greek Historians* (Cambridge: Cambridge University Press, 1998); Paul Cartledge, *The Spartans: The World of the Warrior-Heroes of Ancient Greece, from Utopia to Crisis to Collapse* (Woodstock, NY: Overlook Press, 2003), and his more detailed *Sparta and Lakonia: A Regional History 1300–362 BC*, 2nd ed. (London: Routledge, 2002); Nino Luraghi and Susan E. Alcock, eds., *Helots and Their Masters in Laconia and Messenia: Histories, Ideologies, Structures* (Washington, DC: Center for Hellenic Studies and the Trustees for Harvard University, 2003); Nino Luraghi, *The Ancient Messenians: Constructions of Ethnicity and Memory* (Cambridge: Cambridge University Press, 2008); Alexander Fuks, "Slave Wars and Slave Troubles in Chios in the Third Century BC," *Athenaeum* 46 (1968): 102–11; Kyung-Hyun Kim, "On the Nature of Aristonicus's Movement," in *Forms of Control and Subordination in Antiquity*, ed. Toru Yogi and Masaoki Doi, 159–63 (Leiden: Brill, 1986); Jean Christian Dumont, *Servus: Rome et l'esclavage sous la république*, Collection de l'École Française de Rome 103 (Rome: École Française de Rome, Palais Farnèse, 1987); J. A. North, "Religious Toleration in Republican Rome," *Proceedings of the Cambridge Philological Society* 25 (1979): 85–103; P. Green, "The First Sicilian Slave War," *Past and Present* 20 (1961): 10–29, with objections by W.G.G. Forrest and T.C.W. Stinton, "The First Sicilian Slave War," *Past and Present* 22 (1962): 87–93; G. P. Verbrugghe, "Sicily 210–70 B.C.: Livy, Cicero and Diodorus," *Transactions and Proceedings of the American Philological Association* 103 (1972): 535–59, and idem, "Slave Rebellion or Sicily in Revolt?" *Kokalos* 20 (1974): 46–60; N. A. Mashkin, "Eschatology and Messianism in the Final Period of the Roman Republic," *Philosophy and Phenomenological Research* 10, no. 2 (1949): 206–28; P. Masiello, "L'ideologica messianica e le Rivolte Servili," *Annali della Facolta di lettere e filosofia* 11 (1966): 179–96; and Barry Strauss, *The Spartacus War* (New York: Simon & Schuster; London: Weidenfeld & Nicolson, 2009).

NOTES

[1] For these terms, see Yvon Garlan, *Slavery in Ancient Greece*, rev. ed., trans. Janet Lloyd (Ithaca, NY: Cornell University Press, 1988), 24, 87.

[2] On this subject, see Karl-WilhemWelwei, *Unfreie in antiken Kriegsdienst*, 3 vols. (Wiesbaden, Germany: Steiner, 1974–1988); Garlan, *Slavery in Ancient Greece*, 163–76; and Peter Hunt, *Slaves, Warfare, and Ideology in the Greek Historians* (Cambridge: Cambridge University Press, 1998).

[3] Aristotle *Politics* 1269a36–b6.

[4] For an introduction, see Paul Cartledge, *The Spartans: The World of the Warrior-Heroes of Ancient Greece, from Utopia to Crisis to Collapse* (Woodstock, NY: Overlook Press, 2003), and his more detailed *Sparta and Lakonia: A Regional History 1300–362 BC*, 2nd ed. (London: Routledge, 2001); Nino Luraghi and Susan E. Alcock, eds., *Helots and Their Masters in Laconia and Messenia: Histories, Ideologies, Structures* (Washington, DC: Center for Hellenic Studies and the Trustees for Harvard University, 2003); Nino Luraghi,

The Ancient Messenians: Constructions of Ethnicity and Memory (Cambridge: Cambridge University Press, 2008).

[5] Thucydides 7.27.5.

[6] Thucydides *Hellenica Oxyrhynchia* 17.4.

[7] For an overview of the era of slave wars between 140 and 70 BC, see Brent D. Shaw, *Spartacus and the Slave Wars* (Boston: Bedford/St. Martins, 2001), 2–14; for a more detailed account, see K. R. Bradley, *Slavery and Rebellion in the Roman World, 140–70 B.C.* (Bloomington: Indiana University Press, 1989).

[8] Appian *Civil Wars* 1.9.36.

[9] See J. Vogt, *Ancient Slavery and the Ideal of Man*, trans. T. Wiedemann (Oxford: Blackwell, 1975), 40; Bradley, *Slavery and Rebellion*, 1–15; Peter Garnsey, *Ideas of Slavery from Aristotle to Augustine* (Cambridge: Cambridge University Press, 1996), 75–86.

[10] Constantine, Porphyrogenitus, Excerpt 4, p. 384 (Diodorus Siculus 34.2.38).

[11] Appian *Civil Wars* 1.116.539.

[12] Strabo 14.1.138, 34–35.2.26. See Kyung-Hyun Kim, "On the Nature of Aristonicus's Movement," in *Forms of Control and Subordination in Antiquity*, ed. Toru Yogi and Masaoki Doi, 159–63 (Leiden: Brill, 1986).

[13] Diodorus Siculus 2.55–60.

[14] See the recent argument by Theresa Urbainczyk, *Slave Revolts in Antiquity* (Stocksfield, UK: Acumen Publishing, 2008), 31–34, 75–80.

[15] On the messianic aspects of the Roman slave revolts, see N. A. Mashkin, "Eschatology and Messianism in the Final Period of the Roman Republic," *Philosophy and Phenomenological Research* 10, no. 2 (1949): 206–28, and P. Masiello, "L'ideologica messianica e le Rivolte Servili," *Annali della Facolta di lettere e filosofia* 11 (1966): 179–96.

[16] Athenaeus *Deipnosophistae* 6.266d. The sole ancient source is the gossipy Athenaeus, *Deipnosophistae* 6.265d–66d. For a modern account, see Alexander Fuks, "Slave Wars and Slave Troubles in Chios in the Third Century BC," *Athenaeum* 46 (1968): 102–11.

[17] Diodorus Siculus 34.2.46, 36.4.4, with Jean Christian Dumont, *Servus: Rome et l'esclavage sous la république*, Collection de l'École Française de Rome 103 (Rome: École Française de Rome, Palais Farnèse, 1987), 263–64.

[18] "Enormous strength and spirit": Sallust *Histories* frag. 3.90 (my translation).

[19] Wife or girlfriend: Plutarch *Life of Crassus* 8.4.

[20] Plutarch *Life of Crassus* 8.4.

[21] Claudian *Gothica* 155–56.

[22] Aulus Gellius, *Attic Nights*, 5.6.20, trans. Shaw, *Spartacus and the Slave Wars*, 164.

[23] We depend largely on ninth- and tenth-century Byzantine summaries of the account of Diodorus of Sicily, who in turn relied heavily on the Stoic philosopher Posidonius; see Thomas Wiedemann, *Greek and Roman Slavery* (London: Routledge, 1981), 199–200. For the theory of nationalist rebellion, see G. P. Verbrugghe, "Sicily 210–70 B.C.: Livy, Cicero and Diodorus," *Transactions and Proceedings of the American Philological Association* 103 (1972): 535–59, and idem, "Slave Rebellion or Sicily in Revolt?" *Kokalos* 20 (1974): 46–60.

[24] Constantine Porphyrogenitus, Excerpt 4, 384f. (Diodorus Siculus 34.2.48) (Loeb translation).

[25] Photius *Bibliotheca* 388 (Diodorus Siculus 36.6.1) (Loeb translation).

[26] Appian *Civil Wars* 1.116.540 (my translation).

[27] Revolt of Selouros in Sicily: Strabo *Geography* 6.2.7; nascent slave rebellion in southern Italy in AD 24: Tacitus *Annals* 4.27; possible slave revolt under Bulla Felix in Italy in AD 206–7: Cassius Dio *Histories* 77.10.1–7.

[28] Augustus *Res Gestae* 25.

9. Julius Caesar and the General as State

ADRIAN GOLDSWORTHY

IN THE EARLY HOURS OF JANUARY 11, 49 BC, Julius Caesar led the Thirteenth Legion across the Rubicon and became a rebel. The river—in reality little more than a stream, and now impossible to locate—marked the boundary between his province of Cisalpine Gaul and Italy itself. North of that line he was legally entitled to command troops. To the south he was not. Nineteen months later, while surveying the corpses of his enemies at Pharsalus, Caesar claimed, "They wanted it; even after all my great deeds I, Caius Caesar, would have been condemned, if I had not sought support from my army."[1]

Caesar was more successful than any other Roman general, fighting "fifty pitched battles, the only commander to surpass Marcus Marcellus, who fought thirty-nine."[2] Yet there was an ambiguity about his reputation because many of his battles were fought against other Romans. For more than a year before crossing the Rubicon, Caesar and his opponents in the Senate had engaged in a game of brinkmanship, each in turn raising the stakes. Probably both sides expected the other to back down. There was no profound ideology involved. His opponents were determined to end Caesar's career, and he was equally resolved to preserve it. The price was a war fought all around the Mediterranean that cost tens of thousands of lives. However unreasonable his opponents had been, it was Caesar who crossed the Rubicon and started the civil war of 49–45 BC. Cicero believed that fighting this war was unnecessary and foolish, but was still scornful of Caesar's behavior: "He claims that he is doing all this to protect his dignity. How can there be any dignity where there is no honesty?"[3]

The rebel won the war. Caesar became dictator for life and held supreme authority in the republic. He also had effective control of the entire Roman army. His rule was not especially tyrannical. Enemies were pardoned and many promoted, while his legislation was generally sensible. However, the republican system was supposed to prevent any one individual from permanently possessing so much power. For this and other reasons, a group of senators stabbed Caesar to death on March 15, 44 BC. Just over a decade later, Caesar's adopted son defeated his last rival and became Rome's first emperor. Augustus created a system that would endure for centuries, and was a monarchy in all but name. "Caesar" eventually went from being simply a family name to a title synonymous with supreme power. Caesars would rule Rome for 500 years, and the Eastern or Byzantine Empire for nearly a thousand more. The name would survive into the twentieth century in the forms *kaiser* and *tsar*.

Caesar conquered Gaul and raided across the Rhine into Germany and over the English Channel into Britain. By Roman standards these wars were all justified and for the general good of the state. Successful commanders were expected to profit from victory, and Caesar did so on a massive scale, matching the scope of his campaigns. He was a commander of genius who then turned his army against opponents within the republic and made himself dictator through force of arms. His career was that of a talented man who began as a servant of the state, but then subverted it and became its master.

In a modern democracy, the armed forces are supposed always to remain fully under the control of civil authorities. This has been especially important in Britain since the civil wars, which had led to the rule of Cromwell and the Major Generals. Memories of this same rule by the army influenced America's founding fathers, and George Washington earned almost as much praise for his refusal to stand for a third term as president as for winning the war with Britain in the first place. The United States was to be a better version of the ancient republics, avoiding Rome's slide into military dictatorship and imperial rule. In contrast, France's revolution led to the rise of its own Caesar in the form of Napoleon. At his coronation as emperor in 1804, Napoleon himself placed the crown on his head to emphasize that he had taken power rather than been given it.

Dictators have seized powers in military coups in many countries, although since the Second World War the problem has afflicted only Third World countries and has seemed a distant one in the West. It is important to remember that Caesar did not spring from nowhere. He did not single-handedly destroy the republic, nor did he subvert a democracy that was functioning well and essentially stable. The conflict from 49 to 45 BC was not the first civil war, and others were as willing as he to resort to violence. Sulla had already fought his way to the dictatorship in 82 BC, ruthlessly proscribing his enemies for execution. He is supposed to have had on his tombstone an inscription boasting that no one was a better friend or worse enemy.[4]

Roman public life was very dangerous in Caesar's day. Most important men had lost relatives or friends during the struggle between Sulla and Marius. Senators lived with the knowledge that political rivalries could easily erupt into intimidation, violence, or even warfare itself. Times were less stable than in earlier centuries, and that meant that there were greater opportunities for rapid advancement. Pompey the Great broke almost all the rules in his rise to become Rome's greatest general and one of the dominant figures in the state. Ironically, he would die as a defender of the republic against the rebel Caesar.

The Roman republic was already floundering before Caesar began his career, let alone by the time he crossed the Rubicon. That does not mean that its collapse was inevitable, but it did make it a real possibility. Military dictators do not usually appear unless a state is in serious, usually long-term, trouble. Napoleon could not have existed without the chaos of the Revolution and the Terror. However popular a great and successful military commander may be, the circumstances need to be right for him to turn against the state that appointed him. Caesar's dictatorship was not an instance of the army taking over the state. The republic's political leaders also commanded its army, and in 49 BC they chose to employ the legions to resolve their political rivalry.

There is also another lesson from Caesar's career. For all his military success, he failed to find a political solution, and was murdered. There are limits to what force alone can achieve. Caesar might have preserved both his life and his rule had he taken greater precautions to protect himself, and had he maintained control with greater ruthlessness.

Augustus would do both these things, learning a brutal lesson from the failure of his adoptive father.

POLITICS AND WAR

The same men led Rome in both peace and war. Men entering public life followed a structured career, the *cursus honorum*, which brought them a mixture of military and civil posts. Provincial governors combined supreme military, civil, and judicial power within the territory placed under their command. Magistrates were elected and held office for a single year. Governors were normally appointed by the Senate and did not have a fixed term in the post, remaining there until a replacement was appointed. They were rarely left in a post for more than a few years.

Leading an army in a successful war gave a man glory and wealth. Both brought considerable political advantages, helping him and his descendants to win office in the future. Annual elections meant that competition for the approval of voters was frequent. The comparatively short terms granted to provincial governors ensured that many were eager to fight and win a war before they were replaced. It was a system that had fostered aggressive warfare and expansion throughout the republican period. It did not do much to encourage long-term planning or consistency in relations with neighboring peoples.

Caesar came from an aristocratic family that had languished in comparative obscurity for a long time. His early career was flamboyant but in most respects conventional. He saw military service as a junior officer in Asia Minor in his late teens and won the *corona civica*, Rome's highest award for gallantry, which was traditionally given for saving the life of a fellow citizen. As a private citizen he raised a force to arrest a group of pirates, and on another occasion did the same to repulse an attack on the Roman province of Asia by elements of Mithridates of Pontus's army. Caesar later served as a military tribune, most probably in the war against Spartacus. There is no record of any military activity during his quaestorship. In 61 BC he went to Spain as governor and led a rapid punitive expedition against Lusitanian tribes. His army was equivalent in size to three legions.[5]

By the time he was forty, Caesar had served for at most six or seven years in some military capacity or other. This was perhaps a little below average for a Roman politician, but not excessively so. Although his record was good, many other men could boast of comparable achievements. Caesar's rise up the *cursus honorum* was helped by his military exploits, but other factors were far more important. He championed popular causes, won a reputation as an orator and legal advocate, and spent borrowed money on a staggering scale to advertise himself and win popularity. As Sallust put it, "'Caesar had accustomed himself to great effort and little rest; to concentrate on his friends' business at the expense of his own, and never to neglect anything which was worth doing as a favour. He craved great *imperium*, an army, and a new war so that he could show his talent."[6]

The contrast between Pompey's career and Caesar's career could not be more marked. Only six years older, Pompey raised three legions from his own estates and at his own expense, and rallied to Sulla's cause during the civil war. He had no legitimate authority to do this, but his army was large enough to make his support worth having. All of his early victories were achieved over Roman enemies, as he mopped up Sulla's enemies in Italy and Africa and earned himself the nickname "the young butcher" for the enthusiasm with which he executed senators. In 78 BC the Senate employed him to deal with an attempted coup by the consul Lepidus. After that he was sent to Spain to finish off the last remnants of Marius's supporters. He was given proconsular power by the Senate, but had never held a magistracy and was not even a senator. In 71 he returned to Rome, demanded and was given the right to stand for the consulship, and finally became a senator. In 67 and 66 BC he was given extraordinarily large provincial commands, for the first time winning victories against genuinely foreign opponents. On his return to Rome at the end of the decade, he was fabulously wealthy and enjoyed a record of military success far outstripping any other senator's.

Caesar wanted a war to win glory to match men like Crassus and Lucullus, and ideally Pompey himself. He also needed a war to pay his massive debts. Late in 60 BC, he formed a secret alliance with Pompey and Crassus, both of whom were frustrated by their failure to get measures through the Senate. Caesar became consul for 59 BC, and with their backing he forced through the legislation they wanted, as well as some of his own. He also secured himself a grand military command, combining the provinces of Cisalpine Gaul and Illyria, which won him an army of three legions. This was not allocated by the Senate but given to him by the vote of the Popular Assembly, which at the same time granted him five years in the post. Pompey had gained some of his commands in the same way. The Senate did augment Caesar's province by adding Transalpine Gaul following the sudden death of its current governor. This province included another legion to augment Caesar's army.

THE SHAPING OF WAR

Like many successful statesmen, Caesar was an opportunist. When he went to his province in 58 BC, he needed a war, any war, so long as it was on a grand scale. His initial plans envisaged a campaign on the Danube, most likely against the wealthy and powerful Dacian king Burebista. The unexpected addition of Transalpine Gaul to Caesar's command was soon followed by news of the migration of the Helvetii, a tribe from what is now Switzerland. The migrants wanted to cross through the Roman province and were seen as a threat by tribes allied with Rome. Caesar would have been criticized if he had ignored this problem. In any event, he quickly realized this was an opportunity, and took swift action. He concentrated his army to meet this threat, and repulsed the Helvetii. He then left his province to pursue them, eventually smashing them in battle.

By the end of the campaign, it was too late in the year to think of mounting an operation in the Balkans. Rather than waste the time, Caesar decided to attack the German leader Ariovistus. The latter had originally been invited into Gaul by the Sequani, but had then come to dominate the tribe and its neighbors. Up to this point, the Romans had accepted the situation, and in 59 BC Caesar himself had helped Ariovistus be formally named a "friend and ally of the Roman People." Now he argued that the German leader was a serious threat to allied tribes such as the Aedui. Ariovistus was attacked and defeated. Involvement in the affairs of Gaul offered further opportunities for intervention. In 57 BC, Caesar once again claimed that defending Rome's allies and interests required him to launch another major aggressive war, this time against the Belgic tribes.

Caesar carefully publicized his achievements in his famous *Commentaries*, which seem to have been released as individual books during the winter months after a campaign.[7] These portray a commander always acting for the good of the republic. They do not mention the more personal factors that shaped the warfare but instead present a seamless—and apparently logical—progression from one campaign to the next. The tribes of Gaul were portrayed as unstable and prone to internal revolution, but essentially static. In contrast, Caesar depicted the Germanic tribes as seminomadic pastoralists, always inclined to migrate westward to the better land of Gaul. This invoked memories and fears of the Cimbri and other tribes that had threatened Italy itself at the end of the second century BC. The Rhine was presented as the clear dividing line between the Gauls and the Germans, although Caesar's own narrative acknowledges that things were more complicated. This gave him a clear limit to the land he needed to occupy, and a clear reason for destroying any Germanic groups that moved into Gaul. The expeditions over the Rhine were brief and never intended to lead to permanent occupation. They demonstrated that the Romans could and would cross the river whenever they chose. Doing so by building a bridge—something beyond the capability of the tribes—reinforced the point of overwhelming Roman superiority.[8]

In 56 BC, the fighting was smaller scale, and much of it was carried out by Caesar's subordinates at the head of detachments from the army. This was in part because the largest obvious targets or opponents had already been dealt with, but mainly because political concerns kept Caesar in Cisalpine Gaul, as close to Italy as possible. Tensions between Pompey and Crassus nearly led to the breakdown of their alliance. Both men traveled to meet with Caesar inside his province, at what is known as the Conference of Luca. A new deal was made, one consequence of which was the extension of Caesar's command by five years.

This permitted Caesar far more scope for planning. It is probable that he was already contemplating an expedition to Britain. In 56 BC he defeated the Veneti, a tribe that possessed a fleet and might have hindered the expedition. In 55 BC a campaign against migrating German tribes delayed the attack on Britain, so that only a small-scale operation crossed the channel at the very end of the year. The campaign nearly ended in disaster when much of the fleet was wrecked in a storm. Caesar returned the next year with a much bigger force. He achieved a minor victory, but once again underestimated the power of the English Channel and was nearly stranded on the island. Militarily, the British expeditions achieved very little indeed, at high risk. Politically they were a staggering success, with the Senate voting Caesar twenty days of public thanksgiving to mark the victory—a longer period than had ever been awarded before.[9]

Caesar's campaigns were aggressive and opportunistic. However, in neither their conduct nor their operation were they markedly different from Roman warfare in this and earlier periods. Unlike most commanders, Caesar had larger forces at his disposal and a longer period of command. By Roman standards, his campaigns were justified. The only direct attack on his behavior in Gaul was launched by Cato the Younger in 55 BC, after Caesar had massacred the migrating German tribes. Cato's concern was not with the slaughter itself but that it had occurred during a truce, and so was a breach of Rome's much vaunted faithfulness (*fides*). Even in the build-up to the civil war, Caesar's opponents attacked him for his behavior during his consulship in 59 BC and for what they claimed were his ambitions for the future. They do not seem to have wanted to hold him to account for his activities in Gaul.[10]

DIFFERENT POLITICS

Caesar won almost every battle he fought and never lost a campaign. Yet from the beginning of his time in Gaul, he realized that battlefield success alone was not enough. Rome had existing alliances with many tribes, especially those bordering Transalpine Gaul. Defending these allies provided the main pretext for Caesar's initial intervention and most of the subsequent campaigns. As he advanced farther into Gaul, new allies were acquired. Caesar was always considerably more brutal in dealing with enemies from outside Gaul than with the tribes already established there. Ariovistus, the Helvetii, and the migrating German tribes were treated with extreme savagery and ejected. On the whole,

Gallic tribes that fought against him were treated more generously. Allied tribes provided him with troops and shared in the benefits of victory. The Aedui, a well-established Roman ally, were granted many favors, and expanded their own influence as it became clear that their subordinate allies would also enjoy Roman protection.

Individual chieftains and leaders benefited even more from Caesar's friendship. Every year he summoned the tribal leaders to a council at least once, and frequently more often. He also met and consulted with them individually. Some served with his army for long periods. Commius of the Atrebates played an especially prominent role in the expeditions to Britain, and was rewarded for this and other services, becoming king of his own people and being given overlordship of the Menapii. Diviciacus of the Aedui proved a staunch ally and gained many adherents from other tribes because it was known that Caesar often granted him favors.

Caesar kept a close eye on politics within the tribes and supported the leaders who seemed most likely to be loyal to him. For such men, the arrival of the Roman army was an opportunity to strengthen their own position. It was also a reality they could not afford to ignore. The same had been true of Ariovistus, who had been invited in by the Sequani, but who had then used his army to dominate them as well as their neighbors. Caesar drove out any rival power so that his would be the only outside influence on the politics of the tribes.

Caesar's conquest of Gaul did not introduce large numbers of Roman colonists to the region. The province he created—as indeed was the case with virtually every other Roman province—would be populated by the people already living there. For this to be successful, enough of the inhabitants needed to be persuaded that it was in their best interests to accept Roman rule. The power of the Roman army acted as a deterrent to resistance, but on its own was not enough. Caesar increased his forces from four legions to more than a dozen during the course of the Gallic campaigns, but even after this increase these troops could not be everywhere simultaneously. It was not practical to hold down a province by force alone, nor was it desirable. A large army could easily cost as much as or more than the revenue from the province. The need for such a garrison would also make clear that the war was not really won and would greatly reduce the glory of any victory.

Therefore, from 58 BC on, Caesar devoted considerable time and effort to diplomacy, hoping to win over the tribal leaders. Old allies were strengthened and defeated enemies were shown leniency in order to turn them into new allies. This was the normal Roman method, and indeed it has been that of most successful imperial powers. He was helped by the fact that he possessed both civil and military authority, which meant that in each campaign, his strategy was molded to fit a political objective. This is perhaps harder in the modern world, where things are likely to be less neat and more than one authority is frequently involved. At the time of writing, the United States and its allies are involved in conflicts in Iraq and Afghanistan, where military force in itself cannot achieve victory without the creation of a stable political settlement. However, it is worth remembering that Caesar was not attempting to create a viable democracy and then withdraw. He was engaged in permanent conquest and could be considerably more ruthless in his behavior. The Romans did not have to worry about world opinion.[11]

Yet some factors do remain in common. For every tribal leader who gained from Caesar's arrival, there were others who did not. Politics were as fiercely competitive within and between the tribes as they were in the Roman republic. If a chieftain saw his rivals preferred over him, he had little personal incentive to support Rome. One alternative was to seek aid from another outside source, such as one of the German tribes, accepting their dominance as the price. Alternatively, the chieftain could directly attack and defeat his rival. Ideally this could be done swiftly and so completely that Caesar might be willing to accept the change, although in general, he took care to resist and punish anything of this sort.[12] If not, then the Romans would need to be driven out as well. It is too simplistic to think of purely pro- or anti-Roman factions or leaders within each tribe, in the same way that it is mistaken to speak of a simple divide between pro- and anti-Western groups in modern conflicts.

Men like Commius and Diviciacus had agendas and ambitions of their own. Such leaders felt that they were using Caesar as much as he was using them, adding to their own power through Roman support. Diviciacus's brother Dumnorix looked elsewhere for the support needed to dominate the Aedui. As his sibling became more and more powerful, Dumnorix began covertly to resist Roman rule. Later, probably after Diviciacus's death, Dumnorix encouraged a rumor that Caesar planned to make him king of the tribe. He was eventually killed on Caesar's orders, having tried to avoid being taken on the first British expedition.

Allegiances could change. Personal interest more than anything else dictated whether leaders supported Rome or resisted Caesar. This interest could change. In the winter of 53–52, many Gaulist leaders decided that the Roman presence was hindering their own freedom of action. In the great rebellion that followed, chieftains who had benefited from Caesar's favor joined with those who had consistently resisted to expel the Romans. Vercingetorix, the man who became the main leader of the rebellion, had been a favorite of Caesar, although this is not mentioned in the *Commentaries*.[13] A more conspicuous defection was Commius's.

Caesar came close to defeat in 52 BC, and suffered a serious reverse in his attack on Gergovia. He did not give up, and, after winning a small-scale action, seized back the initiative and cornered Vercingetorix at Alesia. After an especially brutal siege, Vercingetorix was forced to surrender. The war was not quite over. For more than a year, Caesar and his legates launched a succession of punitive expeditions against any tribe that still showed resistance. Leaders like Commius were hunted down, although in his case he managed to escape to Britain. When the walled town of Uxellodunum was captured, Caesar ordered that the captured warriors have their hands cut off as a dreadful warning.

Yet as always, along with reprisals and the use and threat of force came concerted diplomacy. As one of his officers put it, "Caesar had one main aim, keeping the tribes friendly, and giving them neither the opportunity nor cause for war. . . . And so, by dealing with the tribes honourably, by granting rich bounties to the chieftains, and by not imposing burdens, he made their state of subjection tolerable, and easily kept the peace in a Gaul weary after so many military defeats."[14] This task took more than two years. As always, much of the diplomacy was personal. It worked. In 49 BC, Caesar led away almost his entire army to fight in the civil war. Gaul did not erupt into rebellion when the Roman troops left and Caesar was kept busy elsewhere.

Yet this success came at a price. Caesar had misread the situation in the winter of 53–52 BC and had been surprised by the rebellion. Although he recovered and won, it took much time and effort to rebuild the peace. Rumors spread in Rome of serious defeats in Gaul, encouraging his opponents in the belief that he was vulnerable. Caesar had less time to prepare for his return to Rome. Had he been able to spend a year or more in Cisalpine Gaul, closer to Italy, had he been more accessible to messages and visits from influential men, then it is possible that the civil war could have been avoided—possible, but not certain. In the end, much depended on the attitude of Pompey. It was his shift toward Caesar's enemies that gave them the military capacity to wage a civil war.[15]

PRIVATE ARMIES

None of the civil wars could have been fought without the willingness of Roman soldiers to kill each other. By the first century BC the army was effectively a professional force, its ranks filled mainly from the poorest sections of society. For such recruits the army offered a steady, if not especially generous, wage, and fed and clothed them. Unlike the old conscript army recruited from property owners, such men had no source of livelihood once they were discharged from the army. The Senate generally proved reluctant to deal with this problem, and it was usually only with considerable effort that a commander was able to secure grants of farmland for his discharged veterans. This encouraged a bond between general and soldiers that often proved stronger than that between the legions and the state itself. Securing land for his veterans was one of Pompey's chief motives for allying with Crassus and Caesar. The latter brought forward the necessary legislation in 59 BC.[16]

There was more to the bond between general and soldier than simple economic dependency. Shared victories helped create mutual trust but in themselves were not enough. Lucullus was one of the ablest tactical commanders of this period, but nevertheless he was not liked by his men, being seen as mean when it came to rewarding them. Men like Pompey were far more generous in sharing the spoils of victory.

Caesar had immense charisma, and the loyalty of his soldiers during the civil war was almost fanatical in its intensity, in a way matched throughout history by only a few individuals, such as Napoleon. The bond was not instant, nor did it spring out of nothing. In 58 BC, Caesar took charge of four legions raised by someone else. He immediately recruited two new legions, and the following winter he added two more. In twelve months the size of his army doubled. It would soon triple.

At first the soldiers did not know Caesar and did not especially trust him. In the campaign against the Helvetii he made mistakes, notably a botched night attack on their camp that left a force stranded out on a limb while Caesar and the main body sat and did nothing. In the event, the Helvetii were either oblivious to the opportunity or not inclined to take advantage. Later in the summer came the mutiny at Vesontio, where for a while his army refused to march against Ariovistus. Caesar flattered and cajoled them into moving, and then rapidly defeated the enemy. The victories in 58 BC were followed by the hard-won success at the Sambre in 57 BC. During that battle Caesar went personally to rally the most hard-pressed section of the line, demonstrating that he would not abandon his men. Over time, the legionaries came to feel that they could rely on their commander to support them and to win. The fixed belief that they would prevail in the end made Caesar's soldiers extremely difficult to beat.

Confident of victory, Caesar's soldiers were equally confident of sharing in its rewards. These were considerable. One source claims that a million people were sold into slavery during the course of the Gallic campaigns. Another mentions the looting of local shrines and their hoarded treasure. Caesar expected tight discipline on campaign and imposed a rigorous training regimen, but mitigated this by granting the soldiers considerable freedom at other times. Conspicuous gallantry was rewarded with money and perhaps promotion—and also with a mention in the narrative of the *Commentaries*. Caesar and other sources claim repeatedly that Roman soldiers fought better when they were being watched by their commander, who had the power to reward or punish them.[17]

Many of Caesar's senior officers became extremely wealthy during these campaigns, something lampooned by the poet Catullus. Command of an army gave a Roman governor considerable patronage, allowing him to make appointments as legates and tribunes and to a whole range of other posts. He could also award contracts to business-men. The profits of war were also of great value in winning friends at Rome. Caesar gave a loan to Cicero and a legate's commission to his brother Quintus, who is portrayed in a very favorable light in the *Commentaries*. Vast sums were rumored to have been spent to purchase the support of Aemilius Paullus and Curio, respectively consul and tribune of the plebs, in 50 BC.[18]

Caesar's massive expansion of his army was not officially sanctioned at first. He carried this out on his own initiative and authority, funding it through the revenue from his province. He treated the people of Cis-alpine Gaul as if they were citizens and enrolled them in the legions. Later he would do the same in the Transalpine province, eventually forming an entire legion, *Legio V Alaudae*, from this source.[19] In 55 BC, Pompey and Crassus arranged not only the extension of Caesar's com-mand but the retrospective approval and funding from the Senate for the enlargement of the army. It was probably not until the dictatorship that Caesar himself was able to confirm the grant of Roman citizen-ship to the Gauls recruited into his army.

Expanding the army gave Caesar not only greater forces but also much greater patronage. Each new legion raised created sixty com-missions for centurions, as well as half a dozen or so tribune posts. In the *Commentaries*, Caesar notes that he promoted centurions to higher grades for conspicuous service, often transferring men from a veteran legion into a new formation. By the end of the campaigns in Gaul, it is likely that every centurion in the army owed his original commis-sion or one or more steps in promotion to Caesar. By 48 BC, Caesar's legions were on average below half strength, and by the time it reached Alexandria, the veteran Legio VI numbered fewer than 1,000 men, just 20 percent of its full complement. We do not know how often fresh recruits were drafted into existing legions, but it is possible that the preference was always to raise new formations, creating more commis-sions with which to reward loyal followers.[20]

Ordinary soldiers—*nostril*, "our men"—are praised for their cour-age and prowess in the *Commentaries* but are almost never named. Even the eagle bearer of the Tenth Legion who famously jumped over the side of a ship and led the charge up the beach during the landing in

Britain in 55 BC is anonymous. Centurions are singled out and identified far more often. When Caesar was rallying the line at the Sambre, he encouraged the men as groups, but called to the centurions by name. (There were 480 centuries in the army at that time, a number it is not impossible for one man to know. Today, battalion commanders could be expected to recognize each of the soldiers under their command, in a way that would not be possible for leaders of brigades or larger formations.)[21]

Although there is a persistent myth that centurions were promoted from the ranks, Caesar never once mentions doing this. Many, if not all, seem to have been directly commissioned, and probably came from the moderately well-off classes and local aristocracies of Italy. Substantial numbers of centurions were given leave by Caesar to assist in vital elections at Rome. In part this was through intimidation, but given that the Roman voting system gave more weight to the better-off, this also suggests that many centurions were men of consequence. Some were rewarded by Caesar with enough wealth to become equestrians, such as Scaeva, who held an outpost at Dyrrachium against massive odds in 48 BC. The prominence of centurions in the *Commentaries* adds to the impression that they came from a politically significant class that Caesar wished to cultivate.[22]

THE RUBICON AND BEYOND

Crossing the Rubicon was a sign of Caesar's political failure. It was a gamble; hence his famous comment, "the die is cast." It would have been far better to return peacefully, moving smoothly into a second consulship and then a new provincial command, both of which would have secured him against prosecution. Such a victory would also have been far more satisfying, forcing his rivals to acknowledge his deserved preeminence. Caesar's eventual victory should not blind us to the fact that in most respects, the odds were against him. Pompey and his allies were not ready to defend Italy. This was in part because no one would expect a war to begin in January, long before the normal campaigning season, but also because they always expected Caesar to back down. Yet they managed to withdraw with considerable troops to Greece. Once there, Pompey was able to call on the resources of the eastern provinces to mass and train a great army.

Caesar overran Italy quickly but did not have the ships to pursue Pompey. Inactivity would only allow his enemies to grow stronger, and so he led his army to Spain. Pompey had controlled the Spanish provinces since his second consulship in 55 BC, governing them through deputies and remaining near Rome himself. Caesar won another quick victory, outmaneuvering Pompey's generals. He could not afford to suffer a serious defeat. Since the war was fought to protect his career and position, a serious reverse would have utterly discredited him. His opponents were far more able to absorb such losses and blows to prestige. Caesar had to keep attacking and had to keep winning, and even after these early successes his enemies possessed much greater resources.

Pompey waited for Caesar to attack him in Greece. The same strategy was employed by Brutus and Cassius in 42 BC, and by Mark Antony in 31 BC. There was much to recommend it, as each of these possessed a stronger fleet than their opponents. Yet in every case they were beaten and the risk-taking attacker prevailed. Keeping the initiative was clearly a major asset in civil as well as foreign wars. The 48 BC campaign was close and could easily have ended in disaster for Caesar. Despite his soldiers' formidable powers of endurance, Caesar failed at Dyrrachium and was forced to retreat. Pompey then decided that the Caesarean army was sufficiently weakened to be defeated, and so risked battle at Pharsalus. This was not unreasonable, since he was under considerable pressure from the distinguished senators with his army, who accused him of prolonging the war needlessly. Caesar's failure to attract prominent supporters ensured that his leadership was never challenged by subordinates. Waiting to starve the enemy into submission, however, was a difficult strategy to maintain in a civil war. Caesar accepted the offer of battle and proved himself the better tactician, winning an overwhelming victory.

The civil war did not end. Pompey fled to Egypt and was killed. Caesar pursued him and became embroiled in that kingdom's own civil war. He placed Cleopatra on the throne and then stayed for some time, personal reasons mingling with political ones. The time permitted surviving Pompeians to muster again in North Africa. They were defeated in 46 BC. Another force, led by Pompey's son, had to be confronted and beaten in Spain in 45 BC. Caesar had not intended to seize supreme power by force. Once he had done so he had to fight to keep power, and also had to decide how to use it. It is important to remember just how short a time Caesar spent in Rome as dictator. After his murder another spate of civil wars erupted, fought first between his defenders and his assassins. Both sides produced floods of propaganda concerning what Caesar was planning to do. The truth is now impossible to recover with any certainty.

Caesar's immediate plans involved fighting major wars against the Dacians and then the Parthians. These offered the "clean" glory of defeating foreign enemies of the republic rather than fellow Romans. Caesar nominated magistrates for the next three years, which suggests that he planned to be away for at least this time. The Parthians were formidable opponents who had defeated and killed Crassus in 53 BC and would later severely maul Antony's invasion force. Whether or not Caesar would have fared better is hard to say. It is uncertain whether he planned conquest and occupation or simply a grand punitive expedition to gain public vengeance for Crassus.

As dictator, Caesar was head of the republic. Since he had come to power by force, it was important to maintain control of the army. At some point, probably just before or during the civil war, Caesar had doubled the basic rate of pay for a legionary soldier. No doubt higher ranks received proportional increases. Veterans were discharged and given farms. As far as possible this was done without inflicting serious hardship on existing communities. Around the time he celebrated his triumphs, there was a protest by disgruntled soldiers. This was dealt with extremely severely, and several men were executed. As dictator, Caesar continued to be generous but firm with his soldiers. Officers of all ranks received lavish rewards. Caesar enrolled large numbers of new senators, including equestrian officers, some Gauls, and a few former centurions.[23]

Many individuals from the army benefited from Caesar's dictatorship. The army itself was not granted particular privileges, nor was it placed in direct control of any new aspects of life. Caesar had come to power through civil war but, as in Gaul, hoped to create a regime that survived by consent as much as by force. In the last months of his life he dismissed his Spanish bodyguard. Presumably he felt that if his regime was to survive three years of his absence on campaign, then he needed to show confidence while he was in Rome. Sulla had resigned the dictatorship he had taken by force, but Caesar described this as the act of a "political illiterate."[24] Caesar believed he should hold on to power. He misunderstood the attachment of others to tradition, and was murdered.

LIMITS OF FORCE

Caesar was a commander of genius. Like Alexander or Napoleon, he was not a great military reformer and took over a fighting force already improved by others. All of these men honed their armies to a fine edge, inspired them, and led them with a flair and imagination that produced spectacular success. Also like Napoleon, Caesar exploited his military success to seize supreme power within the state. Unlike the French emperor he did not so profoundly shape the entire state around himself. Caesar effectively controlled elections and was himself a higher authority above the magistrates chosen. Yet these still served, the Senate and Popular Assemblies continued to meet and vote, and the courts functioned much as they had before the dictatorship. The conspirators felt that almost the sole thing needed for the republic to function as normal was the removal of Caesar himself.

The dictator fell to internal rather than foreign enemies, unlike Napoleon. Military success was not enough to allow Caesar to create a stable regime; that task would be left to Augustus. He too would seize supreme power through military force. It took decades to create his new regime and to turn the brutal triumvir who had clawed his way to the top so violently into the beloved "father of his country." Augustus took care to keep the army loyal to himself alone. For over two centuries, the republican tradition of the senatorial class holding military and civil power continued. At any time, only a handful of senators were capable of supplanting the emperor. There were civil wars in AD 68–69 and 193–97, but otherwise there was far greater stability than in the last decades of the republic. Augustus and his successors were military dictators, but at the cost of political independence they gave the Roman world internal stability. Senators enjoyed prestigious careers and could still win glory, but simply did so as representatives of the emperor. This and so much more would change in the third century.

Caesar became dictator through force of arms. His exceptionally long and spectacularly successful command in Gaul had turned his army into a ferociously efficient fighting force and created an intensely personal bond between soldiers and commander. Without this he could not have seized and held on to power. Yet his victory in the civil war was not inevitable. Pompey had huge resources at his disposal and had long been acknowledged as Rome's greatest general. The precariousness of reputation—*auctoritas*, for the Romans—is shown by the ease with which Caesar's new achievements rivaled and then surpassed Pompey's past successes in the popular imagination. Few politicians would doubt the need to stay in the headlines, or that respect for achievements can rapidly fade or be pushed aside by newer stories. If anything, the pace of the modern world and the modern media have sped up the process. (For some, there may be the comfort that their mistakes and scandals can also be forgotten faster.)

Much has changed, and few modern leaders, at least in the West, could match Caesar's battlefield achievements. That does not mean that even in our societies, military glory (even if we would not use the word) cannot be transferred to political advantage. Yet it remains, as always, a precarious thing. Military failure, whether perceived or real, can be damaging. Leaders like Napoleon and Caesar who base their rise on military glory need to keep refreshing this glory with more victories if their popularity and their grip on power are not to fade. Caesar was a military dictator, but his behavior was moderate. One of the more depressing lessons from this period of history is that it was the far more ruthless Augustus who was able to hold on to power for more than forty years and ended up dying in his bed.

FURTHER READING

The primary sources for Caesar's career and campaigns must begin with his own *Commentarii* on the conflicts in Gaul and the civil war. The additional books (book eight of the *Gallic Wars* and the *Alexandrian War*, *The African War*, and *The Spanish War*, completing the *Civil Wars*) provide a slightly different perspective on his behavior. Cicero's extensive writings provide a great deal of material on Caesar and attitudes toward his behavior. The biographies of Plutarch and Suetonius contain much material not mentioned elsewhere, and both Dio and Appian supplement these works. All of these sources must be used with some caution, since Caesar was a highly controversial figure during and after his lifetime.

The modern literature on Caesar is extensive. Good starting points are offered by Mattias Gelzer, *Caesar*, trans. Peter Needham (Cambridge, MA: Harvard University Press, 1968), Christian Meier, *Caesar*, trans D. McLintock (New York: Basic Books, 1996), and Adrian Goldsworthy, *Caesar: The Life of a Colossus* (New Haven, CT: Yale University Press, 2006). Almost a century after its publication, T. Rice Holmes's *Caesar's Conquest of Gaul*, 2nd ed. (1911), continues to provide one of the most thorough discussions of the Gallic wars.

Lawrence J. F. Keppie's *The Making of the Roman Army* (London: Batsford; Totowa, NJ: Rowman and Littlefield, 1984) is one of the best and most accessible surveys of its development in this period. Also of interest are Emilio Gabba, *The Roman Republic, the Army and the Allies*, trans. P. J. Cuff (Berkeley and Los Angeles: University of California Press, 1976), Jacques Harmand, *L'armée et le soldat à Rome de 107 à 50 avant nôtre ère* (Paris: A. et J. Picard, 1967), and Richard Edwin Smith, *Service in the Post-Marian Roman Army* (Manchester, UK: University of Manchester Press, 1958). Nathan S. Rosenstein, *Imperatores Victi: Military Defeat and Aristocratic Competition in the Middle and Late Republic* (Berkeley and Los Angeles: University of California Press, 1993), is useful on the behavior expected of a Roman commander in battle, and there is further discussion of this in Adrian Goldsworthy, *The Roman Army at War 100 BC–AD 200* (Oxford: Clarendon Press, 1996), 116–70. The collection of papers in *Julius Caesar as Artful Reporter: The War Commentaries as Political Instruments*, ed. Kathryn Welch and Anton Powell (London: Duckworth and the Classical Press of Wales, 1998), includes a number of useful discussions of Caesar's presentation of his campaigns in the *Commentarii*.

NOTES

[1] Suetonius *Caesar* 30.4.

[2] Pliny *Natural History* 7.92.

[3] Cicero *Letters to Atticus* 7.11.

[4] Plutarch *Sulla* 38.

[5] For a discussion of Caesar's early career, see Adrian Goldsworthy, *Caesar: The Life of a Colossus* (New Haven, CT: Yale University Press, 2006), 65–66, 148–50, 185; Christian Meier, *Caesar*, trans. David McLintock (New York: Basic Books, 1996), 99–189; and Mattias Gelzer, *Caesar*, trans. Peter Needham (Cambridge, MA: Harvard University Press, 1968), 21–24, 28–29, 61–63.

[6] Sallust *Catiline* 54.4.

[7] Peter Wiseman, "The Publication of the *De Bello Gallico*," in *Julius Caesar as Artful Reporter: The War Commentaries as Political Instruments*, ed. Kathryn Welch and Anton Powell, 1–9 (London: Duckworth and the Classical Press of Wales, 1998).

⁸ For the importance of rivers, see David Braund, "River Frontiers in the Environmental Psychology of the Roman World," in *The Roman Army in the East*, ed. David Kennedy, *JRA Supplementary Series* 18 (1996): 43–47.

⁹ Caesar *Gallic War* 4.38.

¹⁰ Plutarch *Cato the Younger* 51; Suetonius *Julius Caesar* 24.3; with Gelzer, *Caesar*, 130–32, and Meier, *Caesar*, 282–84.

¹¹ On Caesar's diplomacy, see the discussion in Goldsworthy, *Caesar*, 315–17.

¹² See, e.g., the career and eventual execution of the chieftain Acco, Caesar *Gallic War* 6.4, 44.

¹³ Dio 40.41.1, 3.

¹⁴ Caesar *Gallic War* 8.49.

¹⁵ For rumors, see, e.g., Caelius's report to Cicero, in Cicero *Letters to His Friends* 8.1.4.

¹⁶ On the army in this period, see F. E. Adcock, *The Roman Art of War under the Republic*, Martin Classical Lectures (Cambridge, MA: Harvard University Press, 1940); Peter A. Brunt, *Italian Manpower, 225 BC–AD 14* (Oxford: Oxford University Press, 1971); Peter Connolly, *Greece and Rome at War* (Englewood Cliffs, NJ: Prentice-Hall, 1981); Emilio Gabba, *The Roman Republic, the Army and the Allies*, trans. P. J. Cuff (Berkeley and Los Angeles: University of California Press, 1976); Lawrence Keppie, *The Making of the Roman Army* (London: Batsford; Totowa, NJ: Rowman and Littlefield, 1984); Jacques Harmand, *L'armée et le soldat à Rome de 107 à 50 avant nôtre ère* (Paris: A. et J. Picard, 1967); and Richard Edwin Smith, *Service in the Post-Marian Roman Army* (Manchester, UK: University of Manchester Press, 1958).

¹⁷ On discipline, see Suetonius *Caesar* 65, 67; Plutarch *Caesar* 17; on the importance of the general as a witness to behavior, see Adrian K. Goldsworthy, *The Roman Army at War, 100 BC–AD 200* (Oxford: Clarendon Press, 1996), 162–63.

¹⁸ See, e.g., the case of Cicero's client Trebatius, in Cicero *Letters to His Friends* 7.5, letters to Trebatius, *Letters to His Friends* 7.6–19; Cicero *Letters to His Brother Quintus* 2.15a, 3 for quotation; see also Gelzer, *Caesar*, 138–39; on plunder, see Catullus 29.

¹⁹ Suetonius *Caesar* 24.

²⁰ On promotions of centurions for gallantry, see *Gallic War* 6.40; Suetonius *Caesar* 65.1; on centurions' command style and heavy casualties, see Goldsworthy, *The Roman Army at War*, 257–58, see Caesar *Gallic War* 7.51, *Civil War* 3.99; on the competition to show conspicuous valor and win promotion or reward, see *Gallic Wars* 5.44, 7.47, 50; *Civil War* 3.91.

²¹ The eagle bearer of the Tenth: Caesar *Gallic War* 4.25; the Sambre: see Caesar *Gallic Wars* 2.25.

²² On Scaeva, see Suetonius *Caesar* 68.3–4; Appian *Civil War* 2.60; Dio mentions a Scaevius who served with Caesar in Spain in 61 BC, Dio 38.53.3. For the *ala Scaevae* *CIL*10.6011 and comments in J. Spaul, *ALA²* (1994): 20–21. For the social status and levels of education among centurions, see J. N. Adams, "The Poets of Bu Njem: Language, Culture and the Centurionate," *Journal of Roman Studies* 89 (1999): 109–34.

²³ Ronald Syme, *The Roman Revolution* (Oxford: Clarendon Press, 1939), 70, 78–79; on the execution of unruly soldiers, see Dio 43.24.3–4.

²⁴ Suetonius *Caesar* 77, 86.

10. Holding the Line
Frontier Defense and the Later Roman Empire

PETER J. HEATHER

ACCORDING TO AN ANALYSIS FIRST OFFERED BY EDWARD LUTTWAK in the mid-1970s, the Roman Empire consciously moved from a frontier policy based on expansion to one based on defense in depth from the Severan era at the start of the third century AD. From this point on, its military effort was directed toward strategically planned belts of fortifications designed to absorb small-scale threats, backed by mobile, regionally based field armies held in reserve and carefully placed to deal with larger-scale incursions.[1] In the summer of 370, for instance, some Saxon raiders used ships to avoid the frontier defenses of the northern Rhine and landed in northern France. Substantial raiding followed, until the local Roman commander gathered sufficient heavy cavalry and infantry units to ambush and destroy the now unsuspecting Saxons, who had been lulled into a false sense of security by a truce that ostensibly permitted them to withdraw unharmed.[2] This is a textbook example of the kind of frontier strategy Luttwak identified, but on closer inspection, and despite the continuing influence of his work, which has remained solidly in print for more than thirty years, his analysis is substantially mistaken.

For one thing, while successive moments of energetic activity along the frontier are detectable in the archaeological record, some of which affected the many thousands of kilometers separating the mouth of the Rhine from that of the Danube, campaigns and fortress building can sometimes be shown to have had rather more to do with internal political agendas than with rational military planning. Keeping the barbarians at bay was the fundamental justification for the large-scale taxation of agricultural production that kept the empire in existence. Not surprisingly, emperors liked to show the landowners, who both paid and levied these comparatively vast sums of annually renewable wealth, that they were tough on barbarians, and tough on the causes of barbarism. In the 360s, for instance, the brother emperors Valentinian I and Valens built fortresses energetically on the empire's Rhine and Danube frontiers to make the point that they were taking proper care of the empire, even though the policy broke some agreements with frontier groups that were currently peaceful.[3] Valentinian also unilaterally lowered the annual subsidies being paid to some Alamannic leaders on the Upper Rhine, in order to be able to claim that he did not buy peace from barbarians.[4] Both lines of policy were highly irrational in terms of maintaining frontier security, because they actually provoked disturbances, but the emperors' internal political agendas came first.[5]

Offensive warfare likewise had not come to end, more or less at the end of the third century, because of any carefully planned, strategically informed decision making, based on the rational analysis of the capacity of the empire's economy to generate sufficient forces to defend its existing assets. Rather, further attempts at conquest had slowly run out of steam on all of Rome's frontiers on a much more ad hoc basis when it became all too apparent that the fruits of conquest—usually measured in terms of the glory generated for individual rulers rather than any rational, strategically minded cost-benefit equation—ceased to be worth the effort.[6]

Politicians' egos and internal political agendas have long interfered with rational military planning, however, and it should come as no great surprise that this was also true in the ancient world. Arguably, therefore, a much greater deficiency in Luttwak's analysis is his lack of attention to how Rome's frontier assets—the combination of fortifications and troops he so insightfully identified—were actually used in practice in the late Roman period of the third and fourth centuries. For right through to the end of the fourth century, Roman forces did not merely wait for the barbarians, sitting behind belts of formidable frontier fortification like some equally doomed precursor of the French and the Maginot Line. Such a sequence of events did unfold along the frontier on occasion, as in the case of the Saxons in 370, for instance, but far too infrequently for it to count as the dominant strategy that the Romans employed for maintaining frontier security. Such a strategy would not in any case have proved very effective. To economize on pay, equipment, and supplies, many units of the mobile armies were kept at such a low state of readiness unless a campaign was actually in the offing, and slow speeds of movement made for such slow re- sponse times, that there was a substantial danger that even quite large barbarian raiding forces would be safely back across the frontier long before any effective counterstrike could be launched. Everything ex- cept messages could move no faster than about 40 km per day, and to ease the problem of supplying them, even the mobile troops were not quartered in very dense clusters. To concentrate a decent force against any attack and then get the troops to a point where they could actually intervene was generally a matter of weeks rather than days, so that a purely responsive strategy would always leave raiders with plenty of opportunity for pillage and withdrawal.[7] I suspect, in fact, that it was precisely to buy the time he needed to mobilize sufficient troops that the local Roman commander went through the sham of concocting his pseudo-agreement with the Saxon raiders of 370.

When the narrative historical sources are added to the evidence of military archaeology and known troop deployments, a very different picture of overall Roman strategy emerges. Forts and armies were only two elements of an approach to frontier management that relied extremely heavily on a manipulative repertoire of diplomatic intru- sions, backed by the periodic deployment of main force. The typical pattern that emerges from late third- and fourth-century sources is that whenever the political-military situation along a particular frontier zone threatened to get out of control, a major campaign, often led personally by a reigning emperor, would be mounted beyond the impe- rial border. The Tetrarchic emperors of the late third and early fourth centuries mounted a succession of such campaigns on all three main sectors of Rome's European frontiers: the Rhine, Middle Danube (west of the Iron Gates), and Lower Danube (to the east). Constantine I cam- paigned on the Rhine in the 310s, and in the Lower and Middle Danube regions in 330s. His son Constantius II (together with his cousin and caesar Julian) led armies east of the Rhine and north of the Middle Danube in the 350s, while in the next decade Valentinian and Valens again led substantial military forces over the frontier in both the Rhine and Lower Danube regions.[8]

As recounted in the surviving narrative sources, these campaigns tended to follow a similar script. Any overly mighty barbarian leaders were first subdued, and then, for a period, the Roman armies set to burning down every settlement they could find.[9] But the deeper purpose of this kind of military action was not destruction per se, although the campaign certainly had a deliberately punitive purpose, as well as being good for military morale, since it allowed the troops to pillage at will. The effects of regular Roman pillaging of frontier areas are also occasionally visible archaeologically.[10] Nonetheless, the actual Roman campaigning was no more than the precursor to the campaigns' main purpose, which was to force all the higher- and medium-level barbarian leaders of the affected region formally to submit to imperial authority. Once a sufficiently dominant display of aggression had been deemed to have occurred, the emperor would typically establish his camp, and the regional barbarian leaders would troop in one by one to make their submissions. This process is again explicitly described on a number of separate late Roman occasions, from the Tetrarchic emperor Maximian in the 290s to Constantius II and Julian in the 350s and beyond.[11] How far into barbarian territory beyond the frontier these campaigns tended to range is not clear. They could certainly last several weeks, however, and I suspect that at least their diplomatic effects—in the form of acquisition of territories belonging to the procession of submitting kings and princes—were felt for a distance of about 100 km beyond the imperial frontier.[12]

The emperor and his advisers then set about turning short-term military dominance into longer-term security, as the example of Constantius II's manipulations in the Middle Danube region in the 350s effectively illustrates. First on the agenda was a survey of current barbarian political confederations in the affected region. If any were too large, posing too great a threat to frontier security, they were broken up, with subleaders being handed back their independence from the overly mighty king to whom they currently owed allegiance. In the

Middle Danube of the 350s, for instance, Constantius was clearly worried about the power of a certain Araharius, and freed some Sarmatian vassals led by Usafer from his control. He also elevated the prince of another group of Sarmatians, Zizais by name, to royal status and renewed the political independence of his following. This independence was backed by guarantees of Roman military support and reinforced by targeted annual diplomatic subsidies to reinforce more favored leaders' positions. It has sometimes been argued that these subsidies were "tribute" and a sign of late imperial weakness. As a diplomatic tool, however, they had been in constant use since the first and second centuries, when Roman dominance was pretty much absolute, and in the fourth century they were granted even to barbarian leaders who had submitted. They should clearly be understood in modern terms, therefore, as targeted aid, designed to shore up the power of Rome's chosen diplomatic partners.[13]

While all this diplomatic maneuvering was under way, any Roman captives held in the region were released, and forced drafts of manpower were taken from the submitting barbarians as recruits for the Roman army.[14] At the same time, these periodic emperor-led interventions were usually undertaken in response to some reasonably sustained bout of frontier trouble. Because campaigning on this scale was expensive, it usually required a major sequence of disturbances to act as a trigger. Even aside from the Roman troops' pillaging, therefore, it was entirely common for the renewed agreements to contain punitive clauses, with those held to be the guilty parties being punished in a variety of ways. On occasion, this could even mean a barbarian king's execution. In 309, for instance, Constantine I executed two kings of the Franks in the theater at Trier.[15] More usually, however, the desire for revenge was satisfied by imposing various financial penalties, most commonly in the form of exactions of labor and raw materials for rebuilding work, along with substantial quantities of food supplies.[16]

From time to time, emperors might use their military superiority to take much more drastic action. Aside from breaking up dangerous political structures on the other side of the frontier, emperors were also concerned to ensure that no frontier region became overcrowded. This was a situation that could and did lead to the internal rivalries of different barbarian leaders spilling over onto Roman soil. One response was to force—at sword point, if necessary—some of the empire's immediate neighbors to abandon their established homes and move away from the frontier zone. In the Middle Danube of the 350s, for instance, Constantius II decided that one particular Sarmatian subgroup, the Limigantes, was to be expelled, and was entirely happy to use force to make them leave. Another response was to allow particular barbarian groups to be received onto Roman soil on strictly regulated terms. The Tetrarchs in particular employed such controlled resettlements on all the major European frontiers in the two decades after 290 AD, but this technique had an established prehistory and continued in use subsequently.[17]

This is not to say that Rome's repertoire of manipulative diplomatic techniques was always deployed as part of an entirely coherent or rational policy for frontier defense in what might be termed a "grand strategy," with the emphasis firmly on "grand." As we have seen, internal political agendas sometimes made emperors pick fights where there was no need, so that they could show off to their taxpayers. In reality, too, all the major cross-border campaigns of the late imperial period tended to be responsive, coming after the breakdown of order within a particular frontier region, rather than because political and military intelligence indicated that order was about to break down. When assessing the overall effectiveness of Roman frontier defense, therefore, it is necessary to factor into the equation that substantial economic losses to outside raiding were also part of the picture, since it took a fair amount of raiding to trigger a response. How substantial that raiding might have been has emerged from an exciting archaeological find made while dredging in the Rhine near the old Roman frontier town of Speyer. Late in the third century, some Alamannic raiders had been trying to get their booty back home across the Rhine when their boats were ambushed and sunk by Roman river patrol ships. This booty consisted of an extraordinary 700 kg of goods packed into three or four carts, the entire looted contents of probably a single Roman villa, and the raiders were interested in every piece of metalwork they could find. The only items missing from the hoard were rich solid silver ware and high-value personal jewelry. Either the lord and lady of the house got away before the attack or else the very high-value loot was transported separately. In the carts, however, was a vast mound of silverplate from the dining room, the equipment from an entire kitchen (fifty-one cauldrons, twenty-five bowls and basins, and twenty iron ladles), enough agricultural implements to run a substantial farm, votive objects from the villa's shrine, and thirty-nine good-quality silver coins.[18] If this haul represents the proceeds of just one localized raid, the magnitude of the more sustained disturbances required to trigger an imperial campaign should not be underestimated. Nonetheless, the overall pattern of the evidence is unmistakable. Late Roman emperors did not leave their troops passively behind the frontier merely waiting for trouble. Periodically, the field armies were trundled out in force to establish an overwhelming level of immediate military dominance, which was then used to dictate an overall diplomatic settlement for the region that was in line with the empire's priorities, to maximize the cost-value ratio of the original campaign.

In addition, a further subrepertoire of intrusive techniques was then used to shore up each diplomatic settlement and increase its effective life span. Targeted annual subsidies, designed to keep favored kings in power, were common. Particularly favored groups would also receive special trading privileges. Normally, trade was allowed only at a few designated points in any frontier segment, but occasionally the empire would throw in an open frontier to sweeten a deal. After his defeat in of the Gothic Tervingi on the Lower Danube in the early 330s, for instance, the emperor Constantine I opened up the entire spread of their sector of the Lower Danube for trade. This was done by the emperor from a position of strength, as something designed to give these Goths, or their leaders who would benefit from the tolls, real reason to keep the peace.[19] It was also customary to take high-status hostages, usually the sons of kings and princes, as a further prop to any peace deal. If things went wrong, these captives could be executed, but there is only one known fourth-century example of this. More generally, these hostages were usually also young, and bringing them up around the imperial court had long been designed to impress on these possible future rulers of Rome's borderlands the power and prestige of the empire, which could act as a deterrent to future misbehavior should the now former hostages ever come to power as adults.[20]

Less positive measures were also available. If a particular barbarian leader's ambitions threatened to destroy or distort the peace arrangements, then imperial commanders were regularly ordered to resort to kidnap or assassination. In just the twenty-four years covered by the dense contemporary narrative of the late Roman historian Ammianus Marcellinus (354–78), these techniques were deployed on no less than five separate occasions.[21] Whether all these tactics amounted to a grand strategy is contestable, but their existence shows the late empire operating on far more than a merely defensive footing. Rather, what emerges with great clarity is that the later empire turned its immediate neighbors into junior client members of a Roman world system, exerting military power to order their affairs in the manner that best suited the empire's interests. The narrative suggests that each major intervention led to diplomatic settlements with an average life span of some twenty to twenty-five years—more or less a political generation. On the Rhine, for instance, the Tetrarchic emperors mounted one major intervention in the 290s, Constantine mounted another in the 310s, and there then seems to have been substantial stability down to the 350s. The Tetrarchs were again busy on the Middle Danube in the decade after 300 AD, Constantine intervened with a major campaign in the early 330s, and peace then prevailed again until the later 350s. The pattern on the Lower Danube was again similar, with the Tetrarchs and Constantine mounting campaigns in the 300s and early 330s, but this time the peace deal—perhaps, among other reasons, because of the special trading privileges granted the Gothic Tervingi—lasted until the mid-360s.[22] This does not amount to an unblemished record of frontier security, but, especially for a premodern state operating at such slow speeds over such vast distances, getting twenty to twenty-five years of peace from each bout of major campaigning represents a decent return on its military investments, and no bad overall record of keeping its possessions secure.

To understand Roman–barbarian relations fully, however, and to grasp the relationship between Roman frontier policies and the eventual processes of imperial collapse, it is necessary to explore one further dimension of the empire's approach to client management and frontier security. In the short term, any particular round of campaigning-followed-by-diplomacy was geared toward generating as much stability as possible on a particular sector of the frontier. Looked at in the long term—and by the fourth century, these rhythms of Roman frontier management had been in operation along the Rhine and Danube for the best part of 400 years—these techniques had had powerfully transformative effects on the empire's neighbors across the border. Diplomatic subsidies and trading privileges, backed up by imperial diplomatic interference, such as providing political and military support for favored barbarian rulers, tended to put money and power in the hands of particular kings. Played out over 400 years, the longer-term effect of this approach was to help concentrate power more generally in the hands of an entirely new type of king. The Germanic world of the first century AD was populated by a host of small-scale sociopolitical units. Well over fifty appear in the pages of Tacitus's *Germania* covering Central Europe, for the most part between the Rhine and the Vistula. By the fourth century, this multiplicity of smaller units had given way to a much smaller number of larger ones, perhaps no more than a dozen. These were certainly confederative overkingships, so that estimates of the degree of political revolution they represent need to be kept within reasonable bounds. But whereas in the Roman period larger confederations disappeared with the defeat of their leaders, these fourth-century counterparts could survive even substantial defeat. The immediate rulers of the Alamanni of the Upper Rhine frontier were a series of canton kings and princes. Periodically, however, these banded together under an overking of particular power, especially when expansionary warfare (against Rome or a neighbor) was in the offing. Even after massive military defeats, such as that at Strasbourg in 357, which brought down the Alamannic overking Chnodomarius, the confederation retained its cohesion and could quickly reform under the leadership of new overkings, of whom Rome faced a sequence in the course of the fourth century. The durability of the larger political structures of the fourth century marks them out their earlier counterparts.[23]

Equally important, the nature of political power had changed out of all recognition. A much stronger hereditary element had invaded the top end of politics. Among the Alamanni the overkingship tended not to be hereditary, not least because Roman policy was geared toward eliminating a succession of its holders. But the canton kings do seem

Other transformations, of course, also played an important role within this broader revolution. The early centuries AD saw the advent of new farming regimes in Germanic-dominated Central Europe, which generated large increases in food production and hence in population. The overall power of the Germanic world, at least in demographic terms, clearly increased in relation to its imperial Roman neighbor, and the new kings presumably used some of this surplus food to support their retinues. Again, Roman economic demand and transfers of Roman technical know-how appear to have played a significant role in this agricultural revolution, and in accompanying economic expansions in some areas of manufacture and trade.[28] I also strongly suspect that the generally aggressive, not to say humiliating, nature of the Roman approach even to its favored client kings—where, after the fashion mastered by the Sarmatian prince Zizais in the presence of Constantius II in 358, groveling accompanied by gentle sobbing while begging for favor was the generally favored protocol for barbarian kings in the imperial presence[29]—likewise played a major role in the ability of the new class of hereditary military kings to build up their control. If this scenario seems far-fetched, one need only remember that part of Roman frontier policy was to burn down the villages of its neighbors once per generation, and that several of the princes taken hostage clearly came back none too enamored of the Roman way.[30] Indeed, one gain that might be had in return for paying the dues necessary to support the new kings' military retinues was surely the hope that belonging to a powerful confederation of the new kind might help fend off the worst effects of Roman imperial intrusion. In short, all the different kinds of relationship—positive and negative, political and economic, diplomatic and military—that had naturally sprung up between the empire and its originally very much less developed neighbors combined to accelerate the transformative processes that turned the large number of small sociopolitical units occupying the imperial hinterland in the first century AD into the much smaller number of more powerful ones that had replaced them by the fourth. And what gave these relationships so much transformative power was the fact that each stimulated its own autonomous response among the Germani. It wasn't just that imperial Rome did things that transformed Germanic society—although it certainly the Greuthungi, and a series of smaller groups across Rome's Lower Danube frontier. The Huns' second move, onto the Great Hungarian Plain, was preceded by another huge exodus of Roman clients from precisely that region: another large Gothic group led by a certain Radagaisus, who moved into Italy, a large coalition comprising two separate groups of Vandals together with Alans and Sueves, who moved across the Rhine, and a further force of Burgundians, who followed them in the same direction. The sources are not explicit that Huns caused this second exodus. But Huns appear in the region vacated by these migrants immediately afterward, and the most likely explanation for this unprecedented demographic upheaval is that it was a repeat of the scenario of the 370s, but this time played out across Rome's Middle Danubian and Upper Rhine frontiers as the Huns moved westward.[32] In effect, the Huns imparted a unity of purpose among many tens of thousands of invaders that is hard to imagine occurring otherwise. And it was the simultaneous appearance of these politically separate barbarian groupings that prevented the Roman Empire from defeating them: as it attempted to do, and as it certainly would have been able to do had not so many come at one time.[33]

The scale of the resulting strategic disaster was made much worse from the Roman point of view by the fact that the empire's attempted military counterstrikes prompted a further phase of alliance building among the migrants. Thus, from half a dozen or so separate units that entered the empire in 376–80 and 405–8, there emerged two much larger units. The Visigoths, who eventually settled in southern Gaul in 418, were composed of the Tervingi and Greuthungi of the first phase, united further with surviving Goths from the attack of Radagaisus on Italy in the second phase. The Vandal force that eventually seized the economically vital lands of North Africa, breadbasket of the western empire, in the 430s (after a lengthy interlude in Spain) were likewise created by the full unification there of both Vandal groups and the Alans, who originally outnumbered them.[34] The crucial point is that these further political reconfigurations created groups big enough to resist even major Roman field armies. Hence the new groups were able to survive on Roman soil in the long term, not least because the intrusive Huns united several of the other frontier Germanic groups under their control beyond the frontier and began to mount campaigns, which meant that the maximum Roman force could not be deployed against the original—now reorganized—migrants.[35] And while the Hunnic Empire proved only a ramshackle and temporary phenomenon, its collapse only increased the problems facing the imperial authorities, as it led several other Germanic groups comparable in scale to the Visigothic and Vandal alliances, not least the Burgundians and Ostrogoths, to end up on western Roman soil as well.

The overall threat to imperial survival posed by these unsubdued immigrants was straightforward. The Roman state funded its armies and other state activities overwhelmingly from a land tax on agricultural production. When the newly enlarged barbarian coalitions formed on Roman territory and proved impossible to dismantle, they ate away at this tax base by seizing control of provinces, with or without imperial consent. The Visigoths, for instance, were originally settled in limited areas of southern Gaul (as were the Burgundians) with imperial consent, while the Vandals seized the richest provinces of North Africa by force. These annexed areas then paid nothing further into imperial coffers. At the same time, imperial consent to these settlements was always extracted at sword point, which meant that substantial tracts of the land that did remain in imperial hands suffered considerable damage and were consequently much less able to pay their customary tax dues. Emperors customarily seemed to have granted damaged areas a tax remission of six-sevenths. Very quickly, therefore, these barbarian settlements pushed the central authorities of the western imperial state into a vicious cycle of decline. Losses of land and revenue undermined the capacity of the state to maintain its armed forces and hence its capacity to resist the further demands of barbarian intruders, whether those already on Roman soil or new ones from outside. Even the Visigoths, erstwhile imperial allies, were quick to take any opportunity to expand their own area of domination, notably under Euric, who launched wars of conquest after 468 that brought most of Spain and much of Gaul under Gothic rule. As this process worked itself out, both Romans and barbarians eventually came to realize that the central Roman state was no longer the major player in the politics of Western Europe, and it is no accident that the final act of imperial dissolution, the deposition of the last western emperor Romulus Augustulus, occurred when the wage bill of the remaining Roman army of Italy could no longer be paid.[36]

The relevance of this story to the modern world turns immediately on the process of imperial collapse. The developed Western world has a marked tendency to see strategic problems in terms of its own policies, of what it has or has not done or might do in the future, as if other parties to any relationship do not have a say in the ultimate train of events. A similar kind of attitude is apparent in traditional approaches to Roman imperial collapse, which largely focus on whether Roman frontier strategies were wise enough or sufficient to combat the outside threat. An overall picture of developing patterns of political, social, and economic organization in Central Europe of the Roman period, however, emphasizes that it is just as important to focus on what the so-called barbarians were doing. So often historians, usually following Roman commentators themselves, have discussed the ultimate fate of the frontier in terms of whether Rome, at different points in its history, found or lost the magic strategic calculus, when in reality, given developing conditions on the ground, the empire's fate was substantially contingent on what was happening across the frontier. Rome was at heart a Mediterranean-based empire that used those resources to exercise domination over large parts of more northerly Europe. The ultimate reason why the empire fell, and why a Mediterranean-based state has never been so dominant in Western Eurasian history since, lies in the fact that the first millennium marks a crucial watershed in the development of Europe as a whole. New farming techniques generated much larger populations, which were then mobilized by much more sophisticated political structures. The result was a fundamental shift in the strategic balance of power, which meant that Mediterranean resources no longer provided a sufficient power base from which to exercise European domination. The accident of Hunnic intrusion may have dictated exactly how and when the empire fell, but it was the unleashing of forces of development in barbarian Europe that meant that it was bound to fall sometime, and, what's more, never return.

Perhaps even more important, I suspect, is what this story has to tell us about the dynamic forces unleashed when originally less-developed economies and political structures come into contact—on a whole series of levels—with larger-scale imperial neighbors. For much of the transformation that generated larger and more powerful socio-economic and political structures on the fringes of the Roman world in the first half of the first millennium AD can be traced to the consequences of unprecedented contacts between barbarian and imperial Europe: military, economic, political, and indeed cultural. Again, this is not just a story of the empire doing things but of barbarians reacting with intelligence and determination to the opportunities and dangers that imperial policies presented. In fact, the development of the Germanic world is only one example of a much more general phenomenon. In response both to the positive opportunities such contacts presented and to the negative factor of aggressive exploitation that empires generally exercise over their originally weaker neighbors, such societies often display a marked tendency to develop and reorganize themselves in such a way as to overturn the original inequalities of power. Highly analogous patterns of development, for instance, are visible among Slavic societies on the fringes of Frankish imperial Europe in the second half of the millennium.[37] And this pattern, I would argue, has held good to a considerable extent in more modern contexts too, where the developed West's economic, political, and even military domination, so evident across the globe in the twentieth century, is rapidly being overturned by outside political structures—modern barbarians, if you will—that it previously exploited but that have taken full advantage of its dangers and opportunities to reorganize themselves. What all of these examples suggest to me, in short, is that there often operates a kind of Newton's Third Law of Empires. The exercise of imperial political dominance and economic exploitation will in the long run stimulate a series of reactions that turns initially weaker neighbors into societies much more capable of resisting or even overturning the aggressive imperialism that set those reactions in train.

FURTHER READING

The most important single work on Roman frontier defense continues to be Edward N. Luttwak, *The Grand Strategy of the Roman Empire from the First Century* A.D. *to the Third*

(Baltimore: Johns Hopkins University Press, 1976). Luttwak is not an ancient historian but a strategic analyst who applied his expertise to the archaeological evidence of Roman frontier fortifications and troop deployments. His cogent analysis—suggesting that the empire moved deliberately from attack to defense in depth at the end of the second century AD—set the agenda for all subsequent work, even if its conclusions have been substantially modified. Three works among other notable titles—J. C. Mann, "Power, Force and the Frontiers of the Empire," *Journal of Roman Studies* 69 (1979): 175–83, C. R. Whittaker, *Frontiers of the Roman Empire: A Social and Economic Study* (Baltimore: Johns Hopkins University Press, 1994), and B. Isaac, *The Limits of Empire: The Roman Army in the East*, 2nd rev. ed. (Oxford: Oxford University Press, 1993)—have among them shown that internal political agendas often adversely affected the working of truly rational foreign policy, and that command and control limitations made it extremely unlikely that emperors were capable of the kind of strategic overview that Luttwak's hypotheses require.

Whittaker's work has also contributed to a second critique, along with sustained archaeological investigations conveniently summarized in such studies as L. Hedeager, "The Evolution of Germanic Society 1–400 AD," in *First Millennium Papers: Western Europe in the First Millennium*, ed. R. F. Jones, J.H.F. Bloehmers, S. L. Dyson, and M. Biddle, 129–44, B.A.R. International Series 401 (Oxford, 1988), and Maureen Carroll, *Romans, Celts and Germans: The German Provinces of Rome* (Stroud, UK, 2001). These works have demonstrated the extent to which the world beyond the frontier was transformed by sustained economic interaction with the empire. My own work, particularly "The Late Roman Art of Client Management and the Grand Strategy Debate," in *The Transformation of Frontiers from Late Antiquity to the Carolingians: Proceedings of the Second Plenary Conference, European Science Foundation Transformation of the Roman World Project*, ed. Walter Pohl, Ian N. Wood, and Helmut Reinitz, 15–68 (Leiden: Brill, 2000), has drawn on historical evidence (little explored by Luttwak) to show both that Rome did not in fact move onto the defensive, as he supposed, and that Roman military and diplomatic activities, in conjunction with economic interactions, played a major role in creating larger and more coherent political structures in neighboring barbarian societies. For the argument that it was this transformation of the north and east that eventually made it impossible for a Mediterranean-based state to extend a Europe-wide domination, see now Peter J. Heather, *Empires and Barbarians: Migration, Development and the Creation of Europe* (London: Macmillan, 2009).

NOTES

[1] Edward N. Luttwak, *The Grand Strategy of the Roman Empire from the First Century A.D. to the Third* (Baltimore: Johns Hopkins University Press, 1976).

[2] Ammianus Marcellinus 28.5, with further comment in Peter J. Heather, *The Fall of the Roman Empire: A New History* (London: Macmillan, 2005), 67–68.

[3] Ammianus 28.2, 29.6; Themistius *Orationes* 10. These moments do show up in the archaeology: James Lander, *Roman Stone Fortifications from the First Century A.D. to the Fourth*, B.A.R International Series 206 (Oxford, 1984); Sandor Soproni, *Der spätrömische*

Limes zwischen Esztergom und Szentendre (Budapest: Akademiai Kiado, 1978); Constantin Scorpan, *Limes Scythiae: Topographical and Stratigraphical Research on the Late Roman Fortifications on the Lower Danube*, B.A.R. International Series 88 (Oxford, 1980).

⁴Ammianus 26.5, 27.1.

⁵John Drinkwater, *The Alamanni and Rome 213–496* (Oxford: Oxford University Press, 2007), has recently argued that all Roman operations on the Upper Rhine frontier were driven by different emperors' needs for prestige rather than by military necessity, but this is to overstate the point. True, the Alamanni did not by themselves (see below) pose a threat to the overall existence of the empire, but they were responsible for substantial raiding (see note 20) and occasionally threatened local annexations of Roman territory: in the 350s, for instance, a band some 50 km wide in the Rhine valley. For more limited—and to my mind more convincing—general critiques of the "rational" Luttwak approach, see J. C. Mann, "Power, Force and the Frontiers of the Empire," *Journal of Roman Studies* 69 (1979): 175–83; C. R. Whittaker, *Frontiers of the Roman Empire: A Social and Economic Study* (Baltimore: Johns Hopkins University Press, 1994).

⁶Mann, "Power, Force"; see esp. Benjamin H. Isaac, *The Limits of Empire: The Roman Army in the East*, 2nd rev. ed. (Oxford: Oxford University Press, 1993), ix. For further comment, see Heather, *Fall of the Roman Empire*, chap. 2.

⁷L. Michael Whitby, *Rome at War AD 293–696* (Oxford: Oxford University Press, 2002), provides an excellent introduction to issues of readiness and mobility; see now John F. Matthews, *The Journey of Theophanes: Travel, Business, and Daily Life in the Roman East* (New Haven, CT: Yale University Press, 2006), on the limited speeds possible even for officially assisted travelers.

⁸Tetrarchic campaigns have to be reconstructed largely from very fragmented narrative sources and the evidence of the victory titles they claimed: see Timothy D. Barnes, *The New Empire of Diocletian and Constantine* (Cambridge, MA: Harvard University Press, 1982). The main sources for the mid-fourth century are the first part of the Anonymous Valesianus and then the full and contemporary narrative of Ammianus Marcellinus for the years 354–78. General commentary and more detailed discussion of the pattern can be found in Peter J. Heather, "The Late Roman Art of Client Management and the Grand Strategy Debate," in *The Transformation of Frontiers from Late Antiquity to the Carolingians: Proceedings of the Second Plenary Conference, European Science Foundation Transformation of the Roman World Project*, ed. Walter Pohl, Ian N. Wood, and Helmut Reinitz, 15–68 (Leiden: Brill, 2000).

⁹Compare, e.g., the Caesar Julian on the Rhine frontier and the Augustus Constantius on the Middle Danube, both in the 350s: Ammianus 17.1, 6, 10, 18.2 (Julian); 17.12–13 (Constantius). But the pattern was the same with Valentinian on the Rhine in the 360s and 370s (Ammianus 27.2, 10, 29.4) and Valens on the Lower Danube in the 360s (Ammianus 27.5).

¹⁰Maureen Carroll, *Romans, Celts and Germans: The German Provinces of Rome* (Stroud, UK, 2001) is excellent on the economically debilitating effects of constant imperial campaigning on Germanic groups of the Weser in the first and second centuries. Drinkwater, *Alamanni*, 9, shows that the Alamannia exhibited marked signs of economic development in the fifth century after Roman raiding stopped.

¹¹Maximian: *Panegyrici Latini* 2 [10].7–10. Julian: Ammianus 17.1.12–13, 17.10, 18.2.15–19. Constantius: Ammianus 17.12.9–21.

[12] See further discussion in Heather, "Client Management."

[13] Ammianus 17.12.9ff. On subsidies, see further Heather, "Client Management," and on the longer-term history, Johannes Klose, *Roms Klientel-Randstaaten am Rhein und an der Donau: Beitrage zu ihrer Geschichte und rechtlichen Stellung im 1. und 2. Jhdt. N. Chr.* (Breslau: Marcus, 1934).

[14] Some examples of forced drafts of manpower: Ammianus 17.13.3, 28.5.4, 30.6.1, 31.10.17.

[15] *Panegyrici Latini* 7 [6].10.1–7; see Ammianus 27.2.9 for another example from 366.

[16] E.g., Ammianus 17.1.12–13, 10.8–9, 18.2.19.

[17] Limigantes: Ammianus 17.13. The Tetrarchs organized substantial resettlements, particularly of Franks and Carpi; see Erich Zollner, *Geschichte der Franken bis zur Mitte des sechsten Jahrhunderts* (Munich: Beck, 1970), and Gh. Bichir, *The Archaeology and History of the Carpi*, trans. Nubar Hampartumian, B.A.R. Supplementary Series 16 (Oxford, 1976). Constantine resettled more Sarmatians in the empire in the 330s: *Anonymous Vaesianus* 6.32. On the terms of such settlements, see Peter J. Heather, *Goths and Romans 332–489* (Oxford, 1991), 4. For all the precautions, resettlement could occasionally go badly wrong: Ammianus 19.11.

[18] Detailed report: *Die Alamannenbeute aus dem Rhein bei Neupotz*, ed. Ernst Küunzl, 4 vols. (Mainz: Verlag des Römisch-Germanischen Zentralmuseums, 1993). A brief English summary can be found in K. Painter, "Booty from a Roman Villa Found in the Rhine," *Minerva* 5 (1994): 22–27.

[19] Heather, *Goths and Romans*, 3. E. A. Thompson, *The Early Germans* (Oxford: Oxford University Press, 1965), shows how rare such an economically open frontier arrangement was.

[20] On the execution of hostages, note the laments of the Alamanni recorded at Ammianus 28.2.8–9. David C. Braund, *Rome and the Friendly King: The Character of Client Kingship* (London: Macmillan, 1984), explores Roman cultural diplomacy more generally. Not that it always worked. The Gothic royal hostage taken by Constantine in 332 seems to have reacted adversely to the experience, advising his son to have nothing to do with the Romans: Ammianus 27.5.9, with Herwig Wolfram, *History of the Goths* (Berkeley and Los Angeles: University of California Press, 1988), 62ff. On the other hand, Ammianus received help from an ex-hostage who had come to love classical learning when on a spying mission on the Persian front: Ammianus 18.6.17ff.

[21] Macrianus: Ammianus 29.4.2–5; Vadomarius: Ammianus 21.4.1–6 (see also 21.3.5; 26.8.2); Vithicabius: Ammianus 27.10.3–4; Gabinus: Ammianus 29.6.3–5; leadership of Gothic Tervingi: Ammianus 31.5.5–8.

[22] In more detail, see Heather, "Client Management."

[23] See now Peter J. Heather, *Empires and Barbarians: Migration, Development and the Creation of Europe* (London: Macmillan, 2009), chap. 2.

[24] Wolfram, *Goths*, 62ff.

[25] D. H. Green, *Language and History in the early Germanic World* (Cambridge: Cambridge University Press, 1998).

[26] Chnodomarius: Ammianus 16.12.60. On the warband excavated at Ejsbøl Mose, see Mogens Ørsnes, "The Weapon Find in Ejsbøl Mose at Haderlev: Preliminary Report," *Acta Archaeologica* 34 (1963): 232–48. For an example of retinue and enforcement,

see Peter Heather and John Matthews, trans., *The Goths in the Fourth Century*, Translated Texts for Historians (Liverpool: Liverpool University Press, 1991), 5.

[27] Heather, *Empires and Barbarians*, 3.

[28] For an introduction, see L. Hedeager, "The Evolution of Germanic Society 1–400 AD," in *First Millennium Papers: Western Europe in the First Millennium*, ed. R.F.J. Jones, J.H.F. Bloemers, S. L. Dyson, and M. Biddle, 129–44, B.A.R. International Series 401 (Oxford, 1988).

[29] Ammianus 17.12.9–11; compare the famous apoplectic fit of the emperor Valentinian I when barbarian envoys failed to show him sufficient respect: Ammianus 30.6.8.

[30] Above note 20.

[31] Drinkwater, *Alamanni*, has recently argued that the Alamanni offered no threat at all, but this is to move from one extreme to another. On the agendas of the Gothic Tervingi, see in more detail Heather, *Goths and Romans*, 3.

[32] The events of 376 are well documented in, among other sources, Ammianus 31.3ff. The events of 405–10 have to be reconstructed, but again, the most plausible reconstruction is that a second westward movement of Huns was the fundamental cause of the exodus onto Roman soil: Heather, *Fall of the Roman Empire*, 4–5, with Peter J. Heather, "Why Did the Barbarian Cross the Rhine?," *Journal of Late Antiquity* (forthcoming, 2009), responding to the arguments of those who have attempted in the meantime to come up with alternative explanations of the invasions of the Roman west in the period 405–8.

[33] As is shown, for instance, by the defeats in 386 and 405 of two Gothic refugee leaders, Odotheus and Radagaisus, who attempted to force their way across the Roman frontier by themselves. These examples, and the aggressive imperial response to the more successful, clustered invasions, show that this period saw no fundamental shifts in Roman policies to outsiders, as was argued famously by Walter Goffart, "Rome, Constantinople, and the Barbarians in Late Antiquity," *American Historical Review* 76 (1981): 275–306.

[34] Visigoths: Heather, *Goths and Romans*, 6. Vandals-Alan alliance: Heather, *Fall of the Roman Empire*, 5–6.

[35] For introductions to the Hunnic Empire and its activities, see Otto J. Maenchen-Helfen, *The World of the Huns*, edited by Max Knight (Berkeley and Los Angeles: University of California Press, 1973), and E. A. Thompson, *The Huns*, rev. ed., People of Europe Series (Oxford: Blackwell, 1995).

[36] The process is examined in more detail in Heather, *Fall of the Roman Empire*, chaps. 9–10.

[37] Heather, *Empires and Barbarians*, esp. chaps. 2, 10, and 11.

Acknowledgments

I wish to thank my fellow contributors for their professionalism and skill in helping to put this volume together—as well as for their shared interest in making the knowledge of the ancient world more accessible to the modern. Robert Tempio, classics editor at Princeton University Press, first suggested to me that I consider editing a prequel to Princeton's hallowed *Makers of Modern Strategy* editions, and he was largely responsible for the conception of the volume. Deborah Tegarden at Princeton did a marvelous job as editor, both in reviewing the manuscript and preparing the essays for publication. Tobiah Waldron compiled an excellent index. My assistant Jennifer Heyne helped with both the copy editing and final proof correction.

Finally, I wish to gratefully acknowledge Bill and Nancy Myers, and their children, Mary Myers Kauppila and George Myers, for their financial support in the preparation of this volume. In addition to their interest in the humanities at the Hoover Institution, Stanford University, the Myers family members have also long demonstrated their appreciation of scholarship in the classics—especially its application to contemporary history.

Victor Davis Hanson
The Hoover Institution
Stanford, California
November 2009

Index

divine sanction, 18–19
Doloaspis, 126
Drangiana, 121
Drauga, 17–19
Drimacus, 188, 193, 197, 201
drones, 2
Dumnorix, 215–16
Dyrrachium, 221

Earle, Edward M., 1–2
Ecbatana, 120–21
Ecclesia, 68, 85n40
economic issues, 132; Athenian Empire and, 5;
    circuit wall and, 151–52; counterinsurgency
    and, 167–68; fortifications and, 58–59;
    frontier defense and, 229, 233, 235, 241–42;
    Greek city-states and, 5; harbor duties
    and, 38; imports and, 38; Julius Caesar and,
    210; naval power and, 69; North Africa
    and, 239; Peloponnesian Wars and, 34, 104;
    Piraeus harbor and, 63–64; preemption
    and, 108–10; private armies and, 217–20;
    satrap system and, 125–26; slavery and,
    196, 200; spice trade and, 133; taxes and,
    163–65, 176–77; trade restrictions and, 233;
    treasurers and, 126; tribute and, 34–35, 38
Egypt, 130, 172–73, 221; Alexander and, 120, 126,
    131–32; Alexandria, 127–28, 134; Athenian
    campaign and, 34–35, 55; Cambyses and, 17;
    Cleopatra and, 221; collapse of Assyrian
    Empire and, 12; Julius Caesar and, 221–22;
    marriage customs in, 131; Pompey and,
    221; Ptolemaic kings and, 131–32, 135; satrap
    system and, 126; segregation and, 131; Six-
    Day War and, 101–2; strategic significance
    of, 14–15; treatment of elderly and, 131;
    Zenobia and, 166
Ejsbol Mose, 236
elderly, 131
Elis, 145
elitism, 15–16, 24, 40, 186, 192
Elpinice, 42
empire building, 13–14; Alexander and, 118–35;
    Athenians and, 34–55, 70, 97; autonomy
    and, 36–37; Boeotia and, 94–99, 103–12;
    class issues and, 40–41; Darius and, 18–19;
    Delian League and, 31–34, 43, 45; expan-
    sionism and, 55; financial gain of, 37–38;
    fortifications and, 58–78 (see also fortifica-
    tions); founding cities and, 127–28; glory

and, 31, 35–36, 43, 49–50; Greek concept
    of power and, 34–38; Hellenization and,
    118, 130–31, 177; intermarriage and, 127–29;
    interstate system and, 59, 63, 69, 71–73, 77,
    86n43, 87n50, 88n58; King's Peace and,
    70–73, 86n43, 88n56, 89nn59,63; mainte-
    nance challenges and, 49; multipolar state
    system and, 69, 73, 86n43; naval power
    and, 51–52 (see also naval power); negative
    connotation of, 4–5, 47; Pericles and, 31, 36,
    38, 40–55; Piraeus harbor and, 65; quality
    of life and, 38–39; religion and, 36; Rome
    and, 118, 163–69; Spartans and, 67–70, 97;
    Thucydides and, 45–47; transpopulation
    policy and, 127; tribute payments and,
    34–35
English Channel, 167, 207
Enna, 191–92, 194
Epaminondas the Theban, 2, 9; aftermath
    of strategy of, 105–7; as agent of change,
    95–96; ancient records on, 99–100; battle
    of Leuctra and, 97, 103, 109; Boeotia and,
    94–99, 103–12; death of, 106, 108; democ-
    racy and, 6, 94; as "first man of Greece,"
    93; frees helots, 6, 93–94, 98, 104–8, 112,
    114n9, 115n11, 116n19, 188; humiliates
    Spartans, 83n25, 93–99, 103–12; inva-
    sion of 370–69 and, 96–100, 104; lack of
    modern knowledge on, 94; Laconia and,
    104, 106–8; lessons learned from, 107–10;
    longer-term aims of, 104–5; preeminence
    of, 93; preemption and, 6, 97–100, 103–12;
    tenure of, 99, 104; unorthodox methods of,
    99–100; urban fighting and, 149, 153–54; as
    zealot, 112
ephors, 67
Ephorus, 93
Eryx, 177
espionage, 17, 24–25, 28
eunomia (good governance), 20
Eunus, 194–95, 201
Euripides, 94, 130
Eurotas River, 98, 104, 149
Eurymedon River, 34
Ezekiel (Biblical prophet), 12, 15

Fallujah, 140
famine, 96
Fertile Crescent, 14
fides (faithfulness), 213

217–18; Spanish bodyguard of, 223; Spartacus and, 209; Thirteenth Legion and, 206;
Veneti and, 212; war strategy and, 211–13

military (*continued*)
fortifications and, 5, 58–78; frontier defense and, 227–42; gender issues and, 152–53, 156; historical analysis of, 1–3; hoplites and, 46, 64, 66, 91nn69,72, 94, 97, 103, 107–8, 114n7, 139–40, 147, 149–53, 156; intelligence gathering and, 7, 24, 53, 156, 232; keeping the initiative and, 221; King's Peace and, 70–73, 86n43, 88n56, 89nn59,63; legionaries, 165, 172–73, 185, 218, 222; light infantry, 151; mercenaries, 92n73, 126, 139, 142, 144, 148, 154, 157; naval power and, 58–59 (*see also* naval power); no-fly zones and, 112; occupational challenges and, 6, 9–10, 15–16; phalanx and, 9, 24, 28, 64, 85n34, 95, 104, 114n7, 150, 154, 185–86; pitched battles and, 27, 92n73, 95–97, 139, 152–54, 196, 199, 206; private armies and, 217–20; provisioning, 98–99; satrap system and, 124–29; seasonal armies and, 98–99; security zones and, 76–77; sling bullets and, 141, 148; status hierarchies and, 152–53; strategy and, 7 (*see also* strategy); thetes and, 64; urban fighting and, 138–57; Western superiority in, 7; world opinion and, 157

Mithridates, 199, 209
Mithridates VI Eupator, 189
Mogadishu, 140, 155
Montaigne, Michel de, 93
Morocco, 171
Motya, 148
Mounichia hill, 144, 147, 151, 153
Mouseion hill, 144
Mt. Ithome, 104
Mt. Taygetos, 98, 105
multipolar state system, 69, 73, 86n43
mutilation, 167
Mycale, 48
Mytileneans, 33

Napoleon, 8, 10, 207–8, 218, 223–4
Naucratis, 126
Naupactus, 188
naval power, 51–53; Athenian, 63–65, 73; British, 77–78; Conon and, 58–59, 69–70, 75, 87n47; economic issues and, 69; fortifications and, 63–65; frontier defense and, 227, 232–33; Julius Caesar and, 212–13; Long Walls and, 65; *ochlos* and, 94; Phaleron and, 65; Piraeus and, 63–65; Spartans and, 62,

86n43; Themistocles and, 58–60, 63–65; thetes and, 64; Thucydides on, 81n16; triremes and, 60, 64, 67, 85n37
nemesis (divine anger), 37
Nepos, 100
Nero, 165–66
night-vision goggles, 2
Nile Delta, 169
Nineveh, 12, 20
no-fly zones, 112
North Hill of Olynthos, 147
nostril (our men), 219
Notium, 142, 155
nuclear weapons, 179
Nysa, 131–32

Oath of Plataea, 61
Ober, Josiah, 73, 92n72
occupational challenges, 6, 9–10, 15–16
ochlos, 94
Octavian, 175
Odeion of Pericles, 145
Oenomaus, 190
Oeum, 147
Old Oligarch, 38–40, 50–51
oligarchy, 6; Boeotia and, 95–96, 105, 108–12, 114n5, 116n21; democracy and, 95–96; fortifications and, 66–68, 83n28, 85n41; Greek empire building and, 38–40, 50; Leontiades and, 95; urban fighting and, 138–47, 151–53, 157
Olynthos, 141, 147–48, 151
On the Fortune or the Virtue of Alexander (Plutarch), 128
Opis, 123, 128–30
Oracle of Zeus-Ammon, 120, 131
Orchomenos, 96
Ortygia, 144
ostracism, 46–47
Oxus, 121
Oxyartes, 121, 129

pacification, 6
Pagondas, 103
Pakistan, 118
Pallantion, 144
Palmyra, 166
pan-Hellenism, 44
Parapamisadae, 129
parents, 131

and, 139; defensible locations and, 145–46; direct assault and, 141; discipline and, 148; Epaminondas and, 153–54; factionalism and, 156; Fallujah and, 140; foreign occupiers and, 142; fortifications and, 143–52; gang warfare and, 141; gender issues and, 156; holding the acropolis and, 144; hoplites and, 149–51; house-to-house, 147–49; intelligence needs and, 156; Iraq War and, 140; lessons from, 155–57; light infantry and, 151; mercenaries and, 157; modern, 140, 155–57; new technology for, 155; Peloponnesian Wars and, 138–42; phalanx and, 150; Plataea and, 138–41, 144, 146; polis environment and, 143–49; propaganda and, 140; public buildings and, 145–46; riots and, 141; roof tiles and, 147, 155–56; sectarianism and, 156; siege engineering and, 141; sling bullets and, 141, 148; *stasis* (civil strife) and, 141–42; street layouts and, 146–49, 155; surveillance and, 157; technology and, 156; terrain and, 140; terrorism and, 7; Thebans and, 141, 144; Thirty Tyrants and, 139; three-dimensional nature of, 147; Thucydides on, 139; topographical issues and, 141, 149, 156; treachery and, 141; trenches and, 146; types of, 141–43; weapons and, 149–51; weather and, 153; world opinion and, 157

U.S. Congress, 102

utopia, 192

Uxellodunum, 216

Valens, 228, 230

Valentinian, 228, 230

Vandals, 239

Varro, 190

Veneti, 212

Vercingetorix, 165, 216

Verres, Gaius, 176–77, 199–200

Vesontio, 218

Vespasian, 165, 173

Vindex, 166

Visigoths, 239–40

Vistula, 235

voting: Delian League and, 32–33; fortifications and, 85n41, 87n47; Julius Caesar and, 209, 211, 213, 220, 223; synods and, 32–33

wars: aggressive vs. defensive, 100–103; civil, 3, 131, 139, 142, 145–46, 150, 163, 165–66, 170, 174, 176, 191, 198, 200, 206–10, 213, 216–17, 221–24; consolidation challenges and, 6; fourth generation, 2; gang, 141; Greco-Persian, 20–28; guerrilla tactics and, 121, 124, 169–70, 196; human nature and, 3, 39, 48; importance of historical perspective on, 2–10; insurrections and, 7–8, 10, 126, 142, 189, 192, 200–201; intelligence gathering and, 7, 24, 53, 156, 232; King's Peace and, 70–73, 86n43, 88n56, 89nn59,63; naval power and, 51–53 (*see also* naval power); occupational challenges and, 6, 9; politics and, 209–11; preemption and, 94–112; revolts and, 7–8, 12, 23–24, 33–35, 82n22, 119, 122–26, 134, 142, 165–73, 182n31, 185–88, 200–202; sectarianism and, 156; slave, 185–202; strategy and, 2 (*see also* strategy); tearless battle and, 105; urban fighting and, 7, 138–57; Western heritage of, 3; world opinion and, 157

Washington, George, 207

weapons, 149–51, 179, 191, 195–96

world opinion, 157

World War II era, 208

Worthington, Ian, ix–x, 6, 118–37

Xenophon, 3, 67–69, 71, 99, 106, 139

Xerxes, 2, 26–28, 37, 59, 100, 120, 132

Yahweh, 15

Yauna, 16, 23–24

zealots, 112, 117n28

Zenobia, 166

Zizais, 231, 237